| DATE DUE | |
|---|---|
| MAR 1 7 2002 | |
| | |
| | |
| | |
| | |
| | |
| | |
| | |
| | |
| | |
| | |
| | |
| | |
| | |
| | |
| | |
| | |

# VILLAGE SPACES

# VILLAGE SPACES

| SETTLEMENT AND SOCIETY |
| IN NORTHEASTERN IRAN |

## LEE HORNE

SMITHSONIAN INSTITUTION PRESS • Washington and London

Copyright © 1994 by Smithsonian Institution.

Designed by Janice Wheeler.
Edited by Joanne S. Ainsworth.
Production editing by Rebecca Browning.

Library of Congress Cataloging-in-Publication Data
Horne, Lee.
Village spaces: settlement and society in northeastern Iran / Lee Horne.   p.
cm.—(Smithsonian series in archaeological inquiry) Includes bibliographical
references and index. ISBN 1-56098-329-9
1. Land settlement patterns—Iran.   2. Villages—Iran.
3. Dwellings—Iran—Khar o Tauran.   4. Ethnoarchaeology.   5. Khar o
Tauran (Iran)—Social life and customs.   I. Title.   II. Series.
GF671.H67   1994
307.76′2′0955—dc20                                                                93-8589

British Library Cataloguing-in-Publication Data is available.

∞ The paper used in this publication meets the minimum requirements of the
American National Standard for Permanence of Paper for Printed Library Materials Z39.48-1984.

Manufactured in the United States of America.

10 9 8 7 6 5 4 3 2 1

03 02 01 00 99 98 97 96 95 94

For permission to reproduce the illustrations appearing in this volume, please
correspond directly with the author. The Smithsonian Institution Press does not
retain the right to reproduce these illustrations individually or maintain a file of
addresses for illustration sources.

# Smithsonian Series in Archaeological Inquiry
## Robert McC. Adams and Bruce D. Smith. Series Editors

The Smithsonian Series in Archaeological Inquiry presents original case studies that address important general research problems and demonstrate the values of particular theoretical or methodological approaches. Titles include well-focused, edited collections as well as works by individual authors. The series is open to all subject areas, geographical regions, and theoretical modes.

# CONTENTS

# TABLES

# FIGURES

# ACKNOWLEDGMENTS

In the summer of 1976 I took a break from archaeological fieldwork in western Iran to help map a small village on the edge of the desert in northeastern Iran. During that summer and the two that followed, the map grew to become a full-fledged study of rural settlement and society in an arid land setting. This book is the result of that study.

My research, funded in part by the UNESCO Secretariat (Paris) as part of its MAB (Man and the Biosphere) Project 11, Integrated Ecological Studies on Human Settlements, was carried out under the aegis of the Iranian Department of the Environment. It had the special advantage of being part of the Turan Programme for Ecological Research and Management in and around the Iranian Deserts. Brian Spooner, as director of the program, organized and orchestrated this complicated multidisciplinary project and encouraged the many publications that have come out of it. By working in cooperation with the other natural and social scientists in the program, I profited from a range of ecological and cultural information not often available within a single region in Near Eastern research. Of particular pertinence was the published and unpublished work of Brian Spooner (especially on the history and cultural ecology of the area), Siegmar Breckle and Helmut Freitag (on the flora), Brian O'Regan (on the fauna), Christopher Hamlin (on monitoring land use through remote sensing), Endre Nyerges (on the ecology of domesticated animals in traditional pastoral systems), Robin Dennell (on the history and prehistory of land use in Tauran), and most especially Mary Martin (on village-based pastoral-agricultural technologies and adaptive strategies). She knows how indebted I am to her for sharing her data, ideas, and friendship with me both in the field and here at home. I hope that I have represented this debt properly within the text itself. William Remson surveyed the village in 1976 and provided the essential outline map on which all further mapping was based.

I am most grateful to Robert Dyson and Brian Spooner for their guidance throughout the entire process that resulted eventually in this book. Richard Zettler, Richard Blanton, and Mary Martin read and made prerevision comments on all or most of the manuscript, as did Carol Kramer, who deserves special thanks not only for providing intellectual stimulation and scholarly information throughout but even more for her unfailing encouragement and friendship. Catherine Cameron, Stuart Fleming, Vincent Pigott, Holly Pittman, and Michael Schiffer made helpful comments on earlier ideas and analyses that eventually found their way into the text. I heartily thank them all for their aid. In addition to the above, Judith Berman, Betty Starr Cummin, Eija Paunila, Bruce Pearson, Gregory Possehl, Jennifer Quick, and Irene Winter, each in a different way, provided just the right kind of support at one or another critical point in the research and writing. Joanne S. Ainsworth edited the final text with skill and grace. And finally, much love and thanks go to my son, Joe, for his tolerance of the repeated absences and distractions of field research.

Writing acknowledgments brings back vivid memories of the field. Among fieldworkers must also be counted the men, women, and children of Baghestan, whose participation in the project included every conceivable task, from keeping weather records to providing our daily bread. Their appearance here as coded household numbers hardly conveys their human qualities as lively, various individuals; nor do the numbers show the unceasing hospitality and cooperation on which we were so dependent. We will always be grateful to them.

# CHAPTER I

# INTRODUCTION

This is a book about the spatial organization of a rural area in northeastern Iran. In it I address problems in the relationships between the material and the sociocultural dimensions of human settlement in a group of small agricultural and pastoral villages in Khar o Tauran, a village district (*dehestān*) on the edge of the great central desert of the Iranian Plateau. I document and explore in considerable detail the processes by which the shape of settlement is tied to the shape of society in this particular area. My approach to the subject matter is ethnoarchaeological, and my primary goal is to assess assumptions and inferences common in the archaeological literature and to propose new ones.

The archaeological record is a material one, composed of tangible artifacts and other kinds of intended and unintended alterations of the physical world. All these material objects and manifestations are of course located in space, and the spatial distributions, patternings, and relationships of a society's remains are among the best kinds of data archaeologists have.

Archaeologists have long used spatial order within sites to discover depositional sequences and associations and to establish chronological relationships. Spatial information has generated numerous hypotheses and interpretations about settlement and settlement patterns, both within and among sites. Reviews of settlement or survey archaeology, such as Chang 1968 and 1972, Crumley 1979, Evans and Gould 1982, and Parsons 1972, show that these endeavors have been largely behavioral and rest on the assumption that spatial behavior correlates with other kinds of

I

behavior, including social behavior. Behavioral approaches are useful because they involve statements about relationships between spatial organization (as found in the material archaeological record, for example) and social organization.

To the extent that archaeology is concerned with material culture as evidence for, rather than as relics from, the past (Wylie 1985), it has never been a freestanding academic discipline. In attempting to understand past societies, archaeologists work within many other disciplines, especially history, geography, and social anthropology. Historians, geographers, and social anthropologists generally have more complete and accessible bodies of data at their command than do archaeologists (in the narrow sense). Contemporary societies usually provide the material for developing and assessing theoretical propositions in these fields.

The archaeologist who looks for analogies or inspiration in existing ethnographic studies of contemporary societies, however, may run against the problem that the material side of the evidence is often missing. At a regional level, spatial studies in sociocultural anthropology frequently parallel the work of archaeologists (Smith 1976 has many good examples) and report and make use of data that could be reported and used by archaeologists. At a community level, however, spatial or architectural studies in sociocultural anthropology have been mostly cognitive in their approach and give priority to the conceptualization, perception, and symbolism of space rather than to the adaptive and social organizational problems (and their material correlates) that interest many archaeologists.[1] Or they may approach spatial behavior as a form of communication, which again does not require the kind of detailed material information that archaeologists routinely analyze. It is not always explicit in these studies whether and how ways of thinking about space and architecture are realized in material form. And whatever their final interpretive goals may be, archaeologists must be able to base their arguments on the physically recoverable characteristics of the societies they study. There is no intrinsic reason why those in other disciplines should feel the same need. Archaeologists who have undertaken research to remedy this lack of existing studies in other disciplines, whether they do it in the library, laboratory, or field, are usually referred to as ethnoarchaeologists.

Archaeologists who concentrate on the Near East have produced good sets of survey data and regional studies; they also have a long tradition of plentiful architectural information from stratified contexts. Yet very little ethnographic information at a larger-than-village scale has been collected and analyzed in the Near East (or anywhere else for that matter).[2] Much of what is known at a regional scale depends on the work of geographers or national census surveys and statistics. And at the village scale, in spite of the number of village ethnographies in the Near East, no more than a handful of detailed village plans have been published, and only two of these (Kramer 1982b and Watson 1979) show ownership of individual structures household by household.[3]

Both of these published plans are the product of explicitly ethnoarchaeological research, which now has a respectable portfolio in the Near East. In Iran, however, this research has been restricted to the western and southwestern parts (for example, Digard 1975, Edelberg 1966/67, Hole 1979, Jacobs 1979, Kramer 1982b, Rouholamini 1973, Watson 1979), which is not surprising, since much important archaeological research has been done in that area.

Kramer and Watson's pioneering studies are especially relevant to the work presented here, both for what they have in common with it and for the ways in which they differ from it. Iran is ethnically, religiously, socially, and geographically a heterogeneous country.[4] At the time of the agricultural census carried out by the government of Iran in 1973, for example, there were 59,000 villages in Iran, with an average size of 51 households each. About half of the villages had between 10 and 100 households (Ashraf 1983). Given these numbers, and Iran's diversity, it was not difficult to find a place and a theme that both extended and offered a contrast to the work done by Kramer and Watson. Aliabad, the village Kramer studied, and Hasanabad, the village Watson studied most intensely, share with Khar o Tauran (and most of the villages of the Iranian Plateau and its fringes) their small size, an agricultural and pastoral adaptation, and a Muslim, Iranian cultural background. They also share a dry environment of winter rain and summer drought. Yet they differ in several important ways. Whereas Khar o Tauran is Persian ethnically and linguistically, Aliabad and Hasanabad are Kurdish and Laki, respectively (although Hasanabadis often refer to themselves as Kurds).

Khar o Tauran is more distant from urban centers than either of the other two. It lies in the sparsely settled, semiarid steppe of the Iranian Plateau rather than in the more densely occupied, wetter hills of the Zagros. It is an area of small, independent landholders rather than (at least until the redistributions under land reform) of large, absentee landlords as in Aliabad and Hasanabad. A closer look at the spatial, architectural, social, and economic differences among these villages will be found in the chapters that follow.

## THE STUDY AREA

Khar o Tauran, the village district where this study took place, lies in the province of Semnan in northeastern Iran (Figure 1). Within Khar o Tauran, my research focused on a group of villages on the Tauran Plain (Figure 2) and in particular on Baghestan, one of the thirteen villages on the plain.[5] The Tauran Plain is roughly 120 square kilometers in area. The nearest towns are Sabzevar (population 42,000 according to the 1966 census), economic center for the area, and Shahrud (population 31,000 in 1966), the formal administrative center. Both are far enough away from the Tauran Plain (100 to 150 kilometers by dirt road and track) that this distance is more or less the same for all the settlements. A sand sea lies to the north of the plain, and a short mountain range separates the plain from Iran's central salt desert to the south. The elevation of the area is about 1,300 meters above sea level. The region can be characterized as arid; mean annual rainfall is less than 150 millimeters and is extremely variable from year to year. Thus, the villagers must cope with a climate that is not only dry but subject to wide short-term fluctuations.

Martin describes these communities as "fully embedded in a cash economy but with production for local needs" (1987, 164n1). Some rain-fed farming with the aid of catchment dams and terraces is practiced, but settlements are dependent on irrigation from qanāts (artificial underground channels) and springs for most of their water. Wheat, barley, melons, onions, tomatoes, and grapes are the main crops grown for local consumption; cotton and tobacco are the main cash crops. The area is heavily pastoral as well. Nearly all villagers have some sheep and goats,

Figure 1. Location of Khar o Tauran in Iran.

and many have flocks so large that in the summer, when the animals produce milk, they must take them to stations at some distance from their home villages to secure enough pasture for the flocks and firewood to process the milk.

Mechanization, with its resultant improvement in communications and extension of area under cultivation, has just begun. Threshing and a certain amount of plowing are done by tractors hired by the villagers from around the city of Sabzevar; some villagers own motorcycles, and a locally owned pickup truck and a bus from Sabzevar make trips at irregular intervals to and from the city in good weather. Nevertheless, Tauran remains relatively isolated and its way of life essentially traditional.

There are thirteen permanent settlements on the plain, and several

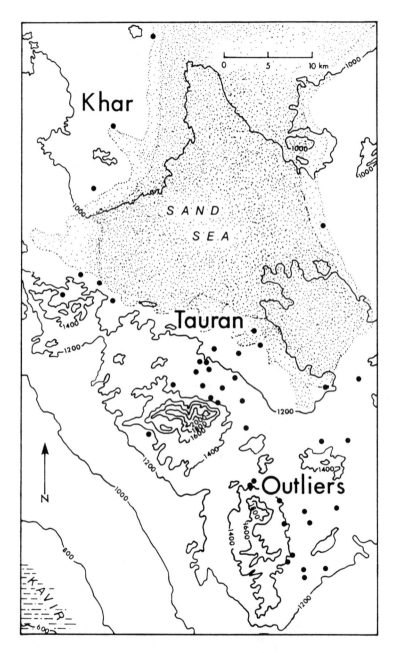

Figure 2. The three groups of settlements that make up Khar o Tauran. Dots represent villages and include some that were abandoned before 1976.

summer milking stations. The villages vary in size from less than thirty to about 250 persons; milking stations are occupied by the members of one or two households, who live the rest of the year in the villages. Land is owned by the villagers themselves, typically in small holdings of less than a hectare, fragmented into even smaller plots. Both agricultural fields and pasture are in short supply (Martin 1980a, 33–34). In spite of the sparseness of settlement, the area is in fact hard put to support its current residents, let alone any increase in numbers.

The resident population speaks Persian. The people are not tribally organized, but shallow kin groups do exist. The most common household unit is the nuclear family, often extended by related, unmarried adults. As Shi'i Muslims, most residents observe the standard requirements of the faith.

Factors external to and beyond the control of the villagers themselves have always been important elements in the social environment. Variations in outside investment, markets, caravan routes, taxation, and security have alternately drawn Tauran to and cut it off from the outside world. These exogenous factors have probably been significant for thousands of years and should figure in any discussion of either short- term or long-term adaptations on the plain.

It must be emphasized, however, that Tauran is only relatively isolated. The central government has established and maintained a strong presence in the area since the 1950s. Many decisions (and their enforcement) that used to be in the hands of local residents are now out of their control. Rangeland and water sources were nationalized, village territories reduced, and restrictions imposed on dry farming, charcoal burning, and firewood collection (Martin 1982b, 167–168).

Yet even though Tauran, like other areas in the Near East, is part of a greater, complex society in the process of becoming industrialized, certain aspects of this particular area made it an especially good prospect for ethnoarchaeological research. It has remained relatively isolated and freer from urban and Western influence than many other parts of Iran. At the time of the fieldwork, no village on the plain had piped water, electricity, or tube wells. Continuities of land ownership were not disrupted during the land reform of the 1960s and 1970s, since a landlord system was never a prominent feature in this area. Many features of the environment and the pastoral-agricultural technology appear to have been part of Near Eastern settlements for at least 8,000 years.

The architectural characteristics of these rural settlements might also be called traditional in the sense that they do not depend on industrial materials or technologies. Although decorative or superficial elements such as glass windows and metal hinges may be purchased, structures are still built effectively of packed mud, mud brick, and other local materials. House construction, a central interest in this study, is in many cases designed and undertaken by the owner himself, with specialists called in only for the roofing. The scale of settlement, locally and regionally, also has a considerable tradition; Neolithic villages around the world, for example, seem to have fallen into this size range of 100 to 150 inhabitants (Johnson 1977, 490–91).

It may be customary in the Near East to choose for ethnoarchaeological research villages that are as "traditional" as possible.[6] But it is not in fact possible to find a village that shares a physical and social environment, a technology, and a demography with a medieval Islamic village, let alone a prehistoric one. The utility of material presented here must be evaluated anew for each case at hand according to the questions and context of a particular theoretical interest or archaeological program.

## THE FIELDWORK

Given the construction of the research design, any one of the villages on the plain, excepting perhaps the smallest, would have been an appropriate choice for study. Because Baghestan had already been chosen as a reference settlement for the Turan Programme, I made my base there.[7] During the three summers of 1976–78, I lived in a compound rented from one of the village households, shared at times with other members of the Turan team. The fieldwork was carried out without an interpreter; I had studied Persian at the University of Pennsylvania (although I was still not prepared for the idiosyncrasies of Taurani dialect) and had previously spent two archaeological field seasons with the Royal Ontario Museum's Project in Kurdistan, directed by Louis D. Levine.

Although most of the data were collected from the village of Baghestan, I did visit at least briefly every village on the Tauran Plain and a number of villages and summer stations in the rest of Khar o Tauran. I also visited abandoned villages and archaeological sites and walked several transects across the plain to observe evidence of past occupation and to gain some idea of the history of settlement in the area.

In addition to the field data recorded by myself and others of the program, what little documentary material applies to the area in the form of travelers' reports, medieval geographies and histories, aerial photographs, maps, censuses, and other kinds of statistical reports has also been consulted.[8]

I have not used personal or family names in the book. Households are coded by number, and family names are simply Family A, B, or C (most of the households share one of three surnames). All the men I asked gave (rather enthusiastic) permission to publish their real names, although both men and women said women's first names could not be used. In view of the problematic nature of "informed consent," I decided not to use real names. Besides, I found no compelling reason to use names rather than numbers in a book such as this. The repetitious nature of many of the names would surely confuse the reader. I chose number and letter codes rather than pseudonyms because it seemed to me less intrusive than renaming people whose names are so much a part of their identity.

Baghestan has about 150 residents. There are advantages and disadvantages to working in such a small village. All fieldwork, of course, involves sampling, whether consciously or not, and all fieldwork is done within a time constraint, whether self-imposed or not. Often, because of such constraint, a sample must be made to stand for the whole. In this case, because of the small size, I found it was possible in much of my work to collect data on every house and every household. On the other hand, the small size meant that some important events did not occur during the three seasons of observation. I never saw a marriage, a funeral, or a house completely constructed or dismantled. What I missed in the way of a full cycle of social and economic activity by not being present in the winter, I gained in comparative detail by being there during three sequential summers. The work of others, particularly that of Mary Martin, who did observe holidays, funerals, and seasonal change throughout Khar o Tauran, has been invaluable in filling in the missing pieces.

Fieldwork was stopped in 1978, one season short of completion, by the Iranian Revolution. Although that fourth season would have brought closure to some of the questions being pursued, increased the amount of detail, and provided better comparative information from neighboring villages, it would not, I feel, have substantially altered the direction or conclusions of the final product.

## ORGANIZATION OF THE BOOK

The chapters that follow are organized to progress from the general to the specific both spatially and analytically. Thus the discussion proceeds from region and "study area" to single village settlement and individual households and from the natural and social environments to the particular material expressions of interaction and organization.

Chapter 2 is an introduction to the natural environment, the climate, topography and hydrology, and vegetation and fauna of Khar o Tauran. All of these elements, directly or indirectly, affect the shape of settlement. In a sense, the whole area is a site; all of it has been affected by human settlement and activities. I discuss the biological and physical characteristics of four topographic zones—mountains, plains, sand sea, and *kavir* (playa)—plus the special environment of settlement in their roles as context, natural resource, and hazard to be accounted for in the organization of life and livelihood in Khar o Tauran.

Agriculture, pastoralism, fuel production, building construction, and historically known activities such as smelting and charcoal burning all depend either directly or indirectly upon the local environment. In Chapter 3 I present technological strategies, tools of production, the organization of production, and, generally, the ways in which the villagers of Khar o Tauran manipulate particular resources in order to secure a livelihood. I consider ways by which "off-site" subsistence activities might be recognized and recovered archaeologically in this kind of natural and social environment.

In Chapter 4 I take up the shape and nature of settlements in Khar o Tauran—the kinds of activities that take place within them, their distribution across the landscape, and their relationship to the physical environment and to one another. I then focus on the environmental, social, and historical factors that affect locational and occupational stability and instability in this area.

Chapter 5 contains descriptions of village layouts in this area and analyses of the village of Baghestan as workplace, shelter, social setting, and cosmological setting. I show how historical, environmental, social, and cultural factors shape the final compromise that is the physical entity of the village today.

In Chapter 6 I look closely at the built environment of the village: the materials and techniques of construction, and the arrangements of activities and objects within structures. Architectural variation is explored through its relationship to the social, demographic, and economic spheres of the village.

Then, in Chapter 7, the village is considered as the archaeological site it will become. I draw upon the processes that shape and maintain a village to show how the social processes that lie behind physical ones determine the form an archaeological deposit takes. Processes of site formation are as much a product of technology, settlement density and stability, and the life cycle of the built environment as they are of natural physical laws.

In the final chapter I pull together the findings of previous chapters to test, at three different scales of analysis, the "fit" between selected spatial and social aspects of settlement. I discuss methodological and interpretive implications of the ways in which space is used at different scales of settlement, from rooms and activities to houses and households to the entire village and its fields. These three kinds of "fit" were chosen to match those of current interest in the ethnoarchaeological and archaeological literature. They recapitulate the approach taken in this book and make the results relevant to students of settlement in other parts of the world.

# CHAPTER 2

# THE NATURAL ENVIRONMENT

The *dehestān* of Khar o Tauran is an elongated area oriented slightly north-northwest by south-southeast at the eastern border of Semnan Province, Iran. Its geographical center lies at about latitude 35°35' north, longitude 56°45' east. Raised 800 to 2,300 meters above sea level, it comprises some 3,300 square kilometers of mountains, piedmont, seasonal rivers and wadis, moving and stable sands, barren playa, and several areas of alluvial fans and plains that support clusters of small mud brick villages. This surrounding environment is both natural and man-made. Hardly any part, no matter how inaccessible, has not felt the effect of human occupancy, although the degree of alteration by human activity varies dramatically according to the type and intensity of use. One of the tasks of the Turan Programme was to assess in what ways and for what reasons the environment, especially the vegetation and landforms, has been deflected from its natural condition and processes.[1]

In this chapter, I present the environment as it is, with little reference to how it came about. I concentrate on natural resources and other factors that determine or otherwise influence the location of sites and the distribution of population in Khar o Tauran. Although four topographic zones—mountains, plains, sand sea, and *kavir*—represent the distinct natural and cultural habitats of the area, I will make finer divisions where relevant.

## CLIMATE

Climate affects settlement both directly and indirectly. Its direct effects are felt in the need for shelter from the elements—whether achieved by location and orientation of settlements and activities or by architectural or structural means. Indirectly, climate affects settlement through its interaction with the rest of the natural environment. In this case, the effects of climate on water systems and vegetation are the most important. Khar o Tauran's most outstanding climatic feature in this respect is its aridity; it receives only 100 to 200 millimeters of precipitation per year. Under virtually any conditions, this amount is too low for reliable dry farming, although it is adequate for a substantial pastoral economy.

All of the Iranian Plateau lies within a rain shadow cast by the mountains that embrace it to the west and north, the direction from which low pressure, precipitation-bearing weather systems arrive. The climate on the plateau is temperate to hot, semiarid to arid, and Mediterranean in its seasonality (winter precipitation and summer drought). The nature of the climate on the plateau is of course relevant to the availability and kinds of resources, to the ways those resources are exploited, and to the physical comfort and health of those who exploit them.

Arid land ecosystems such as this have been called "water-controlled" (Noy-Meir 1973, 26). Annual rainfall statistics frequently are used to characterize the degree of aridity within a region, but where water availability to local populations is at issue, mean annual rainfall figures tell us little about conditions as they are experienced and how those conditions fluctuate. Temperatures, topography, soils, soil radiation, ground cover, and many other factors affect where the water goes after it falls to the ground. Ideally, local, long-term measurements of these factors are needed to characterize the climatic conditions found in Khar o Tauran. Unfortunately, such ideal statistics exist for relatively few parts of the world, and rural Iran is not one of them. By any measure, however, the study area experiences a deficit of water every year. The villagers must manage water to ensure adequate amounts for both crops and livestock. The ways in which water is managed will be described below.

The evidence for local precipitation, temperature, and climatic conditions in Khar o Tauran comes from recent short-term and intermittent observations made by members of the Turan Programme, in conjunction with extrapolations based on information from the nearest recording stations that had relatively complete runs of data—Semnan, Shahrud, Sabzevar, and Tabas. The nearest of the stations is more than 125 kilometers from the Tauran Plain.

The following comments apply primarily to Khar o Tauran, and specifically to the Tauran Plain, where most of my own observations were made. Microclimatic differences exist on the plain, however, and are recognized by both local villagers and researchers. Differences between the plain and other areas within the district are even more pronounced.

Precipitation in Khar o Tauran is scanty, variable, and seasonal. Published maps of annual precipitation in Iran show the 100-millimeter isohyet passing through the area, with increasingly moist conditions found to the north (the 200-millimeter isohyet follows the foot of the Kopet-Dag range) and increasingly dry conditions to the south, where the central salt *kavir* begins. Nearly all the precipitation falls between November and May. Although 100 millimeters per year is probably a good estimate on the average, year-to-year variation is likely to range between 50 and 300 millimeters and can take the form of sprinkles, steady drizzle, heavy downpours, thunderstorms, snow, or hail. Comparisons for the cities of Semnan, Shahrud, Sabzevar, and Tabas appear in Table 1.

A rain gauge set up at Baghestan by members of the Turan Programme

TABLE 1. TEMPERATURE AND PRECIPITATION FOR SELECTED TOWNS OF THE IRANIAN PLATEAU, 1961–73

| Station | Altitude (m) | Mean maximum temp. (°C) | Mean minimum temp. (°C) | Absolute maximum temp. (°C) | Absolute minimum temp. (°C) | Mean annual temp. (°C) | No. of frost days | Precipitation (mm) |
|---|---|---|---|---|---|---|---|---|
| Sabzevar | 944 | 23.9 | 9.0 | 44.5 | −19.8 | 16.4 | 74.0 | 160 |
| Semnan | 1138 | 24.3 | 11.0 | 44.5 | −12.5 | 17.7 | 42.9 | 129 |
| Shahrud | 1366 | 20.9 | 7.4 | 40.0 | −14.0 | 14.2 | 84.7 | 149 |
| Tabas | 691 | 29.1 | 12.8 | 48.2 | −9.3 | 20.9 | 38.1 | 73 |

*Source:* Iran 1973b.

recorded precipitation during all of 1976 and from October 1977 to May 1978. The latter period included the entire rainy season for that year. In 1976, the gauge recorded 82 millimeters of rain; it fell on a total of eighteen days spread from January to November. During 1977–78, 96 millimeters fell in twenty-five separate events, ranging from two to seven events per month. Some events lasted for more than twenty-four hours, and one covered a period of two and a half days. Three were snowfalls. The mean amount of rain that fell during any one period was 3.8 millimeters, and the range was from a barely measurable 0.4 to 8.8 millimeters (which fell in six hours). Although no agriculturally useful rain falls out of season, each summer there was a day or two of light rain. In July 1977 a steady downpour, lasting several hours, caused flooding in the wadis and dampened but did not damage the uncovered grain harvest on the threshing floors.

Residents claimed that both years were average ones. The figures may seem somewhat low for "average" years, given the data presented in Table 1 and the fact that local dry farming was undertaken during those years. It should be remembered, however, that the timing of rain is at least as important as the amount. Both affect local perceptions, agricultural decisions, and crop yields (see Martin 1982b).

Temperature, the only other variable actually measured during the period of field research, was measured over periods too brief and interrupted for detailed conclusions to be drawn. Compared with the heat of southern Khuzistan or chill of the Alborz Mountains, Khar o Tauran is temperate in climate, neither unbearably hot in summer nor bitterly cold in winter. Table 1 shows mean and absolute temperatures for Shahrud, Semnan, Sabzevar, and the desert oasis of Tabas. By altitude alone, Khar o Tauran's temperature should fall between the piedmont towns (Shahrud, Semnan, and Sabzevar) and Tabas, but differences in exposure to the elements and in topography can skew relationships between altitude and climate. Semnan, for example, lies in a protected basin, so even though it is 200 meters higher than Sabzevar, it is perceptibly warmer.

A mean annual temperature of about 15 degrees centigrade probably characterizes the Tauran Plain accurately; the southern plains and the sand desert are much hotter, and mountain heights in the area much cooler. Good records are available for the summer months of 1976, 1977, and 1978.[2] The absolute high during these months was 40 degrees centigrade;

the absolute low, 14 degrees centigrade. Less can be said about the winter months. January and February are said to be the coldest months, and in 1976, temperatures as low as -8 and -11 degrees centigrade were recorded. Differences in temperature between day and night are probably on the order of 13 to 18 degrees centigrade in the summer and less than 10 degrees centigrade in winter.

No local data are available on relative humidity. See Table 1 again for conditions in Semnan, Shahrud, Sabzevar, and Tabas.

Another weather factor especially significant to human settlement is wind. The direction and speed of the local winds vary according to the time of day, the season, and atmospheric conditions. In addition to the continental-scale movement of large air masses, the large body of sand to the north and the mountains to the south of the Tauran Plain influence local air movements by alternately absorbing and radiating solar heat. The prevailing winds are from the north and northwest. The alignment of fossil sand dunes on aerial photographs (Iran 1956) confirms the antiquity of this wind pattern.

The summer wind typically blows gently from the south (when it is called the *bād-e qebla,* or south wind) through the southeast and east (the *bād-e ruz,* or wind of the day) beginning at dusk through the following morning. At noon it begins to shift, and updrafts and dust devils (*chehel bād,* or forty winds) swirl across the ground and through courtyards. By two o'clock in the afternoon the wind settles to a strong steady northwesterly breeze (*bād-e shomāl,* or north wind, and *bād-e yeilāq,* or wind of the high pasture) that often reaches enough force to make it difficult to walk. At dusk it drops, shifts again, and the cycle repeats itself.

In winter the morning wind also blows from the south and east, but the afternoon and evening winds are likely to be replaced by rainy westerlies (*bād-e siāh,* or black winds) that may continue for several days. Winter winds generally are said to be stronger than summer winds.

Dust-filled windstorms (*bād-e tufān,* or storm winds) occur mainly in the dry season: the drier the weather the more likely they are, according to local accounts. They resemble rainless thunderstorms; in fact lightning and thunder sometimes appear over the *kavir.* Windstorms approach from the west or southwest and move quickly eastward across the plain, usually lasting only a few hours, although sometimes they blow all through the night. They appear to be rather local in nature. Highly visible because of the quantity of yellow dust they carry, they can frequently be seen passing several kilometers away, missing Baghestan but engulfing villages at the edge of the sand sea. In August and September 1978 I counted eight wind-storms during a period of five weeks in Baghestan; a number of others passed in the distance. All but one were in the late afternoon, evening, or night. After they pass, the air is especially clear, and mountains ordinarily hidden by haze stand out on the horizon. The temperature usually drops dramatically, bringing a brief respite from the summer heat.

## TOPOGRAPHY AND HYDROLOGY

The four very different topographic zones of Khar o Tauran—mountains, plains, sand sea, and *kavir*—provide mineral resources and life-sustaining water. In combination with the climate, they support the vegetation and wildlife of the biological environment and the domestic crops and animals of the local economy. Moreover the shape of the terrain has in turn shaped communications within the area and to the outside world. It also shapes settlement, which responds in various ways to situations of protection from and exposure to the elements.[3]

### Geological Situation of Turan

The greater Turan area lies in the Alborz foredeep, a tectonically active area whose surface rocks are mostly of Paleocene origin (Harrison 1968).[4] Far to the north lies the Kopet-Dag Range of the Alborz mountains; a sunken basin (the Mazinan, or Sabzevar, Kavir) and a sea of sand inter-vene between the main east-west route along the piedmont at the base of the range and the inhabited plains of Khar o Tauran. A salt river that drains the kavir marks the western edge of the area; an arm of Iran's great central salt desert, Dasht-e Kavir, effectively cuts off communication directly southward; and a vast stretch of broken terrain unmarked by permanent settlement reaches eastward toward the towns of Doruna and Kashmar and southward toward the city of Tabas. Routes of communica-tion, both historically and at the present time run east-west at the south of the sand sea and north-south on either side of the sand; they depend on both terrain and service settlements for their alignment.

## The Mountains

Broken country and mountains run in a diagonal belt through the lower center of Khar o Tauran (Figure 2). Foothills begin at an altitude of about 1,300 meters and rise to peaks of 1,600 meters and more. The highest points are at 2,000 to 2,300 meters. The western part of the range is mostly limestone, although the lower ridges and outcroppings are frequently conglomerate or shale. In the southeast, toward Asbkeshan, the geology becomes more complex, and a variety of minerals (copper ores, iron oxides, iron pyrites) and rock types (igneous and metamorphic) appear. Stone is used to a minor extent in construction (especially in areas where water and silt for mud bricks are scarce) and for tools such as pounders, querns, and mortars. Copper ores have a history of economic exploitation but are no longer mined or smelted. As of the late 1970s, however, no one had studied the geomorphology or petrology of these ranges.

Snow appears on the peaks of Peighambar, the mountain that rises on the southeast border of Tauran, as early as November, where it remains long after it disappears from the plain. The accumulation, however, is neither deep enough nor persistent enough to support perennial runoff from melting snow. Permanent springs from crevices in the heights are common. On Peighambar these occur at about 1,400 to 1,600 meters and can undoubtedly be found even higher. Although this mountain spring water is in several cases abundant enough to irrigate several hectares of fields and support small settlements, in every case the water disappears through percolation and evaporation without reaching much lower than the alluvial fans. These springs are important for vegetation, animal life—both wild and domestic—and for agriculture and ritual life as well.

## The Plains

Between the mountains and below the alluvial fans lie a series of plains, sloping from the rolling country of the lower outwash fans down to the edge of salt flats or sand sea. The largest of these is the Tauran Plain. A narrow tongue of sand separates this central plain from that of the villages of Hojjaj and Talkhab, from which an extension narrows around between the hills to the south, eventually opening out onto the *kavir*. Another corridor opens out onto the Asbkeshan Plain at the most southeastern corner of the area. On the other side of the Tauran Plain, a corridor leads north and west to the plains of Ahmadabad and Rezabad, blocked by the Salt River on the western border of Khar o Tauran and the Sabzevar Kavir on the northern border.

Lying at about 1,200 to 1,400 meters in altitude, the upper plains and lower alluvial fans are dissected or deeply undulating, with surfaces of stone and gravel. Because of the soil's absorbent qualities, the lower alluvial fans are the prime area for replenishing ground water from rainfall. Below them, at altitudes of about 800 meters to 1,300 meters, the slopes become more gentle, and the surface soil becomes finer and more saline, although it is still coarser than the lowest reaches. At the southern side of the area, the lowest slopes of the plains gradually merge with the clay and salt flats of the *kavir*—formations that are highly saline, finely textured, and frequently crusted with salt. The *kavir* in this region begins at altitudes of about 700 to 900 meters above sea level. In other parts of Khar o Tauran, sand of unknown depth covers the lower plains, beginning at altitudes of about 1,100 meters.

In many of these plains areas, deposits of ceramic-quality light green clay are found—apparently derived from the many low shaley hills nearby. Deposits of gypsum-rich earth are also common. The green clay (*gel-e sabz*) is likely to have been the clay used in a local pottery-making industry attested to by scatters of overfired sherds and wasters that mark kiln sites of earlier periods. This clay is still used today to make the hard center cores of bread ovens. According to one villager, Baghestan is the only source on the plain for this clay and people come from far and wide to dig it, at no cost. Both green clay and gypsum are used for sealing and finishing walls. Gypsum plaster also waterproofs animal feed bins.

In the southeastern part of the area, there are several shallow copper mines, along with deposits of iron oxide, iron pyrites, and other minerals. In the past both copper and the minerals were mined and processed locally.

As noted above, runoff streams fed by mountain springs disappear without providing water for the villages below on the plains. The wadi beds down on the plains themselves fill with seasonal and isolated storms but tend to dry up between rains. Some of the larger and lower beds, such as those of the Dahana and Hojjaj rivers, hold water in the middle of the summer—a result of local springs or seepage rather than distant runoff. Only the Kal-e Shur (Salt River), one of the main rivers that empty into the Great Kavir from Iran's surrounding highlands, runs perennially, supplied ultimately by sources as distant as the hills west of Sabzevar, but its water is far too saline to be drinkable either by people or domestic animals. It is therefore also too saline for crops, which have an even lower tolerance for salt than do people and animals. In May 1933 Alphons Gabriel, a botonist studying the deserts of Iran, measured its salinity to be 12 percent and its temperature 25 degrees centigrade, about 9 degrees cooler than the air temperature (1935, 120).

Springs also arise on the plains and the *kavir,* although they are smaller and less spectacular than the splashing waters of the rocky mountain sources. There are only a few on the Tauran Plain.

The most significant water sources in the area are the artificial ones in Iran called *qanāts* (see English 1966; Goblot 1979; Lambton 1953; Lambton 1969; McLachlan 1988; Sajjadi 1982; Spooner 1983). Subterranean, man-made channels that bring underground water to the surface, *qanāts* are the main source for irrigation, watering animals, and supplying domestic needs in Khar o Tauran. How a *qanāt* works is shown in Figure 3. The outlets look very much like natural springs. In fact, many "springs" on the plain are probably leaks from breaks in old *qanāt* systems.

Like springs, *qanāts* depend on precipitation and runoff for recharge. The water level in subterranean aquifers is therefore susceptible to seasonal and year-to-year variations, although the ground's ability to store the water lowers the amount of the variation (see Hartl 1979). The quality of *qanāt* water and the reliability of flow varies by location too; those lowest on the plain are said to maintain their flow better than those higher up because they have a greater catchment for capturing rain and runoff. On the other hand, these lower systems tend to be more saline, although not so saline as wells in the same vicinity. Light salinity is sometimes praised, however, on the grounds that although it is not so good for drinking straight, it makes better tea.

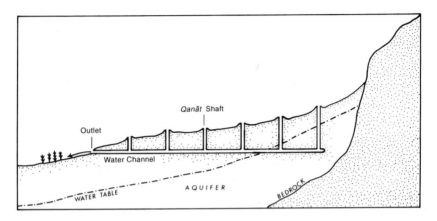

Figure 3. Diagram of a *qanāt* (not to scale).

Wells require lifting mechanisms; *qanāts,* being gravity flow systems, do not. Because of this, and because they tap distant ground water before it becomes overly saline and carry it down to areas where the local ground water is too saline to be usable, *qanāts* permit irrigation in areas that would otherwise be left unirrigated.

Although not used for irrigation in this area, wells are still an important adjunct to other water sources. They are simple affairs, with hand winches for winding up buckets on ropes. Without more efficient lifting techniques they are suitable only for domestic purposes or for watering livestock and not for irrigation, which requires great quantities of water. Wells can be dug only at lower altitudes, where the water table is high—as it is around Khar or at the edge of the sand sea. These wells frequently tap into collapsed *qanāt* systems.

### The Sand Sea

Fifteen hundred square kilometers of sand dominate the north-central part of Khar o Tauran—a deep sea of stable and shifting dunes some 50 kilometers long and 30 kilometers across from east to west. On aerial photographs (Iran 1956), the dunes of the southern part appear to be mostly of the transverse type, simple or reticulated and lying across the dominant north-northwest winds; occasionally they are drawn into long ridges and troughs running parallel to the wind direction. Here and there piled into deeper spits projecting onto the plains, a thin sand cover spreads away from the sea, especially to the south and east. On the west side of the sand sea the wind has shaped the bared silt into ridged forms called *yardangs* by geologists. On both the western and eastern margins, beds of reddish, consolidated sand have been exposed by wind erosion. These may be exposures of the Miocene sedimentary base from which the sand sea presumably has developed, blown during the Pleistocene out of the Sabzevar Kavir to the north and west (see Krinsley 1970). This sand sea, called the Sands of Mazinan by Bobek (1959), ranks fourth of the five largest dune fields in Iran.

Most of the sand sea lies at an altitude of between 900 and 1,200 meters, rising gradually toward the southeast. From the upper Tauran Plain, the southern dunes appear as a ridge on the horizon, over which rise the Parvand Mountains, 35 kilometers in the distance. Two major seasonal riverbeds channel through the sand sea, one (the Hajjaj) at the southern edge running first west and then north; the other (the Sabri) cuts in from the eastern edge of the sand and runs toward the north. Both drain into the Sabzevar Kavir, where they meet the larger Kal-e Shur as it turns south to drain into the Dasht-e Kavir, the playa that bounds the area on the south and forms an arm of the great central Iranian *kavir*. The two rivers swell periodically with winter rain but ordinarily are dry during the summer, although they may contain marshy seepage or even short stretches of water in an especially wet year. These wadis do not drain the sand sea—the sand itself does not shed water—but are part of a drainage system that extends back to the hills and mountains south and east of the sand sea. With origins so far away, flash floods constitute a serious hazard. Local people and even whole families have drowned when caught unaware in a wadi bed. The western side of the sand sea has a high water table; its poor drainage, frequent springs, and marshy areas make it impassible with the winter rains.

### The *Kavir*

The mountains and plains of the western part of the Iranian Plateau drain into a system of closed basins or *kavirs*. Properly speaking, a *kavir* consists of highly saline, fine grained soils and sediments, barren of plant and animal life. It contains a variety of surfaces—crusts, puffy extrusions, salt formations, and so forth. The term is often extended, however, to include less extreme states, especially those along the raised fringes of the playa proper, which do support a sometimes dense halophytic vegetation and the wildlife that may venture down to exploit it. Here the term is used in the stricter sense.

Two *kavirs* figure in the topography of Khar o Tauran at altitudes below 800 meters. The largest is an extension of the Dasht-e Kavir, which dominates the heart of the Iranian Plateau. Khar o Tauran stretches along its northern edge. The Sabzevar Kavir, a playa to the north of Khar and the sand sea, has been open since the end of the Pleistocene (Krinsley 1970); it drains via the Kal-e Shur into the larger Northeastern Basin. The two *kavirs* help mark the area's boundaries on the northern, western, and southern borders.

With the exception of some small patches of especially low land, Khar o Tauran itself contains no internally drained basins. The area is instead a raised system of mountains and plains that drain outward onto the two exterior playas by way of wadis and broad intermontane gullies. The largest of these wadis is the Kal-e Shur, one of the two main rivers that empty into the Great Kavir from Iran's surrounding highlands.

The *kavir* is poor in economic resources. Salt is the only product, albeit a vital one for food processing, especially for making cheese. Although lacking natural resources, these *kavirs* are important geomorphologically. They set the base level for the drainage systems in Khar o Tauran, and from perhaps the Pleistocene on they have supplied the sands that created and maintain the sand sea.

## VEGETATION

The local vegetation figures in nearly every sphere of village and pastoral life. All domesticated animals depend to a greater or lesser extent on the natural range. Wild fodder is collected and fed to domesticated animals within settlements; some of this is weeds (for example, *Medicago sativa*) pulled from between crops, but some is gathered out on the range itself (for example, *Salsola orientalis*). People gather wild plants for their families to eat as well, whether as seasonal delicacies (like some greens), as herbs for seasoning, or as basic subsistence in times of famine.

Until recently, when kerosene became available, all domestic fuel for cooking and heating depended on firewood and brush. Even today a substantial portion of fuel derives from woody vegetation (Horne 1982a and b).

Although very little wood is used in village houses, the support posts, roofs, and fences of human and animal shelters at pastoral stations are of wood and brush. Local plants fill many utilitarian household needs as well. They serve as cooling platforms, pot scourers, brooms, and fasteners for tying up loads on donkeys; they are made into small pieces of homemade equipment such as bird traps and adze handles. Most wooden tools, however, are made by specialists and bought in the city; these include necessities such as plows, spindles, and butter churn paddles. Ingredients for soap, tanning, chemicals, dyes, and probably a great many other materials used in a more self-sufficient past can all be extracted from local species.

The local vegetation also plays an important role in physical and spiritual health. Herbal medicines prepared from roots, leaves, flowers, or seeds of wild plants are widely used. As a deterrent to the evil eye, the seed pod of the wild rue (*Peganum harmala*) is a constant accompaniment to village activity, worked into decorative wall hangings, for example, or burned.

Local communities of vegetation are affected by a number of factors, including altitude, soil, exposure, and destruction or alteration through human activity. The availability of any particular species of vegetation for economic purposes also has a temporal dimension; it varies both seasonally and from year to year. Overall, the impression is of a shrubby rather than a grassy or forested landscape. In part this is to be expected in a desert and semidesert setting.It is also a result of the intensity of exploitation, which removes some species entirely from their preferred habitats, where they would reach maximum development, and cuts down others before they can reach their full height.[5]

## The Mountains

Although from a distance the hills and mountains look barren and rocky compared with the stable sands or the unoccupied plains, the high slopes and valleys of Khar o Tauran provide grazing and firewood over areas wide enough to complement types of land use in the lower regions. The vegetation on pediment and lower slopes (from about 1,300 meters up) consists of communities of *Artemisia herba alba–Ephedra intermedia–Amygdalus lycioides.* On higher slopes and peaks the common vegetation communities are either *Astragalus strobiligerus–Cousinia mesh-hedensis* or *Astragalus strobiligerus–Amygdalus,* with *Onobrychis cornuta* dominant on the very highest northern peaks of Peighambar.

## The Plains

The plains of Khar o Tauran run from altitudes of about 1,300 meters down to about 800 meters or so where they meet the *kavir* and salt marsh. The various vegetative communities vary from 5 to 40 percent in cover with community biomasses estimated to range generally between 1.0 and 6.0 tons (aboveground dry matter) per hectare. The higher reaches of the plains support mainly communities of *Salsola–Zygophyllum,* varying in composition according to the salt content and texture of the soil, which themselves vary with altitude.

Toward the *kavir* and the saltier drainages, the number of halophytic and chenopodal species increases, *Seidlitzia rosmarinus* communities become frequent, and stands of *Haloxylon aphyllum* are common. *Tamarix* communities dominate in wadis and gullies with permanently high water tables.

## The Sand Sea

It frequently comes as a surprise to those unfamiliar with arid landscapes that the stable dunes of a sand sea and the sandy surfaces of its margins are capable of supporting a luxuriant vegetation. Even in Khar o Tauran, where the vegetation is seriously degraded from its pristine state, the sands support a greater plant biomass than almost anywhere else in the area—perhaps as much as 8,000 kilograms per hectare, with a cover of about 40 percent. In remote areas of the sand or where afforestation has been undertaken, these figures rise even higher. A feathery forest of saxaul and grasses on sandy dunes is a beautiful sight, alive with gerbils, lizards, and birds.

Sand vegetation comprises mostly communities of *Stipagrostis–Calligonum*. On low fixed dunes, these communities are dominated by shrubby and herbaceous perennials such as *Stipagrostis pennata, Calligonum leucocladum, C. cf. comosum, Haloxylon persicum, Artemisia eriocarpa;* and by annuals, including *Agriophyllum minus, A. latifolium,* and *Euphorbia cheirolepis.*

Shifting sands support a much sparser vegetation (only up to 5 percent cover), dominated by species different from those that characterize stable dunes. These are *Stipagrostis karelinii, Smirnovia turkestanica,* and *Heliotropium acutiflorum.*

Psammophilic, or sand-loving, types of vegetation, have not been well studied in Iran. The community descriptions above are generalized from observations made at the fringes of the sand sea rather than deep in the interior. Still, they show a wealth of plant material—for supplying wood and for grazing—that justifies the long history of habitation of the margins of the sand sea. Plant communities in these combinations are found in Khar o Tauran only on the sands, although particular species are found on other types of soil as well. Conversely, some useful species common to other habitats (such as various *Salsola*) may also be found on sandy soils.

## The *Kavir* and Its Borders

The *kavir* itself is barren, but areas around brackish springs, seasonally wet watercourses, and the slightly higher fringes of the *kavir* support specialized types of halophilic plant communities able to exploit the extremely wet and salty conditions of such locations. Clay flats may have a cover of up to 90 percent, dominated by *Petrosimonia glauca* or *Cressa cretica,* among others. Salt marsh communities include *Seidlitzia rosmarinus, Halocnemum strobilaceum, Halostachys belangeriana,* and *Tamarix.*

## MAMMALS

In the past, hunting was an important pastime in Khar o Tauran. Animals were taken for food or other products, for sport, and to protect livestock. Hunting has been prohibited since 1975, when the Department of the Environment established the Turan Protected Area; the prohibition has continued under the aegis of the Turan Biosphere Reserve. There is now little except local memory to document the real economic significance of hunting in the more distant past. No matter how popular hunting may have been, or how necessary during hard times, it probably has been only of secondary dietary significance. For centuries, perhaps several thousand years, domestic animals have been the primary means of converting local wild vegetative resources into protein.[6]

### The Mountains

The more hilly and mountainous country in Khar o Tauran supports several species of wild game and their predators. The largest of these are wild sheep and goats. The Persian ibex, or wild goat (*Capra aegragrus*), prefers rocky cliffs and slopes, although it will sometimes descend to foothills and neighboring plains for food or water. Males are much larger than females and may weigh up to 90 kilograms. Based on the distributions described by Harrington (1977, 34, 52), the wild sheep of the area is presumably the Alborz red sheep (*Ovis ammon orientalis*) rather than the closely related Urial sheep (*O. ammon arkal*) found to the north.

Sheep are not as skilled at heights as ibex, and will run rather than climb to escape from predators. Consequently, their preferred habitat is rolling hills and slopes rather than the rocky cliffs and peaks of the ibex. When silhouetted at the top of a ridge, sheep are easily identified by the great outward sweep of their horns; trophy horns are sometimes installed on rooftops in the villages. Traditionally, both wild sheep and goats were in great demand for sport and food. A small amount of hunting continues, in spite of the prohibition on it.

Natural predators in the hills and mountains are the wolf (*Canis lupus*) and leopard (*Panthera pardus*). The wolf, especially, is a constant winter threat to domestic flocks. In northern Iran a large wolf may weigh as much as 70 kilograms (Harrington 1977, 34).

## The Plains

Large game animals of the plains and foothills of Khar o Tauran are the goitered gazelle (*Gazella subgutterosa*), the jebeer (*Gazella dorcas*), and the onager, or Persian wild ass (*Equus hemionus*). Both gazelles and jebeers are hunted and eaten in Iran, as is the onager, although its meat is *haram*, forbidden under Muslim law. The onager is also killed for the folk-medicinal properties of its oil. Once spread widely throughout the Iranian Plateau, it is now an endangered and protected species, restricted to a few wildlife preserves. The Turan Reserve contains one of the world's few remaining populations of this animal.

The goitered gazelle and the jebeer are more securely established at present, especially where they are protected, or where grazing by domestic flocks is controlled. Their main constraint is the encroachment of their territories from spreading human settlement and domestic flock grazing. Although frequently spotted in many parts of Turan, their population here is in fact sparse in relation to that of places such as the Kavir Protected Area to the west, where grazing by domestic animals has been forbidden for more than ten years.

These two kinds of gazelles are in more or less complementary distribution in the Turan Reserve. Goitered gazelles prefer the flat plains to the north of the mountains, especially those around Ahmadabad on the west of the sand sea and in the sparsely settled areas of the southeastern plains. Jebeer range south of the mountains onto the gravel fans leading down to the *kavir* and the broad gullies of the foothills; they sometimes even move down into the salt-tolerant vegetation of the *kavir* fringe.

Of the two, jebeer are smaller and more slender, averaging 17 kilograms in weight (up to 25 kilograms for large males). In some areas they form herds of 20 to 30 animals, although no more than 11 were ever seen together in the Turan Reserve, and 2 to 4 were most common. Goitered gazelles, on the other hand, are the largest of the several species of gazelle in Iran, averaging about 22 kilograms; some males are as heavy as 50 kilograms (Harrington 1977). They tend to form much larger herds than do jebeer (sometimes hundreds of animals), although, again, in the Turan Reserve groups larger than 7 have not been reported and average group size is only 1.8 (O'Regan 1977).

Onagers are larger animals than either of these gazelles; they stand as high as 140 centimeters at the shoulder, compared with 75 centimeters for goitered gazelles and 65 centimeters for jebeer. They eat more roughage than do gazelles, which are delicate feeders. In the Turan Reserve, onagers have been spotted on the plains both to the north and to the south of the mountains. In general they form herds of up to thirty animals, although these sometimes merge into groups of several hundred; details of their behavior in the area are not yet available, but according to local reports, their range shifts with the season and the time of day. Gazelles were also observed to shift their range: for example, jebeer will move into the foothills and springs in the middle of the day, and goitered gazelles will seek more secluded areas in the spring season when they drop their fawns.

Besides human predators and competition for range, these animals are also threatened by wild predators—hyenas (*Hyaena hyaena*), jackals (*Canus aureus*), wolves (*Canus lupus*), and cheetahs (*Acinonyx jubatus*), all of which come out on the plains to hunt. These predators are considered to be an economic menace, and many domestic animals are lost yearly, especially to wolves and jackals. In the winter, when wolves are in the area, not only must flocks be properly sheltered or penned, with shepherds in attendance, but watchdogs are essential to warn of their presence and attack them. Even so, stories are told of wolves who broke into winter sheepfolds and slaughtered dozens of animals before they could be stopped. Endre Nyerges informed me in conversation in 1977 that in the winter of 1976, thirty animals were lost to wolves at Sanjari.

Jackals, although milder natured and more of a nuisance than a danger, are actually more likely to approach or enter settlements. They are said to be fond of grapes. During my stay in 1977, jackals ran through a village courtyard and carried off two lambs. The yipping and baying of jackal packs are common summer night sounds on the Tauran Plain.

Although both are found in small numbers nearby, hyenas and cheetahs are said not to come onto the central plain. Like the hyena, the cheetah appears to be hunted but not eaten in Iran.

### The Sand Sea

Those fauna restricted to the sand sea proper offer little in the way of economic resources. They consist mostly of small burrowing animals, such as gerbils (*Gerbillus* spp.) and jirds (*Meriones* spp.), and the larger cats that prey on them. There are some species of ground game birds as well, and the ubiquitous small owl. Species from the plains (for instance, the goitered gazelle) use the margins of the sand sea but do not penetrate into the interior.

### The *Kavir*

The *kavir* proper cannot support animal life, although many species venture down onto the peripheral saline flats to exploit the vegetation there or to drink at the springs that appear here and there on the edge of the *kavir*.

## BIRDS

Except for the 158 species identified between 1974 and 1976 by the Department of the Environment (Harrington, n.d.), the ecology of birds in Turan has not been studied. Most of the listed species are migrants, passing through on their way to winter or summer areas. The bird species in Turan tend to be widespread, and many are familiar to Europeans (for Iran's avifauna, see Scott, Hamadani, and Mirhosseyni 1975).

Habitats for birds include not only desert and mountain sites, but also aquatic sites that appear during the rainy season or persist year-round at springs, storage ponds, and *qanāt* systems. Those birds that feed on crops (grain and melons especially) are deterred by scarecrows or children during critical periods in the productive cycle.

Game birds include partridges and sand grouse, sometimes captured and fattened by force-feeding, as are domestic pigeons. The Hubara bustard, a large migratory species that breeds in this region, is a popular game bird in southern Iran. It is also the featured prey of falcon hunting in Arabia.

## HERPETOFAUNA

Of Khar o Tauran's numerous lizards and amphibians, most subsist on insects and rodent pests and are harmless or beneficial to the human population. Among these harmless or beneficial species are green toads (*Bufo viridia*), marsh frogs (*Rana ridibunda*), and at least twenty-eight kinds of lizards and snakes, including several species of geckos and the large desert monitor (*Varanus griseus*). Among poisonous species, the Levantine viper is the only one that has been positively identified, but the Persian horned viper and the saw-scaled viper are widespread in similar Iranian environments and will undoubtedly be documented here as well. Snake bites, according to local shepherds, are annually responsible for the death of many sheep and goats. In 1976, for example, seven animals from the Sanjari herd died from snake bites (Endre Nyerges, conversation, 1977).

## FAUNA IN THE SPECIAL ENVIRONMENT OF SETTLEMENT

Most of the larger animals in the area avoid human settlements, and with good reason, since they may be hunted and in any case would have a difficult time finding food to eat. Many of the smaller mammals, insects, and reptiles, however, attracted by water and easy living, thrive in the concentration of resources found in human settlements. Some of these creatures are beneficial, but many become economic or health hazards to be coped with or endured.

Reptiles are generally despised by Iranian villagers, not only from a belief that snakes are highly poisonous (as indeed some are), but also from a general belief that reptiles may be jinn (spirits) in disguise. In any case, even beneficial species of snakes that eat rodents (which themselves eat stored grain) are killed on sight. The populations of house mice, rats, and other kinds of rodents, which frequent houses and storerooms, are kept down to some extent by feral domestic cats. Rat poison is a more prevalent remedy for overpopulation, and tightly sealed containers are a common preventive measure. As mentioned above, wolves and jackals will enter transhumant stations and even villages to catch sheep and goats.

Mosquitoes, flies, ants, and spiders abound, frequently bringing disease and discomfort with them. Bats and the government's malaria squad battle mosquitoes, but ants and flies are mostly ignored or picked out of food. When infested with other kinds of vermin, rice and grain are exposed to sunlight and air to kill or blow the culprits away. Sheep and goat pens become so infested with sheep mites that to control them the pens must be chemically disinfected or burned. Still, many pests and hazards common elsewhere in Iran are not especially bothersome here: I saw only two scorpions during my fieldwork period, although they are reported to be a serious danger at a nearby milking station (Mary Martin, personal communication, 1989). Houses do not appear to be flea-infested, nor are white ants a destructive menace, although they might be if wood were more widely used in construction.

Among the most insidious and destructive kinds of animal life are the parasites that dwell in or on the human population. They cause skin and internal diseases or act as vectors for other diseases, sapping human strength and well-being where they do not kill outright.

The natural environment has been described in some detail for several reasons. The populations of Khar o Tauran are primarily food producers who depend on the primary and secondary products of their surroundings in order to earn a living. Their settlements—the main focus of this book—are an integral part of the way in which they manipulate the environment to obtain food and nonfood products. Through their settlements they come to terms with the hazards and discomforts of an environment that is hot in summer, cold in winter, and dry all year round. In part, the physical setting of the area can explain settlement morphology and location.

# CHAPTER 3

# SUBSISTENCE

Except for a small percentage of residents who migrate part of the year to work in the brickyards or factories of the city, or who are full-time specialists of one sort or another, virtually all local people live more or less directly off the land. Khar o Tauran has been occupied since pre-Islamic times, although perhaps not continuously and not necessarily by forebears of the present-day occupants. Residents claim various origins and times of arrival. Some say they (or their ancestors) have always lived in the area. Many tell of origins in other plateau districts, Fars and Khorasan provinces especially.

Tribal organization is not characteristic of Khar o Tauran today, although it obviously has been in the past, at least for some residents. (The tribally organized Chubdari, who have settled at Rezabad, are an exception in this as they are to many of the rules that apply in the area.) Although individuals or households sometimes cooperate in aspects of production, the product is not pooled beyond the level of the household. Land, animals, and even tools are owned privately by individuals, although arrangements can be made for mutual aid, borrowing, and renting.

Most residents are herders and farmers (whether self-employed or for hire), but there are other ways to make a living in Khar o Tauran. Some can be done at home, and some require separation from the family for short or long periods of time; some are supported by local demand only, and some depend on a market or are otherwise supported by an outside economy. The economic base of the area nevertheless is agriculture and pastoralism. Both men and women work in the fields and with the animals. Generally speaking, men plow, plant, fertilize, spade for grape and melon cultivation, herd flocks outside the village area, and negotiate sale of products locally or in town. Women weed, sift winnowed grain, do the final picking of large tobacco leaves, and milk the sheep and goats. Both men and women plant and cultivate melons, harvest grain, pick cotton and small tobacco leaves, stack dried tobacco leaves, and tend animals locally (Martin 1976 and 1977). Some of these tasks are done for hire.

Fifty animals (sheep and goats) and a hectare of irrigated land could provide an adequate living for a household in a good year, with cash left over for bought necessities (Martin 1980a). Not all years are good, however, and land and pasture are not sufficient to support the current population of the Tauran Plain (Martin 1982b, 146). The most common occupational alternative to farming or herding is shepherding for wages (paid in cash and in kind). A smaller percentage of men and an even smaller percentage of women are part-time specialists who work locally as brickmakers, shopkeepers, seamstresses, and so forth. Only a very few men are full-time specialists; these are mostly government employees such as the gendarmes and the game guards.

Below is a list of the part-time and full-time occupations pursued by residents of the Tauran Plain.

### Occupations Found in the Village of Baghestan

Producer of agricultural products

Producer of pastoral products

Shepherd

Agricultural wage laborer

Miller

Sun-dried-brick maker

General builder

House and roof builder

Quilt maker

Seamstress or cutter

Religious specialist (sheikh, dervish)

Formal complaint writer

Shopkeeper

Teacher

Carpet weaver

**Additional Occupations Found Elsewhere in Tauran**

Plow mender

Saddlemaker

Saddlebag maker

Storage bin (*kondu*) builder

Bread oven (*tanur*) builder

Wooden spoon maker

Midwife

Prayer writer

Letter writer

Kerosene and gasoline distributor

Hauler

Gendarme

Game guard

The teachers; gendarmes; religious specialists, such as sheikhs and der-vishes; and some of the game guards are not natives of Khar o Tauran, nor as a rule is their residence in the area permanent. The rest are all local residents. When no one is available in the area to perform a certain service (such as castrating animals or driving tractors) or produce a certain prod-uct (such as felt coats or copper pots), residents can turn to the city (usually Sabzevar or its surrounding villages) or to another area specializ-ing in the product or service (for example, Sangesar, in the mountains to the northwest of Khar o Tauran). Some kinds of city specialists (such as house and roof builders, or *ostāds*) are often said to do better work than their local equivalents, but they are also more expensive and more difficult to contact because of the distances involved. A few itinerant traders and craftsmen do circulate around the area; their services are especially valuable to those who find it difficult or impossible to get away from home, women in particular. Some of these—for example, a quilt maker and a *tanur* builder—are women themselves. (See also Spooner et al. 1980, Table 4.8, for a listing of occupations that includes specialists who come into Tauran from the urban areas.)

Permanent and temporary migration out of the villages has a significant economic and demographic effect back home, especially in the ratio between males and females, marriage patterns, population growth, and cash input to household budgets. Eleven household heads are hired shepherds who are away for months at a time. Jobs taken by young, single men include working in a city brick or rug factory, driving a truck, and military service (Mary Martin, personal communication, 1988).

Although many—probably most—households practice a combination of strategies to earn a living, in the rest of this discussion I focus on those that depend most heavily on local resources. These activities are divided as follows: food production technologies (the several kinds of pastoralism and agriculture), fuel production, and technologies no longer practiced but important for their effect on the landscape and on settlement patterns (especially metallurgy and transportation-related services). Access to the resources on which these activities are based and the organization of labor vary both within the present-day system and historically. Building activities are described in detail in Chapter 6, but they could as well be included here because of the role that built features play in food production and processing; more than half the structures in these villages are used for such purposes, pastoral as well as agricultural.

## AGRICULTURE

As noted above, agriculture and pastoralism dominate the productive activities of Tauran residents. Yet in spite of the prevalence of pastoralism, only a minority of households in Khar o Tauran depend on it for their sole support. Most practice mixed farming—they combine agriculture and pastoralism in varying degrees in order to supply themselves with their basic food requirements and with the cash to buy what they do not themselves produce in the way of goods and services. Crops are either staples (wheat, barley, melons, garden vegetables, grapes, and tree crops), fodder (barley, alfalfa, and millet), or cash crops (cotton and tobacco, plus any surplus from the staple or fodder crops).

The basic resources of agriculture are land and water; in arid lands, both must be manipulated in order to produce crops in sufficient quantity and with sufficient reliability to make a settled population possible. In Khar o Tauran some simple rainfall farming of barley and melons is undertaken in those years when enough rain falls at appropriate times to make it worth the gamble, but this is by far the most risky and least common form of agriculture.

Less risky and more common are water management systems in which surface water is held in *bands* (check dams, or low earthen walls) that are constructed around an area to be cultivated. Because of the walls, the water is spread over the area and its loss into drainage gullies is prevented. This technique, although less risky than simple rainfall farming, still fails to produce sufficiently reliable annual yields to be used other than as a supplement.

Every permanent agricultural settlement in Khar o Tauran, however, relies on ground water supplies, which are much less sensitive to yearly or seasonal fluctuations in precipitation and which provide a greater and more concentrated supply of water. In a few cases, ground water emerges in natural springs; most often it is led to the fields via *qanat* channels. Altering the terrain for agriculture includes leveling, terracing, building *bands,* and of course constructing and maintaining the channels and storage ponds of the irrigation system. Of the 120 square kilometers of the Tauran Plain, 250 hectares, or 2 percent, are irrigated, whether gardens or open fields, and a fluctuating amount—probably not more than 8 percent—is dry-farmed (Horne 1982a, 203).[1]

Martin (1982b, Figure 3) distinguishes four types of fields in Khar o Tauran. In order of distance from where the ground water surfaces, they are walled gardens, irrigated fields that are double-cropped yearly, irrigated fields that lie fallow in alternate years, and dry-farmed fields, in which water-spreading techniques may or may not be used. Crops in walled gardens include grapes, pomegranate, pistachio, herbs, tomatoes, tobacco seedlings, and onions. Crops in double-cropped fields and in fields that lie fallow in alternate years are wheat, barley, millet, sorghum, alfalfa, cotton, and tobacco. Dry-farmed fields provide wheat, barley, and melons. Not all these crops are food crops, and even food crops generate important by-products such as straw. Cotton, tobacco, sesame seeds, melon seeds, and cumin are cash crops. Agricultural products of other kinds, such as grape syrup processed from surplus grapes, are also sometimes sold.

Although each has gardens, irrigated fields, and dry-farmed fields, all villages do not grow the same crops or experience the same yields. Some are better suited for cotton than tobacco; others cannot grow tobacco at all and grow more barley than wheat. Nor are permanent villages the only locations where crops are grown. Some sites with water but abandoned as living quarters are operated from a nearby settlement; some pastoral stations occupied only in the summer also contain gardens or fields (melon fields especially).

As was generally true of other relatively unproductive and sparsely occupied stretches on the edges of the Dasht-e Kavir, Khar o Tauran was never an area of absentee landlords and residential tenant farmers. The national program of land reform (instituted in 1963) therefore did not change the existing pattern of small holdings owned in most cases by those who worked them. Before the recent period of centralized control, there was certainly a greater concentration of land in the hands of local khans. These tribal leaders probably organized relatives and clients to work their land, but none of them appears to have risen to more than local control. The shift in the distribution of fields and settlement types from the turn of the century to the present pattern of smaller holdings, fewer holders, and larger settlements occurred as a result of economic and political changes in the country as a whole rather than as a legislated change in local land tenure.

Whatever the situation may have been in the past, most agricultural land is now owned by individuals (male or female) who farm the land with the labor of their own household, occasionally supplemented with labor hired locally. When siblings inherit land, the land is split and each receives his or her own share individually. The land is likely already to have been held in discrete small parcels by the deceased, and the fields are divided into a patchwork of small units of ownership as well as of crop management (see Martin 1982b, Figure 4).

Spooner and his colleagues (1980) and Martin (1982b) discuss the seasonal and multiannual scheduling of agricultural tasks. In brief, the cycle begins in November with the first rains, when winter wheat and barley are planted. In the winter the main tasks are plowing and sowing. Irrigation and weeding go on throughout the spring and summer until the crops are harvested. The wheat and barley harvest is over by July, but cotton is not harvested until November. Irrigation cycles vary between weekly and fortnightly waterings, depending on the crops and the soil. The most lax time in the agricultural cycle is midwinter, after the wheat is planted but before close attention must be paid to the irrigated crops. Dry-farmed crops need very little attention once they have been plowed and planted, although the dams and terraces may need work.

People and animals provide nearly all the labor. The only work that is mechanized is threshing by hired tractor and driver, some plowing by tractor, and, increasingly, carting crops from field to house by motorcycle rather than donkey. Long-distance hauling of farm produce into and commercial products and materials out of the urban centers has for some time been handled by privately owned bus and pickup truck (neither frequent nor regular in their service).

## PASTORALISM

Pastoralism is the most spatially extensive food-producing strategy. Khar o Tauran is almost entirely rangeland. In spite of the economic and social importance of agricultural villages, their sites and fields take up very little space in relation to the entire area. They occupy under 10 percent of the Tauran Plain and even less elsewhere (Horne 1982b, 203).

In Khar o Tauran, pastoralism takes a variety of forms. Goats, sheep, and camels are raised for food and other products. Cattle, donkeys, and dogs are also kept, but (except for the occasional milch cow) as work animals rather than food producers.

Nearly every household owns at least one or two animals. (Animal ownership is in fact individual, and a household figure refers to the sum of animals owned by household members.) The mean number of sheep and goats held throughout Khar o Tauran are about 45 to 50 animals per household (Iran 1969 and 1973a). Households with several hundred animals can form their own flocks. In some cases, although the household may not itself own many animals, male household members hire themselves out as shepherds to flock owners whose labor needs cannot be met within their own family labor pool. Moreover, the area is pastorally important to several hundred Sangsari pastoralists based in and around Sangesar, who bring their animals down to winter pasture from the mountains above Semnan.

Martin (1982b, Table I) finds four kinds of grazing patterns in Khar o Tauran: (1) Sangsari long-range transhumant flocks that only winter in the area, (2) locally owned flocks that graze year round at sheep stations, (3) locally owned flocks that spend summers at sheep stations and winters in villages, and (4) pooled flocks that remain based in villages year round and graze on the village common pasture. In addition, nearly every household keeps a few animals out of the flock to fatten for sale or home consumption, feeding them on weeds pulled from the fields or on grown fodder such as millet or alfalfa. The particular grazing location of any individual flock also depends on the species and age of the animals in the flock. Goats, for example, do better than sheep at the topographic extremes of the area—the sand dunes and the mountain heights. Thus, depending on the composition of the flock, the season, the time of day, and the owner or owners' options, flocks will be located in a variety of settings throughout Khar o Tauran.

Sheep and goats need watering points, vegetation, winter shelter (especially for the newborn), protection from predators, and, frequently, agriculturally supplied fodder to carry them through the winter until the pasture freshens again. The availability of drinking water is not as critical a factor as it might seem in such an arid landscape; vegetation is the limiting factor in stock size. Where there are no existing natural water sources, such as springs or wadis, wells have been dug; the water is raised in buckets and poured out into stone-lined troughs. Village-based flocks water at *qanāts* and storage ponds. Animals also get water from the vegetation they eat, and their needs vary, depending on the season and whether they are lactating or not. In the summer they are watered daily; in winter every other day suffices and they need not stay as close to the water source as they do in summer. In summer they must return to their base camp daily for milking and watering. In winter they are not milked, and they spend their nights in semisubterranean or aboveground shelters.

## Grazing Patterns

In 1966, rangeland in Iran was nationalized, and the traditional patterns of rights and control were superseded by government arrangements—including prohibition of any grazing at all in selected areas of research or ecological concern. Although this change in land tenure has economic and social implications for the local residents, it so far has probably not had much effect on the location of pastoral sites and water holes. (The water holes have been nationalized along with the rangeland, but the shelters, or *aghols,* at pastoral sites are still privately owned.) It is, rather, the flockowners and organization of labor that have changed (Martin 1982b). In the past, pastureland in Khar o Tauran was controlled by local tribal groups and private individuals. The rights these individuals once held are now in the control of the central government. Access to pasture can be obtained legally in only two ways. Villages can still have nearby common land where village-based flocks (usually pooled from the holdings of several households) may graze; outside of village-controlled land, access can be obtained only through government permit, and pastureland can no longer be sold or rented. This shift, coupled with an improvement in the economy in general, enabled a greatly increased number of Sangsari pastoralists from outside the area to rent the water holes and pastures that were once in the hands of local tribal khans. The Sangsari, moreover, often patrol the range in the winter to keep village animals from grazing, so that owners of small flocks who once negotiated with local owners of large flocks for access to pasture, winter and summer, are now forced to keep their animals on the Tauran Plain, where the pasture was always poorer and where increased grazing can only make it worse (Martin

1982b). It is, in part, against this background that villagers in Tauran decide their pastoral strategies.

Because animals are raised for meat and not only for milk, pastoral activities vary temporally as well as spatially. Kids and lambs are dropped in the late winter and early spring; out-of-season breeding is prevented by the physical separation of males and females of the same species until the autumn (rams are put in the goat herds, buck goats in the sheep flocks [Nyerges 1982]). From the Persian New Year (the vernal equinox) until mid-summer the animals are milked, and the milk is processed in a number of ways both for immediate consumption and for storage and sale. Until the milk starts giving out, the animals are milked twice a day. It is during this period that many of the animals destined for the outside market (most of them males born either that or the previous year) are sold. In addition, from the New Year on, other animals are put aside to be fattened for home consumption, including Muslim sacrificial feasts for the whole village. Generally, the animals will be fattened until the autumn, when they will begin to be butchered. The meat is either eaten at the time or preserved for later in the winter. Other products are the tail fat from sheep and skins from goats. Animals are also butchered during the Islamic months of Ramadan and Moharram for ritual meals; during the years 1976–78 these fell in August/September and December/January, respectively (they move back ten days each year). Shearing of the large flocks is done in the early summer; individual animals may be sheared at other times.

As has been mentioned earlier, a seasonal but important use of rangeland derives from the yearly presence of the Sangsari (Martin 1982a and 1982b). The Sangsari bring their flocks to the area only for the winter; they walk their animals—mostly their own breed of sheep—down from their summer pasture above Tehran in the autumn and begin the trip back about the time of the Persian New Year, often taking Tauran animals with them to sell for local owners. Sangsari flocks are raised for the commercial Tehran market; they are bred and managed for the production of meat and wool rather than dairy products. In contrast, the Tauran flocks are mostly goats, and the management of both goats and sheep is geared to maximizing milk yields.

From the perspective of the household rather than the flock, there are several degrees of involvement by local people in animal ownership. In villages on the Tauran Plain some households have no animals at all or have only the animals they are fattening. Most households have animals in one of the pooled village flocks, which shepherds are hired to tend. Some have anywhere from a single animal to several flocks that are kept off the plain at sheep stations for part or all of the year and are tended either by household members, other relatives, or hired shepherds. In many cases a male member of the household is himself a shepherd hired by fellow villagers, residents of other settlements in or near the area, or distant Sangsari.

The activities, personnel, equipment, and structures associated with sheep and goat pastoralism are distributed differently across the area, according to combinations of factors that affect pastoral strategies. These factors—the physical environment, the location and availability of pastureland, the needs of the animals, and the economics of domestic and commercial pastoralism—vary from zone to zone, from settlement to settlement, and from household to household.

Until about twenty years ago, the raising of camels was a widespread and important element in the economy of Khar o Tauran. Today, because of the drop in demand for camel meat and products and the introduction of vehicular forms of transportation, only three settlements continue to raise camels, and in far fewer numbers than was once the case. Moreover, nomads who formerly entered the area with their camels for seasonal exploitation of the pasture have in many cases ceased to do so because of increased sedentarization, difficulties in obtaining grazing permits, and changes in the demand for camel products and services.

At the present time there are only about a thousand camels left in Khar o Tauran, all of them in Khar. At one time there were said to be about five hundred camels on the Tauran Plain alone; now there are only a handful. As usual elsewhere in Iran, camels are kept for their meat and hair and for transport and draft. They are not milked (nor, except at Rezabad, even herded) but are left to range free until they are needed for sale.

The camels still in the area are kept in and at the edge of the sand sea, at the edges of the Sabzevar Kavir, and on the flat lower plains adjacent to these areas. They move easily over sandy areas, even in the summer, when the ground temperature is extremely high. They withstand other climatic extremes as well, such as blowing dust and sand. They are the least reliant on water sources of all the domestic animals and thrive on shrubby vegetation, especially *Calligonum, Tamarix,* and *Haloxylon,* and they eat a greater proportion of branches and thorns than do goats or sheep. Sheep and goats also do well at the edge of the sand sea year round but can be taken into the interior only in the winter, when temperatures fall to tolerable levels. Although camel raising is no longer an element in the economy of villages on the Tauran Plain. It is included here because of its role in the economy of the past and because the economy of the past still influences the present-day settlement pattern.

Cattle are kept for plowing and sometimes for milking. The mean number of animals per household is less than one (Iran 1969 and 1973a). They are not kept in herds. For control, they are either tied to stakes or kept in village stables (as are donkeys). Off season, they are sometimes released to graze on annuals and grasses around the low sandy part of the plain until they are needed again back at the village. They may also be penned and fed with gathered wild plants such as *Stipagrostis pennata* on which they graze as well. The upper plains and mountain villages are too far from the sand to make wild fodder feasible, and cattle there are fed fodder crops or agricultural by-products (such as straw) instead.

Like camels, donkeys are beasts of burden. They are also used to plow, sometimes teamed with oxen. Their village life is much like that of cattle, although they are never allowed to range far from a settlement.

As is true elsewhere in the Near East, the flocks in Khar o Tauran are managed by people and goats rather than dogs. In general, Near Eastern dogs, unlike European sheepdogs, are used to guard the flocks against human and animal predators rather than herd them, a job that is left to goats. Recent studies suggest that the difference between the two kinds of dogs is primarily one of breeding; guard dogs such as those in Tauran could not easily be trained to herd even if herding were required of them.

The best guard dogs in Khar o Tauran are said to come from the Kurds who live in the mountains to the north of the area. A good Kurdish dog is expensive; in 1978 a transhumant family paid the equivalent of $150 for one, even though the family had little cash to spare. I never made a systematic count, but my impression is that there were only just enough dogs for the number of flocks to be guarded. Thus, each village or transhumant station had only a few dogs in residence, sometimes only one.

Among the domestic animals in Khar o Tauran, only the dog is considered ritually unclean. They are not touched with the hands unless the act is unavoidable. People pat them with their feet. Still, the village dogs are well treated, fed scraps and gruel, and allowed to cool off in the *qanāt* stream where women draw water and wash their dishes. Probably partly as a result of this kindly treatment, all but one of the dogs I encountered were indifferent or friendly, even when I entered a new village as a stranger. Only when they were out with the flocks would their guarding instincts and training take over. Such behavior is in marked contrast to that of the dogs in other parts of Iran, where rural dogs are notoriously vicious, sometimes even with their own masters (Digard 1980). Dogs are the only domestic animals to receive names. Domestic cats in these villages are feral. They are not kept as pets and are tolerated only because they keep down the rodent population in storerooms, feeding themselves on what they can catch.

## FUEL PRODUCTION

As we have seen, the most important food-producing strategies in Khar o Tauran are agriculture and pastoralism. Tauranis depend on agricultural land, water, and pasture as their primary resources. But they also depend on the availability of fuel for processing their products into edible and storable forms and for heat in the winter, when temperatures frequently drop below freezing. Without a reliable fuel supply, the land could not support a permanent population.

There are three main types of fuel in Khar o Tauran: kerosene, farming by-products such as dung or cotton stalks, and locally collected firewood. Of the three, firewood is by far the most important. Unlike many other parts of Iran, where prepared dungcakes are the main fuel source, here dung is used primarily as fertilizer and only incidentally for fuel. Kerosene has recently been introduced and is popular, but it must be purchased. For the most part it is used within the house—for preparing meals, in lamps, and to some extent for heating.

Firewood is used for a number of different purposes, mainly, as mentioned above, for food preparation and winter heating. It is also used to heat laundry and bathing water and for such miscellaneous and infrequent activities as burning gypsum plaster. Within the village, fires are usually lit at all meals, if only to prepare tea. Nearly all foods are eaten cooked, even in the summer. But the importance of heat-processing of foods goes beyond everyday meal preparation. Both milk and agricultural crops are seasonal and must be put aside in some storable form in order to carry residents through the fall and winter, when crops have been harvested and sheep and goats have stopped giving milk. Grain seeds can be stored without further processing, but nearly everything else must be dried or cooked for preservation. (There is of course no refrigeration.) Surplus products of all kinds, when preserved in transportable, imperishable form, are also more easily sold or exchanged. Milk is especially perishable and must be processed immediately if it is not to spoil.[2] Fresh milk in fact is never drunk, except medicinally as a laxative.[3]

Fuel needs vary spatially and temporally (Horne 1982a). The average village household's consumption was estimated at 5.3 metric tons per year for all purposes. Transhumant households, which need to process large quantities of milk products, use 12.1 tons of firewood per year. Firewood collection is not a commercial activity (indeed, much of it is illegal, given the prohibition against cutting green wood of any kind). It is usually the job of adult male household members, who go out from the village perhaps six times a month, returning with great bundles of brush balanced on donkey back.

Fuel production has not always been intended only for local consumption, however. In the past, firewood collection and charcoal production were significant commercially as well.

## HISTORICAL ACTIVITIES USING LOCAL RESOURCES

Judging from archaeological evidence, several other kinds of productive activity, based on local resources, existed in the past. For example, a large kiln site with wasters and production debris at the village of Zamanabad, along with several smaller areas of pottery and brick wasters on the Tauran Plain testify to a local ceramic industry at some earlier period in Turan's history. No one any longer remembers these activities. Nor does anyone have any memory of metallurgical activity, although copper-smelting sites, marked by glassy slag and occasionally crucible or kiln fragments, abound throughout the area. Shallow mines, now abandoned, indicate that ores were obtained locally, as was fuel (Horne 1982b).

As important as these industries were in the past, little is known about their relationship to settlement and subsistence in the area. Judging by the locations of slag sites, copper smelting was carried out away from village settlements, although temporary camps could have been set up for the metalworkers. These workers need not even have been local residents. The copper itself most likely was sent into the city (Sabzevar, for example), where coppersmiths worked it into utensils to be sold in the bazaar. Ceramic production, in contrast, appears to have been settlement-based; the several kiln sites are either immediately next to or mixed with other kinds of scatter from village sites with long histories of occupation.

While both these industries depended on the local vegetation for fuel, smelting presumably exploited it in the form of charcoal, which is especially destructive to the environment because of the caloric inefficiency of conversion from wood (Horne 1982a and 1982b). The charcoal industry in Khar o Tauran has been discontinued only since 1966, when, in the interest of rangeland productivity, it was prohibited by the Iranian government. It is thus better documented and its social context better understood than either ceramic or copper production.

Throughout the earlier part of this century and perhaps for centuries before that, the production of charcoal in Khar o Tauran appears to have been entirely commercial; very little was used by the villages, which instead depended then, as now, on firewood. Rural areas like this have long supplied Iran's urban areas with fuel. In the city, charcoal was preferred over firewood because of its compactness and storability, its smokeless qualities, and its low transport costs. Charcoal was exported from the area in quantities that were sometimes enormous, both absolutely and in relation to the local biomass. Tauranis told us that just before charcoal was prohibited, it was being sent out of the area at the rate of 100 to 150 camel loads (as much as 30 tons) a day. To produce such an amount would have consumed six to nine times the weight in wood.

Converting the local vegetation into urban fuel, whether it went to the city directly as charcoal or indirectly as copper or milk products, was an economic alternative to the more obvious strategies of agriculture and pastoralism. It would still be, in spite of the increase in fossil fuel use, were charcoal production not banned. It is an alternative that underscores not only how urban demand on the hinterland affects the ways and intensity with which local populations exploit their environments but also how urban demand contributes to the very size of local populations so that the land takes on a carrying capacity that might not be predicted from its agricultural and pastoral technologies alone.

## ARCHAEOLOGICAL RECOGNITION AND RECOVERY OF AGRICULTURAL AND PASTORAL SYSTEMS

Now let us consider how the Tauran Plain might appear archaeologically, focusing on what would be considered "off-site" activities, even though they are in fact based on settlements. The central plain, which covers an area of about 120 square kilometers, is the most densely occupied area in Khar o Tauran (about ten persons per square kilometer); the nearest neighbors on the Tauran Plain live about 1.8 kilometers apart on average. The plain is the most intensively exploited portion of Khar o Tauran and the most effectively altered by human activity. Off the plain, populations are less dense and settlements farther apart; Khar o Tauran as a whole contains only 0.8 persons per square kilometer.

Irrigated agricultural fields are distributed only patchily over the surface of the landscape. Land suitable for dry farming is more widely available. Pastures are more nearly continuous throughout the area, although the degree of natural vegetational productivity and palatability to livestock varies considerably. This "oasis" pattern of nucleated village and field, separated by stretches of pasture or wasteland, is typical of subsistence or undeveloped agricultural settlement in the Near East.

On the Tauran Plain, thirteen of the twenty-seven irrigated field systems have residential year-round villages based at the *qanāt* source (see Figure 29 for those on the main part of the plain). The remaining fourteen systems have associated residential areas only in the summer or not at all. There are occasionally, however, ruins or scatterings of sherds from past occupation nearby. Some dry-farmed fields lie in close proximity to a

village or its irrigated fields; other dry-farmed areas are removed, sometimes a considerable distance, from any kind of settlement. The rest of
the plain is largely pasture with a few wadi bottoms and mini-*kavirs* that
support no vegetation at all.

Less land is under cultivation off the plain than on it, and a greater
proportion is used for pasture. But, as noted above, even on the densely
occupied central plain, only a relatively small percentage of land is currently cultivated, although at one time or another a much higher percentage of the plain appears to have been plowed and sown. Most of the plain
is exploited for pasture, fuel, and construction material.

The area irrigated by any single ground water source is limited by
flow, slope, crop type, and rotation system; no single system in Khar o
Tauran is larger than about 30 hectares. Many of them are within a range
of 2 to 5 hectares. Even with *qanāt* sources, water flow is variable, and the
amount of land actually cultivated varies from year to year. Dry-farmed
systems are constrained as well, but by the size and placement of *bands*,
the natural terrain, and the rainfall in any given year, rather than by the
supply of local ground water. In recent years dry farming has also been
constrained by government decree that froze the amount of land planted
to what it was in the early 1970s.

### Recognition of Off-Site Productive Activities

Aside from the presence of crops themselves, the most obvious physical
alterations to the environment that are directly associated with ongoing
agricultural activity in Khar o Tauran are step terraces with stone or mud
walls, low field enclosure walls to contain and spread water (whose
source may be rainfall, *qanāts,* or springs), check dams perpendicular to
wadi drainage courses, high garden exclosure walls to keep out human
and animal predators, conical spoil heaps that protect the access shafts of
*qanāt* chains, artificial storage ponds, and the irrigation channels themselves. Less visible are plow marks and the shallow patterns of high and
low surfaces that serve to raise or submerge a particular crop during
irrigation. In Tauran these features are mostly built of or dug into earth
and clay, but fieldstone and river cobbles are also sometimes used.

All these modern features, if well-enough preserved, would be visible by a survey taken on foot. Of uncertain age, but still visible today are many out-of-use features. Not only are there abandoned examples of all the above, but also there are scatters of broken ceramic *qanāt* hoops (used to reinforce *qanāt* conduits) and a vegetation cover that differs from similar areas that have not been plowed and cultivated. Even less obvious evidence can, with perseverence, yield results. Dennell (1982), for example, has painstakingly analyzed the varves at the side of a wadi cut in order to reconstruct an abandoned check dam system next to the village of Baghestan. Coupled with observations of other existing cuts and sections, the evidence points to the existence of a widespread system of silt-forming dams by at least the tenth century. These and subsequent silt deposits contribute significantly to the fertility of present-day irrigated fields.

In other parts of the Old World, potsherd scatters have been used to identify ancient fields (see, for example, Wailes 1970 or Wilkinson 1974 and 1982). In Khar o Tauran, however, the fields rarely exhibit such scatters, primarily because the materials used to fertilize fields do not contain potsherds (see below) and because some fields are fertilized infrequently or not at all. Irrigated fields—especially those planted with tobacco or cotton—are manured with a mixture of earth, dung (from cattle, donkeys, sheep, and goats), and straw dug out of pens and stables. Courtyard and house floor sweepings, and ashes from hearths and bread ovens are also carried down to the fields. Irrigated grain fields are less likely to be manured and more likely to be allowed to lie fallow the farther they are from the top of the water source. Dry-farmed grain fields are not manured at all. In the past few years, chemical fertilizer has been used on irrigated grain fields as well as on fields of tobacco and cotton.

Most of the manure used on Tauran's fields comes from pens and stables. In sheep and goat pens, virtually no activity takes place except getting the animals in and out and perhaps de-ticking them with chemicals. Sometimes agricultural equipment is stored in large animal stables, but again, there is little activity not directly associated with animal care. Thus these structures are not used as trash sites. Most broken or discarded items are thrown over courtyard walls or into gullies or pits, and no attempt is made to carry the resulting accumulations of animal bones, broken pottery and glass, and other broken objects out of the village and onto the fields. In addition, at least on the several occasions when I watched farmers load up midden material or dung from unroofed pens, they picked out bones, plastic shoes, stones, and other material that was not wanted in the fields and would have only added unnecessary work to an already laborious hauling task. It may be that these practices are typical only of situations in which a farmer is manuring his own fields from his own supplies of dirt and dung, and that debris, manure, and night soil in larger towns and cities are both accumulated and collected less discriminately, presumably by intermediaries (compare English 1966, Grønhaug 1978). It should be pointed out that Iranian villages today in any case use much less pottery than they did in the past. Many dishes and all cooking vessels are made of metal (and copper retains a value as scrap even when damaged); many other kinds of containers are plastic. These materials do not break easily into small fragments and are easy to pick out. It should also be pointed out that in Baghestan areas of melted down mud brick structures or earlier occupational deposit such as is found in archaeological mounds elsewhere are not dug out and put on the fields.

Pastoral sites also leave their mark on the surroundings in Khar o Tauran (Nyerges 1982). Trampling, grazing, and dung deposition create a peculiarly characteristic area within a 500-meter radius around a winter or summer station. The vegetation that springs up on abandonment of winter stations is visibly different within this range. Degradation of a less marked kind generally reaches out 1.0 to 1.5 kilometers from a purely pastoral site (Nyerges 1982, 244). The length of time for reestablishment of the original vegetation is not known. If the damage is widespread enough, the vegetation may never recover.

Theoretically, these changes in the composition of soil and vegetation from productive activities, if preserved well enough and for long enough, could become good archaeological indicators for site discovery and reconstruction. Techniques such as chemical and pollen analysis that make use of information in the soils and sediments in and around villages were not tested in the field but surely ought to be productive in identifying the presence or absence of different kinds of land use (see, for example, Eidt 1984). Although Mary Martin and I collected soil samples from agricultural and residential contexts, the project was terminated before sampling and analysis could be completed. Other members of the Turan Programme analyzed the fossil pollen collected in a cored sample of sediments from the nearby *kavir* (Moore and Stevenson 1982). Their results indicate that evidence of increasing human interference in the form of agricultural and pastoral activities is indeed preserved in the sedimentary pollen record, although in the absence of organic material, absolute dates could not be determined. In general, however, a systematic study of soils and deposits in this area still remains to be done.

Besides these above- and below-ground means of sampling agricultural and pastoral activities, there are other, less direct techniques, such as aerial photography. Aerial photographs were available for most of the Tauran Plain at a scale estimated to be about 1:22,000 (Iran 1969) and 1:57,000 (Iran 1956)—nominally 1:20,000 and 1:50,000. These show well the irrigated field systems plowed or planted in the spring and early summer of those years. From the photographs it is also possible to identify remnant irrigated field systems that are no longer in use at the abandoned villages of Baba Kuh and Deh-e Nau. Dry-farmed areas can sometimes be picked out where there are check dams or regular geometric terracing but not otherwise. These dry-farming locations appear not to have been planted in the years the photographs were taken; it is likely that little or no dry farming had been possible because of inadequate rainfall during the previous winter.

## The Potential in Off-Site Archaeology

As discussed in Chapter 2, human occupation has altered the entire landscape of Khar o Tauran. As has just been seen, although some effects are ephemeral, many are permanent enough and visible enough that they can be used to reconstruct the kind of activity that took place. Pastoral activities, for example, can be distinguished from agricultural ones on the basis of the changed soils in texture and composition and concomitant changes in vegetation cover. How long the remnants of these or other activities will remain readable and how they are to be dated is another question, but their magnitude and extent suggest that the arid landscape retains evidence of past activities that is potentially of great use to archaeologists.

As in other dryland areas, the irrigation and water management practices of Khar o Tauran, along with the absence of gardens or fields within residential settlements, mean that a great deal of the evidence for agricultural activities and technology lies outside of the settlement itself. Field systems in particular carry social information as well as agricultural information of great interest to archaeologists.

In the off-site archaeology of the Near East, there is an understandable emphasis on the study of water management systems and techniques and their histories (see, for example, Evenari 1958 and Stager 1976 for the Negev and Judaean deserts; Adams 1981, Helbaek 1972, and Oates and Oates 1976 for Mesopotamia; Neely 1971 and Prickett 1979 for Iran). Water management techniques tend to leave a greater impression on the terrain than do field divisions, cropping patterns, or plow and hoe marks, and river systems and the organization of irrigation have long figured in discussions about complex societies.

The great antiquity of occupation and reoccupation in the Near East, however, makes recovery of ancient field forms more difficult than in, say, the relatively younger systems of the New World. Even if good recovery were possible, interpreting the evidence might not be easy. In the absence of accompanying ethnographic or historical data, even the patterns observed in contemporary field systems are subject to various interpretations, to judge by the historical and geographical literature. Regularities in form, especially strip and block forms, have been linked, for example, to one or more of the following: (1) the nature of the water supply, (2) the topography of the land, (3) the age of the system, (4) whether the land being put under cultivation is newly colonized or was previously occupied and whether the settlers are farmers or (former) nomads, (5) whether plot holdings are fixed in tenure or are periodically redistributed, (6) whether the farming community is egalitarian or stratified in organization, (7) whether tenure is collective or individual, (8) whether land is held in large or small holdings, and (9) inheritance patterns. (For fuller discussions, see Bobek 1976 and 1977; Bonine 1989; Boyce 1969; Ehlers and Safi-Nejad 1979; Hartl 1979; Hütteroth 1968; Lambton 1953; Lienau and Uhlig 1978; Loose 1980; and Nitz 1971.)

So far, I have focused on production, land use, and off-site activities, without much reference to the settlements themselves. Given the thesis that settlement is, at least in part, a strategy used in the technology of production, and that food production is the major subsistence activity for nearly all Khar o Tauran residents, the location of productive resources in relation to the technologies for exploiting them should play an important role in the location and shape of settlements. As I discuss in later chapters, many essential productive activities take place back in the settlement, such as storage of food and tools, processing of food and other resources, and sheltering animals.

# CHAPTER 4

# SETTLEMENT IN KHAR O TAURAN

Herding and farming have a long and continuous history in the Near East. In spite of the dramatic increase in urbanization during the past fifty years, they were and still are the occupations of a significant number of the people who live there. A major goal of the ecologically or economically minded Near Eastern archaeologist is to be able to read the nature of pastoral and agricultural technologies from archaeological sites. A broader goal is to understand how these technologies are tied into the greater social and political environment. Making basic inferences such as estimates of population and of carrying capacity depends on the correct identification of subsistence activities and estimations of site size and density of occupation. The ability to make such inferences, however, also depends on the accurate assessment of relationships between sites, such as their relative contemporaneity amd whether they are home bases or satellite stations.

In one sense, of course, the entire area of Khar o Tauran is a settlement. Virtually all of it has economic utility or is somehow the scene of human activity or occupation. Against this diffuse general use of the land, clearly distinguished loci of concentrated activity or meaning stand out. Nearly all these loci have some kind of material or observable alterations that identify them as sites or settlements. Population, activities, and built structures are neither uniformly nor randomly distributed in Khar o Tauran. They are shaped according to resource location and social factors. Explaining these configurations is a complex task, which must take into account the confounding effect of history. The first step is to describe the present distribution of settlement in relation to the environment.

The entire Khar o Tauran area covers about 3,300 square kilometers, and population density is only about 0.8 persons per square kilometer. Settlement in this area takes a number of minor forms and three main forms: year-round permanent villages (*deh*), summer milking stations (called locally *kalāta* or *jā-ye gusfand*), and winter sheep and goat stations (*āghol*). The traits that distinguish them, both in local usage and in this analysis, are seasonality of occupation and the kinds of productive activities undertaken. The three types usually differ from each other in a number of other ways as well. They vary in size and composition of social groups, degree of investment in structures, size and layout of the settlement, building forms, and construction materials.

Settlement types also vary in distribution pattern and locations. Winter stations are the most uniformly distributed; summer stations less so. Compared with villages, both are relatively unstable in their continuity of occupation. The village settlement pattern in contrast can be characterized as stable, clustered, and, within those clusters, evenly distributed.

Some locations are shared by all three settlement types. All three kinds of sites are found on the plains, especially in the outlying regions. The outlier Tau Chah, for example, has a permanent village, a summer station, and a winter station all within a few hundred meters of each other. No settlement of any kind is found at heights greater than 1,400 meters.

Nevertheless, the three types of sites do tend toward complementary distribution. With the exceptions of Tejur and Nur (villages) and Sanjari (a summer station), only winter stations are found south of the mountains, on the *kavir* side. Again, only winter stations are found within the sand sea. Whereas summer stations are likely to be as near to villages as their requirements allow, winter stations are often far from any kind of year-round settlement at all. To understand these and other trends, let us first consider the relation of each kind of settlement to its surroundings.

## LOCATION AND RESOURCES

### Villages

The thirty-seven villages of the area are small, highly nucleated, and irregular in plan (see Appendix). They range in size from one to more than ninety-five households; the mean population size is 69.7 persons. On the Tauran Plain, where village areas were measured from aerial photographs, they range in area from less than 0.5 to 2.23 hectares. Population and area are highly correlated (Table 2).

Roughly half the structures in a village are used for human shelter and activities. The other half shelter animals and agricultural equipment. Buildings are mostly of mud, mud brick, or stone with mud brick vaults or domes (Figure 4). Brush-roofed stables and other less permanent structures are also built. In addition to its fields and gardens, each village has threshing floors and usually a cemetery. An architecturally "complete"

### TABLE 2. POPULATIONS, AREAS, AND DENSITIES OF CENTRAL TAURAN VILLAGES

| Village | Population | Area (ha)[a] | Density |
|---------|-----------|----------|---------|
| Baghestan | 148 | 1.89 | 78.31 |
| Barm | 124 | 1.56 | 79.49 |
| Eshqvan | 174 | 2.23 | 78.03 |
| Faridar | 80 | 1.06 | 75.47 |
| Jafarabad | 82 | 1.09 | 75.23 |
| Kariz | 104 | 1.24 | 83.87 |
| Nahar | 39 | 0.76 | 51.32 |
| Nauva | 36 | 1.15 | 31.30 |
| Salehabad | 112 | 1.94 | 57.73 |
| Taghmar | 27 | 0.39 | 69.23 |
| Zamanabad | 178 | 1.86 | 95.70 |
| Hojjaj | 82 | 1.06 | 77.36 |
| Talkhab | 49 | 0.97 | 50.52 |

Sources: For the villages of Hojjaj, Ravazang, Talkhab, and Zivar: aerial photographs, 1956 series and 1969 series, supplied by the National Geographic Centre, Tehran. For the rest, aerial photographs, 1969 series, supplied by the National Geographic Centre, Tehran, and Iran 1973a.

Note: Mean village population, 95.0 persons; mean village area, 1.32 hectares; mean density, 69.50 persons/ hectare. For correlation between population and area, Pearson's product-moment correlation coefficient $r = .905$, $r^2 = .82$, $p = \leq.0001$.

a. Column 3 includes all space within the village perimeter, including courtyards and unroofed areas.

Figure 4. View over Baghestan, looking northeast. The courtyard and living room of household 27 is in the foreground. The long building just beyond it is the *hoseiniya*, a building used for religious services. Beyond lie walled gardens and irrigated fields. The sand sea stretches across the horizon.

village in local terms would also have a community bath house (*hammām*), a religious building (*hoseiniya*), and a government school house. In the mid-1970s, however, only a handful of the villages in Khar o Tauran were so equipped.

All thirty-seven villages lie between 900 and 1,400 meters in alititude, although the terrain itself drops below 800 meters and rises to nearly 2,300 meters (Figure 2). All are situated on well-drained land, which excludes *kavir* or marsh. Immediately joining each are a water supply and the irrigated gardens and fields on which village economy depends. Between villages lies only sandy or gravelly pasture with occasional stretches of dry-farmed land. Most villages lie on the upper side of their gardens and fields but not necessarily at the upper side of the water source, which often emerges above the village. With only two exceptions, all villages are on the eastern or northern side of mountains or raised slopes rather than on the side facing the *kavir* and are thus exposed to the storm winds that blow from the west. The two exceptions (one of which is to the west of the area shown on the map) are both in fact protected by slopes on their western sides.

As has been noted, the villages are both agricultural and pastoral. They therefore require flat land, suitable soil, and adequate irrigation water to produce their crops. They also require pasture for their animals, firewood for cooking and heat, and construction materials of mud, stone, or brushwood for the buildings.

Water is the most critical resource because the main productive activity for the majority of households in villages is agriculture. Because of the sparse and highly unpredictable nature of rainfall in Khar o Tauran, crops must be irrigated in order to support a permanent sedentary population. Rainfall farming alone, even when enhanced by water management techniques such as damming and terracing, is too risky (with failures at least two years out of three) to provide more than a windfall during those years when the risk pays off. The incorporation of various words for water in nearly a third of Khar o Tauran village names testifies to the intimate association of permanent water sources and villages, to wit, Kariz, Nahar, Chah-e Mer'i, Derazu, Ferinu, Garmab Pain, Garmab Bala, Salamrud, Talkhab, and Tauchah (*kāriz* means underground water channel, or *qanāt; nahr* means "stream"; *chāh* means "well"; *āb* and *u* mean "water"; and *rud* means "river").

The two sources of irrigation water are natural springs and artificially constructed *qanāts,* both exploited through gravity-flow distribution systems. There are no permanent rivers from which water can be led, and what seasonal water flows is saline. Diesel-pumped tube wells, frequently seen in some parts of Iran, have not been installed in Khar o Tauran. Neither does local technology include lifting water by simpler but extremely laborious mechanical means such as the *shaduf* (a weighted pole and bucket device) or bucket brigades.

Springs have the advantage of being available naturally, and usable with very little investment. They have the disadvantage of being most common in the more hilly terrain, which provides little flat land for spreading the water. At lower altitudes springs tend to be too weak and too salty for irrigation.

*Qanāts,* in contrast, can within certain limits be introduced where they are needed. They do, however, require special configurations of terrain, soils, and drainage. The terrain must be flat enough to hold the irrigation water and fertile enough to support crops on a yearly or at least short-term fallow basis. Few locations meet these requirements naturally, and improvements are usually necessary. Terraces are built to facilitate irrigation, to prevent erosion and to build up the soil through silting. Dung mixed with earth is applied to fertilize and condition the soil. Even on the flat land down near the sand sea, soil improvement is important because the natural soil is light and sandy, and the *qanāt* water is saltier than it is higher up.

Thus, a *qanāt* system combined with land engineering (leveling, filing, damming, and ditching) directs the water to exactly where it is needed and ensures its availability throughout the year and across years instead of only a short period following a rainfall. It takes advantage of the natural storage facility of the land by tapping an underground aquifer. It enhances natural storage by means of artificial ponds that are filled and emptied to match the schedule of labor available for irrigating; ponds also increase the strength of the flow.

It is not easy to say to what degree *qanāt* technology makes the entire area suitable for irrigation.[1] After studying topographic maps and data collected in the field, I concluded that agricultural sites depend not so much on variation in hydrology (whether artificially or naturally supplied) as on topography. Water for *qanāt* construction is widely available below certain heights (that is, below the water table in the gravel fans). Whether or not it has been tapped and drawn to any particular point has more to do with the suitability of the terrain for an aboveground, gravity-flow irrigation system than with the nature of the underground hydrology.

### Summer Milking Stations

In many parts of Khar o Tauran, villages are so close together or the pasture that surrounds them is already so heavily used by pooled village-based flocks that villagers who choose (or are forced) to live primarily from pastoralism are obliged to take their animals away from the village to outlying stations. Here they find the grazing they need to maintain larger flocks and higher milk yields than is possible around villages.

These stations correspond to Martin's second category of grazing pattern (given in her list in Chapter 3), in which locally owned flocks spend their summers at sheep and goat stations and their winters back in the villages. There were about eight summer stations on the Tauran Plain at the time this study was made. Most were on the lower reaches of the plain, where space and pasture were available.

On account of the demands of tending the flock and processing milk products, the station must be adequately staffed at all times. Sometimes, however, male members must return to their village periodically to irrigate fields or attend to other business at home.

Summer milking stations constructed to serve that purpose are smaller than permanent villages and very different in appearance (Figure 5). The

Figure 5. The living room at Sanjari, a summer pastoral station owned by a household in the Tauran village of Salehabad. Brushwood fuel, essential for processing milk, is stored on the roof and behind the house. In the foreground is a rug-covered *tālār*, where skins of yoghurt and cheese are kept cool. Summer station *tālārs* are several times larger than those in villages.

few structures, which house perhaps one to three households, are typically round rather than square, with mud and stone walls and brush and mud roofs supported by wooden center posts and cross beams. The structures are primarily for human shelter and activities, since it is not necessary to keep flocks under roofed shelter in the warm, dry summer months. Labor is sometimes shared between households, but in all else they remain economically independent of one another.

People at summer stations frequently reuse the more permanent structures of otherwise abandoned villages. Occasionally they do a small amount of gardening (usually of melons), but their main activities are herding, milking, and processing milk products in large quantities. They must draw water frequently to wash dishes, pots, and other equipment used in milk processing, and for drinking, cooking, washing clothes, and other domestic purposes. Flocks must also be watered. Sometimes the water source is an abandoned *qanāt,* but more frequently it is a small spring or dug well from which water must be raised by hand or with winches. The settlement is always as close to the water source as possible.

Occupation runs from May through August, the period when pastures are freshest and milk yields highest. At the end of the summer, transhumant households return to their home villages, although the flocks may move on to winter stations, accompanied only by male shepherds.

Most summer stations are located without regard to agricultural resources except that a nearby water source is essential. The other prime requirement, besides pasture and water, is firewood: The transhumant households at one summer station with about 250 milking animals used an estimated twenty-one tons of firewood per summer season, most of it for processing the milk into storable and salable products (Horne 1982a, 206; Martin 1982b, 154). Wherever there is pasture, however, there is also firewood within a reasonable distance of the station, because the species used for fuel and those grazed by sheep and goats are either found in association with each other or are actually the same ones.

Pasture and firewood are diffuse resources. Water supplies on the other hand are discontinuous or patchy. The particular location of a summer station within its pasture has more to do with water than either pasture or firewood.

The last environmental factor in summer station location is topography. Both for the quality of the range in hot weather and for human comfort, summer stations tend to be located on high terrain and to avoid both the fringes of the *kavir,* its low plains, and the sand sea proper. Winter stations make use of all these areas.

### Winter Stations

*Āghols,* or winter stations, are more limited in their layout, size, and number of people than are either villages or summer stations. Today, most of them correspond to Martin's first category of grazing patterns, in which long-range transhumant flocks from Sangesar winter in the area. Thus, although these flock owners exert a significant pressure on the environment and hire local shepherds who leave their families for the winter to tend the flocks, they are not themselves part of the local population. When a mobile, frequently long-range strategy such as pastoralism is involved, regions may have to be defined quite differently from the usual criteria.

Typically, winter station structures are semisubterranean shelters (for winter warmth) of either stone or slabs of packed dung, with roofs of brush, dirt, and dung (Figure 6). The roof is supported on wooden poles, sometimes in several rows when the structure shelters a large number of animals. Winter stations are used only as sheep herding bases, usually for two separate flocks, as shelter for men and animals, and as foddering points for animals. Only men stay in winter stations; usually five of them, two for each flock and an extra hand who goes where he is needed. Winter stations are occupied from October through April.

Like those at summer stations, activities at winter stations require water and pasture, but in winter the animals are watered only every other day. Also, the few men who tend them need less water for domestic purposes than do families at summer stations with their milk processing and household chores. Sources for firewood are less important at winter stations because milk is not processed and fires are built only for warmth and cooking. The animals are penned in the winter, and dung is available for fuel to supplement brushwood.

Winter stations tend to be found at lower, warmer altitudes and are more carefully protected from exposure to the elements than are summer stations. They are usually dug into southerly slopes. Many are close to

Figure 6. Āghol Taguk, a winter pastoral station in an isolated area west of the Tauran Plain. It is built of stone and dung-earth slabs and roofed with mud and dung-plastered brush supported by forked poles inside. Virtually nothing has been left behind from the winter's activity.

the sand sea or *kavir,* locations that are unbearably hot in the summer for both animals and people, but tolerable in temperature and productive of pasture in the winter. Winter stations are frequently as far as 4 kilometers away from water, which may be of any fresh source, including wells needing lifting devices such as winches.

Bryan Spooner and Christopher Hamlin located a total of about seventy winter stations in the entire Turan Biosphere Reserve in 1976 (personal communication, 1977). Active stations were spaced about 6 kilometers apart. The Iranian government road maps show far more stations than are ever actually occupied in any one season. The practice of burning winter stations at frequent intervals to destroy sheep vermin means that at least as many are abandoned as are in use, which makes the maps highly misleading.[2] In spite of this, those marked on Figure 7 give some idea of the zones where winter stations are found.

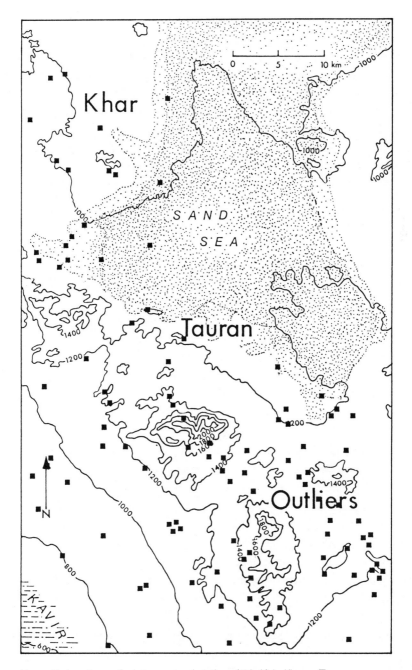

Figure 7. Locations of winter pastoral stations (*āghols*) in Khar o Tauran.

## Year-Round Pastoral Stations

There are, in addition to seasonally occupied winter and summer stations, a few year-round pastoral stations in the area, corresponding to
Martin's second category, in which locally owned flocks graze throughout the year at sheep stations. These year-round stations combine the
activities of both types of seasonal stations. Drawing a strong dichotomy
between types of pastoral stations is probably misleading historically.
Separate winter and summer stations are most likely a recent phenomenon brought about by reduced access to pasture on the part of local
residents; the reduced access, as discussed earlier, was brought about by
nationalization of rangeland and its increased use by commercial, nonlocal shepherds (Mary Martin, personal communication, 1989).

## Other Types of Settlement

Black tent encampments once were common in Khar o Tauran; at the
present time only two groups use them.[3] One winter tent camp is set up
on the east of the sand sea near the summer station of Chah Molla Ali. It
belongs to a group of Kurds who come from the area around Sabzevar, to
the north, to take advantage of Tauran's winter pasture and who move
back out again at the end of the spring. The other group still using black
tents is based in Rezabad, a village of recently settled Chubdari nomads
on the west of the sand sea. Virtually all Rezabadi households abandon
the village in summer to be out near their flocks and pasture during the
productive milking and fattening season. The location of their camps has
not been mapped.

*Bandkhānas* (field houses; literally, dam houses) are single-room houses
built on or next to dry-farmed fields to provide shade and shelter during
periods when crops at a distance from the owner's village need tending or
protecting. They vary from simple irregular huts of mud and brush to
packed mud or even mud brick structures with well-built roofs of pole
and brush. They are not very common; I saw only three.

Shepherds periodically stay out with the flocks overnight, especially at
times when the animals are grazing more or less around the clock, as they
do when there is a full moon. On these occasions they build fires for

cooking or warmth, which leave little trace and may never be revisited. These camps are *shab gomāri* (night-duty sites).

At least five locations in Khar o Tauran (Pai-ye Pir, Khar Kohna, Peighambar, Posht-e Asman, and Abol Hasani) and probably others are the sites of shrines. The shrines vary a good deal in their physical appearance. The building, when there is one, is built in as permanent a fashion as possible, given the likelihood that there may not be enough water for making mud bricks. At Khar Kohna, the shrine is built largely of potsherds picked up from the pre-Islamic and Islamic scatters in the vicinity. When built at the grave of a holy man (as all these local shrines are said to be), they are called *emāmzādas*.

There are also nonresidential sites of concentrated activity. In a number of places, springs and *qanāts* supply water for irrigated fields, although no one lives there; these are called *mazra'as* and are included in the government's *Village Gazetteers*. Check dams and other water management structures for rainfall agriculture are also found detached from settlement. As mentioned above, winter watering points need not be at or even very near the base station. It is better for the pasture and for the animals that they be at a distance, in fact, so that on cold days the sheep may drink at noon after a few hours' walk to warm up.

## LOCATION AND SUBSISTENCE

While the preceding summary description of material and locational similarities and differences among the three main types of settlements freezes the types into somewhat idealized forms, it also describes well most actual examples. If it were not for the makeshift reuse of structures originally intended for other purposes, the formal distinctions would hold almost perfectly.

Villages and transhumant stations clearly differ in productive specialization. But given the amount of environmental variation throughout the area and the dependence of productive activities on the environment, might not variously located villages also differ from each other in the ways they exploit their surroundings? In part they do, although not to the extent that might be predicted by location alone.

TABLE 3. ANIMAL OWNERSHIP IN
KHAR O TAURAN

| Village | Sheep and goats | | Cattle | |
|---|---|---|---|---|
| | 1966 | 1973 | 1966 | 1973 |
| Central Tauran | | | | |
| Baghestan | 400 | 600 | 8 | 20 |
| Barm | 1,500 | 200 | 6 | 10 |
| Eshqvan | 5,300 | 750 | 20 | 12 |
| Faridar | 1,200 | 100 | 9 | 0 |
| Jafarabad | 700 | 450 | 4 | 6 |
| Kariz | 1,000 | 1,320 | 6 | 10 |
| Nahar | 40 | 440 | 3 | 4 |
| Nauva | 200 | 350 | 5 | 5 |
| Ravazang | 1,500 | 600 | 2 | 3 |
| Salehabad | 7,300 | 7,000 | 25 | 20 |
| Taghmar | 200 | 400 | 5 | 6 |
| Yaka Rig | 300 | n.o. | 0 | n.o. |
| Zamanabad | 1,500 | 500 | 10 | 17 |
| Zivar | 300 | 230 | 0 | 0 |
| Outliers | | | | |
| Abol Hasani | n.o. | 250 | n.o. | 0 |
| Asbkeshan | 500 | 400 | 0 | 0 |
| Chah–e Meri | 500 | 600 | 0 | 0 |
| Cheshma Mer'i | 0 | 200 | 0 | 0 |
| Derazu | 300 | 900 | 0 | 0 |
| Ferinu | 200 | 1,320 | 2 | 5 |
| Garmab Bala | 300 | 245 | 4 | 2 |
| Garmab Pa'in | 500 | 1,500 | 3 | 1 |
| Hojjaj | 500 | 900 | 2 | 0 |
| Jorjis Peighambar | 0 | n.o. | 0 | n.o. |
| Kalagh Zili | 250 | 230 | 2 | 2 |
| Kalata Div | 600 | n.o. | 5 | n.o. |
| Kalata Rei | 600 | 560 | 8 | 6 |

TABLE 3. *cont.*

| Village | Sheep and goats | | Cattle | |
|---|---|---|---|---|
| | **1966** | **1973** | **1966** | **1973** |
| Kalata Reza Qoli | 400 | 0 | 2 | 0 |
| Mer'i | 100 | 350 | 0 | 0 |
| Narestana | 50 | n.o. | 0 | n.o. |
| Nur | 20 | 630 | 5 | 8 |
| Posht-e Asman | 50 | n.o. | 0 | n.o. |
| Salamrud | 200 | 210 | 3 | 2 |
| Talkhab | 900 | 900 | 7 | 0 |
| Tauchah | 450 | 545 | 4 | 1 |
| Tejur | 40 | 175 | 1 | 2 |
| Khar | | | | |
| Ahmadabad | 800 | 2,000 | 80 | 50 |
| Darbahang | 1,000 | 800 | 80 | 3 |
| Rezabad | 1,500 | 2,500 | 4 | 0 |

*Sources:* Iran 1969; Iran 1973a.

*Notes:* n.o. = not occupied. In addition to the animals cited, in 1973 Ahmadabad had 200 camels, Darbahang had 45 camels, and Rezabad had 200 camels.

The animals listed in Table 3 are sheep, goats, and cattle, with no distinction made (or available) among different breeds of either. Camels in large numbers are kept only by villages along the sand zone, although villages elsewhere may keep a handful or so. By local report, the same was true in the past, when camel populations were much higher.

Most residents in every village, regardless of its location, raise sheep and goats, including those who also raise cattle. Given the fact that goats fare better than sheep in the sand and in the hills, it would appear reasonable to expect that there would be a greater proportion of goats over sheep in outliers than in villages. There is, however, no consistent difference between areas in the proportions. The census statistics (Iran 1969b and 1973a) that report these ratios are probably not very accurate, and, as discussed below, they are confounded by the fact that although the counts are attached to a home base village, the animals are frequently herded in another ecological zone altogether.

Villages differ considerably in the relative roles farming and herding play in their economies. Some are much more pastoral than others. As might be expected, the total number of sheep and goats raised per household is greater in the outliers (both on the east and west side of the area) than central Tauran, where poor pasture (on account of crowding) and good agricultural conditions prevail. The total number of such animals in the outliers is also greater per household than in Khar, where the town of Ahmadabad provides other kinds of work and skews the pattern.

Even so, villages on the Tauran Plain, for example, raise many more sheep and goats than might be predicted by the amount of pastureland available to them on the plain itself. The reason, of course, is that the major part of pastoral activity is not based in the village but is carried out from satellite stations. Because of the social and political nature of access to pasture and water, these stations can only rarely be associated with their parent villages by locational factors (such as proximity).

Agriculture is also susceptible to environmental variation. As seen above, the purely ecological variables in agricultural production include altitude, water, soils, and terrain—factors that tend to be interrelated. Even within this small area, minor differences in environment are reflected in production. For example, villages at the lower altitudes have longer growing seasons and earlier harvests of grain than those at the higher altitudes. They also tend to have sandier, more saline soils, in which barley does better than wheat, and cotton does better than tobacco. In years of adequate rain, dry-farmed melons thrive on the abundant stretches of flat land near these villages. Villages at the higher altitudes (1,200 to 1,400 meters) can grow tobacco, garden crops, and tree crops more successfully than can the villages below.

Aside from the very good data for the village of Baghestan and some partial data for a few of the villages nearby, there is only the *Village Gazetteer* (Iran 1969b) from the 1966 census to provide data on agricultural production, and it is probably not very reliable. Taking it and the 1973 sample survey (Iran 1973a) at face value, there appears to be much less variation in production than would be predicted if agricultural choices were made solely on the basis of location.

The relationship among location, agricultural land, and settlement is confused by the fact that field ownership is open to nonresidents and many people own fields in other village systems. Furthermore, over half of the irrigated field systems and an unknown but even larger amount of dry-farmed land are not attached to any village at all, nor are they necessarily owned by those who live in the nearest occupied village. Fields in Tauran are privately owned and alienable; villages are not closed corporate communities in which residence is required for land rights. Marriage patterns, inheritance patterns, and the nearness of settlements to one another all contribute to the ownership pattern.

If there is only a partial fit between economic activities and settlement location, other factors must influence the location of sites and the choice of adaptive strategies in spite of site location. Some of these factors are historical. Others spring from the complex economy in these villages. The villagers have social and economic relations with each other and with a national market that is in turn part of an international market system. Some of these relations are new, but others are probably long-standing.

## LOCATION AND INTERACTION

No matter how remote the settlement, none in Khar o Tauran is isolated socially or economically. Communications may be slow or difficult, but they are essential to economic, social, and indeed demographic survival. Most of these villages are too small to be biologically self-sufficient, even if that were an aim, which it is not.

Khar o Tauran villages provide social and economic resources for one another that should be considered along with environmental resources when analyzing the character of settlement in the area. Villages compete as well, especially for water and pasture. This combination of cooperation and competition produces a complex patterning of interaction between villages.

Data collected for Baghestan, in the middle of the Tauran Plain, show interaction to be most intense with other villages on the plain (Table 4). It drops off sharply beyond the plain, and thereafter appears to correlate with settlement size and function rather than with proximity. It does not

TABLE 4. INTERACTION BETWEEN BAGHESTAN AND OTHER CENTRAL
TAURAN VILLAGES, 1976

| Village and no. of households | Ethnicity[a] | Distance from Baghestan (km) | No. of kin claimed by Baghestanis[b] | No. of marriages into Baghestan | No. of times visited by Baghestanis[b] |
|---|---|---|---|---|---|
| Faridar (20) | Ajam | 1.4 | 14 | 0 | 7 |
| Jafarabad (20) | Ajam | 1.5 | 10 | 0 | 9 |
| Nauva (12) | Arab | 1.5 | 8 | 1 | 11 |
| Barm (30) | Arab | 1.6 | 13 | 0 | 8 |
| Eshqvan (50) | Ajam | 2.1 | 2 | 1 | 9 |
| Zamanabad (45) | Ajam | 2.9 | 4 | 0 | 7 |
| Nahar (15) | Shekari | 3.3 | 2 | 2 | 8 |
| Salehabad (30) | Amri | 3.4 | 16 | 0 | 14 |
| Zivar (15) | Shekari | 4.1 | 3 | 0 | 4 |
| Kariz (24) | Shakri | 4.3 | 9 | 2 | 5 |
| Taghmar (8) | Shekari | 5.2 | 1 | 0 | 7 |
| Ravazang (5) | Amri | 5.4 | 1 | 0 | 0 |
| Nur (12) | ? | 10.8 | 14 | 2 | 3 |

a. Baghestan calls itself an Arab village.

b. Data were obtained by interviewing adults living in Baghestan. No verification of reported figures was possible; therefore data may reflect perceived connections as much as actual ones.

appear to follow the gradually decreasing curve predicted by the simple gravity or distance decay models proposed by geographers, which archaeologists have sometimes used to predict interaction between settlements (Hodder and Orton 1976).

Neither do those models describe what happens on the plain, where social interaction does not necessarily entail proximity. As evidenced by kin connections, marriages, and visiting patterns, for example, interaction tends not to favor nearest neighbors. Indeed, in several cases there may be nearest neighbor aversion instead.

Technology, scale, and the social nature of interaction help explain these findings. First, when villagers visit back and forth on the plain, they travel on foot or donkey. When they leave the plain, they usually take a bus or ride in the local pickup truck and head for the city. When traveling in this mode, they tend to bypass settlements in between. (Before motorized transport, the trip to the city took five days with five overnight stops in settlements along the way.)

Second, villages on the plain apparently are simply too close together for distance to exert much friction on interaction. All thirteen lie within a circle 6 kilometers in radius; as noted earlier, the closest neighbors are only 1.8 kilometers apart. From Baghestan, none of the other villages is more than one and a half hours away by foot, and most are less than an hour away. The nearest are within a fifteen- or twenty-minute walk. The result produced is what Plog (1976) calls a "plateau effect," within which, distance has no effect on the intensity of interaction. The radius of this effect here is about 6 kilometers (in his discussion, Plog finds it generally to be within 5 miles, or 8 kilometers). In these circumstances, *who* other villagers are has more influence on interaction than *where* they are. This factor may help to account for the only moderate interaction between Baghestan and Eshqvan, a near neighbor. From what can be reconstructed of local history (Mary Martin, personal communication, 1978), Baghestan's relations with Eshqvan in the past were competitive rather than neighborly; hostile actions between the two villages were frequent. The same was true of some other pairs of villages. In part these enmities were fueled by competing groups of khans and their followers—the ethnic labels attached to each of the villages are remnants of past allegiances if not actual tribal segments (Table 4). As noted above, the political organization of the plain has changed considerably since those days, yet a social coolness appears to persist, seen in the lack of intermarriage and visits between particular pairs.

Given this history, why are villages so crowded together in Khar o Tauran—to the point that in many cases there is not enough room for sufficient fields and pasture within the village limits? The clustered pattern is certainly influenced to some extent by the distribution of agricultural resources (including water, soils, and topography), which are more favorable on the upper plains. When the initial *qanāt* or agricultural investment decisions were made, however, another factor appears to have influenced the spacing of settlement: the presence of through-traffic caravan routes.

Khar and Tauran lie along a minor east-west caravan route that follows the northern border of the central Iranian *kavir*. Its traffic has for centuries fluctuated with politics and security in the mountains and plains to the north, along the base and in the highlands of the Kopet-Dag. For much of the time, it was a poor third choice, used only when insecurity kept the northerly routes blocked (Aubin 1971). By the nineteenth century, renewed governmental investment in caravansaries and postal relays along the Khorasan Road set the main route through Abasabad and Sabzevar to the north of Khar o Tauran; it has remained there ever since.

The meager historical and archaeological evidence also suggests that this southern desert route was once more important than it is today. Tomaschek proposed it as a link in his reconstruction of the Roman route preserved in the Peutinger Table (Tomaschek 1883, 228), and it is in fact the shortest of the alternative paths leading east to Herat from Shahrud. The area's main sherd scatters of pre-Islamic and Islamic date appear at intervals of roughly a day's march, 20 to 30 kilometers. Thus the original *qanāt* investment that provided the basis for settlement in the area may have been made, at least in part, to serve and to be served by those traveling across northeastern Iran.

The clustering of villages is a long-standing characteristic of settlement in the area, judging by frequent comments in the few traveler's reports available (Clerk 1861; Forster 1970 [originally published in 1798]; Vaughn 1893). Even so, in the nineteenth century, settlements were probably more closely matched in size and more dispersed than they are today (compare the *qal'a* [fortified dwelling] and village distributions in Figure 8). The persistence of a clustered pattern and the current trend toward a drawing back of settlement into fewer, larger, and more centrally located sites are at the present time due largely to the location of modern-day services, such as schools, bath houses, and kerosene supplies. If motorized vehicles become common throughout the area and roads improve, settlement may again become more dispersed.

## SETTLEMENT STABILITY

The dynamic nature of settlement in Khar o Tauran is apparent both from the frequency of present-day changes in settlement location and type and

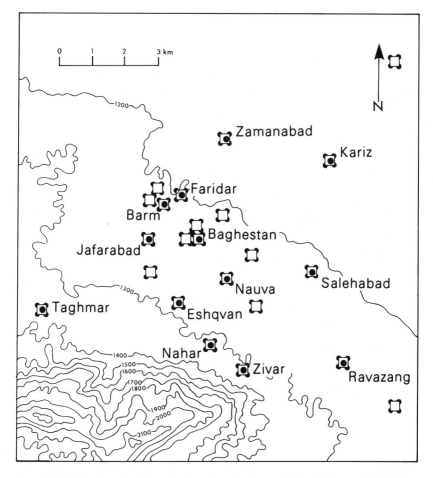

Figure 8. Distribution of *qal'as* and villages on the Tauran Plain. *Qal'as* are indicated by squares, villages by dots.

from the number of abandoned ruins and other archaeological remains in the area. Settlement stability and instability, here or elsewhere, can be spatial, temporal, or both. *Locational stability* is a spatial term that refers to the repeated reuse of particular sites. A locationally stable area has a limited number of locations that are used for settlement. New settlements tend to be established on top of (or very near to) abandoned sites rather than at virgin locations. I use the term *occupational stability* for the temporal dimension of settlement. An occupationally stable area is one in which sites tend to be continuously occupied in a particular time period.[4] These terms emphasize sites rather than people, even though, as shall be seen later, settlements and residents do not necessarily correspond in simple ways. The two concepts are useful not only for reconstructing the history of settlement in the area but also for laying out the processes through which settlement decisions are made.

The locational stability of villages and field systems in Khar o Tauran appears to be relatively high. Sherd scatters at villages such as Baghestan, Zamanabad, and Asbkeshan are 2,000 years old, if not older. The nature of investment in agricultural land in this area contributes to both locational and occupation stability. The initial expense of building a *qanāt* is high. Both the water system and land at a site that is not continuously maintained will deteriorate and require extra effort for rehabilitation. Moreover, the cumulative effects of alterations to the landscape (terracing, soil conditioning) make an older site more desirable than a newly established one. Sites also need the protection that residence provides: when the law was in local hands, an unoccupied site and water source were at high risk of takeover by hostile neighbors.

Working alongside conditions that promote locational stability are those that promote occupational instability, as people and activities circulate around a limited number of available sites. Judging from what is known of the history of Iran elsewhere (see especially Kortum 1975) and from the absence of occupational deposit of any sizable depth in the area, periods of repeated settlement abandonment seem highly likely historically. Some of the abandonments have probably lasted for centuries. (Shallow occupational deposits here are also the result of the tendency to rebuild *next to* rather than directly *on top of* earlier settlement. See Chapter 7 for more on the causes of mound formation here and elsewhere in the arid world.) Kortum (1975) counts climatic conditions, dependency on fragile irrigation works, cyclical swings in the degree of nomadic pastoralism, and political unrest among the reasons for the frequent abandonment of settlements and, indeed, whole regions in Iran. These factors have all been present in Khar o Tauran.

Over short periods of time, one obvious way in which settlement stability varies in Khar o Tauran is with the cycle of the seasons. Most villages in Khar o Tauran are occupied throughout the year by most of their inhabitants (the heavily pastoral village of Rezabad is an exception, as it is to many other aspects of village life). Summer stations are occupied from May into August, depending on the condition of the range; winter stations, from October through April.

Over longer periods of time, occupational stability varies not only according to settlement type but also according to location and size. These variables are themselves interrelated. Quantified information is not available for winter and summer stations, but Table 5 summarizes population size and occupational stability for villages in the three parts of Khar o Tauran during a twenty-year period (see also Horne 1993).

Random fluctuations in demography have their greatest effect on very small settlements, making them inherently less stable than larger ones, and individual settlements in this area have, for the most part, always been small. In addition, summer stations, like small villages in the outlying areas, appear to come and go more frequently than larger, central villages and are more sensitive to swings in economic and climatic conditions. Winter stations, until recently, were very short-lived on account of their periodic infestation with vermin and consequent burning and relocation. Abandonment in bad years and reoccupation in good years is another mark of the flexible nature of agricultural and settlement strategies in areas like this.

Some of the factors in settlement instability, such as the deterioration of pastureland, are long-term, directional trends that may not be reversible. Others, such as attention to or neglect of agricultural investment, appear to be cyclical in nature. *Qanāt* irrigation gives a special twist to these cyclical processes of settlement. Although in the short term the improvements to the agricultural landscape that accompany a successful *qanāt* system promote occupational stability, in the long term the system

## TABLE 5. OCCUPATION AND ABANDONMENT OF PERMANENT SETTLEMENTS IN KHAR O TAURAN FROM 1956 TO 1976

| Village | 1956 | 1966 | 1973 | 1976 |
|---|:---:|:---:|:---:|:---:|
| Central Tauran | | | | |
| Baba Kuh | + | + | − | − |
| Baghestan | + | + | + | + |
| Barm | + | + | + | + |
| Eshqvan | + | + | + | + |
| Faridar | + | + | + | + |
| Jafarabad | + | + | + | + |
| Kariz | + | + | + | + |
| Nahar | + | + | + | + |
| Nauva | + | + | + | + |
| Ravazang | + | + | + | + |
| Salehabad | + | + | + | + |
| Taghmar | + | + | + | + |
| Yaka Rig | − | + | − | − |
| Zamanabad | + | + | + | + |
| Zivar | + | + | + | + |
| Outliers | | | | |
| Abol Hasani | − | − | + | + |
| Asbkeshan | + | + | + | + |
| Chah-e Meri | + | + | + | + |
| Cheshma Harbi | − | − | + | − |
| Cheshmaha-ye Mer'i | − | − | + | + |
| Derazab | + | + | + | + |
| Ferinu | + | + | + | + |
| Garmab Bala | + | + | + | + |
| Garmab Pa'in | + | + | + | + |
| Hesar Bala | + | − | − | − |
| Hesar Pa'in | + | − | − | − |
| Hojjaj | + | + | + | + |
| Jorjis Peighambar | − | + | + | − |

TABLE 5. *cont.*

| Village | 1956 | 1966 | 1973 | 1976 |
|---|---|---|---|---|
| Kalagh Zili | − | + | + | + |
| Kalata Div | + | + | + | − |
| Kalata Rei | + | + | + | − |
| Kalata Reza Qoli | − | + | + | + |
| Mer'i | − | + | + | + |
| Narestana | + | + | − | − |
| Nur | + | + | + | + |
| Posht-e Asman | − | + | − | − |
| Salamrud | + | + | + | + |
| Talkhab | + | + | + | + |
| Tauchah | − | + | + | + |
| Tejur | − | + | + | − |
| Khar | | | | |
| Ahmadabad | + | + | + | + |
| Darbahang | + | + | + | + |
| Rezabad | − | + | + | + |

*Sources:* Author and Iran 1969 and 1973a.

*Notes:* + = occupied; − = abandoned. In 1966 mean village size in Central Tauran was 21.3 households, ranging from 3 to 50; in the outliers, 7.0 households, ranging from 1 to 18; in Khar, 60.3 households, ranging from 44 to 95.

runs down. Maintenance, major and minor, is essential in order to keep up the strength of the flow of water. Blockages and seepage are chronic problems; earthquakes and intentional destruction occur less frequently but are devastating (Melville 1984). According to one estimate for the edge of the Dasht-e Kavir, a *qanāt* that is not maintained will in theory dry up in thirty years (M. Mahdavi in McLachlan 1988, 279n59). Ideally, routine maintenance should be undertaken yearly and major maintenance every ten years or so (Hartl 1979; Holmes 1975).

*Qanāts* in rural Iran are owned and maintained by those who hold shares in them. In the traditional systems of tenure, which have in most places been altered by land reform and government development projects, a single wealthy landlord could own a great many *qanāt* systems, along with the fields and villages they irrigated. The peasants who farm the land would be charged with maintaining the *qanāt*. In some places, however, particularly in desert fringe areas such as Khar o Tauran, the villagers themselves own the land and the water with which to irrigate it. They must rely on their own organization to maintain the water on which their livelihood depends. Short of truly disastrous events, prompt and continuous reinvestment in a *qanāt* system could keep it running almost indefinitely. *Qanāts* run down for social and economic reasons rather than technical ones.

A study by Holmes (1975) in a region to the north of Khar o Tauran demonstrates how the social context of *qanāt* irrigation leads to cycles of investment and decline (Holmes 1975). In her model, after the initial construction of the *qanāt* by an urban entrepreneur, the number of shareholders and their interest in the system soon fragments through inheritance. Small shareholders with diminishing returns cannot easily be mobilized to repair the aging system. If the site is desirable enough, it may be purchased and revitalized by another investor. If, however, it is unused for too long (more than five years), it may fail to attract investors and become permanently abandoned. Holmes estimates that this process occurs within a period of twenty-five to forty-five years—perhaps thirty to thirty-five on average, or within the lifetime of the original investor's grandchildren.

Shareholdings in Khar o Tauran are also small, although the owners are not absentee landlords as they are in Holmes's study (1975). In other parts of Iran, however, large landholders or khans (tribal leaders) had the power and the wealth to maintain and rebuild their *qanāts* when disaster struck (Spooner 1974). Powerful men of this sort appear to have controlled land and pasture in Khar o Tauran in the recent past (Martin 1982b). The size and quality of architectural ruins and *qal'as* on the plain certainly attest to greater social stratification and wealth in the past (Horne 1991).

One might surmise that settlements organized by such powerful men would be more occupationally stable than the more susceptible ones described by Holmes. The proposition deserves archaeological and ethnohistoric investigation, for while successful khans provided leadership, protection, and a measure of economic security for their clients and relatives, they also attracted competition. Without a strong central authority to keep peace, water sources and agricultural fields and flocks were reputedly in continuous jeopardy from neighbors as well as outsiders. During the nineteenth century, Turkmen brigands raided the area on horseback for animals and slaves, and villagers lived in constant fear. According to one early nineteenth-century observer, these raiders would sweep down from 200 miles above to 200 miles below the high-road towns of Shahrud, Sabzevar, and Nishapur on forays lasting a week or more (Fraser 1984). The road directly to the north of Khar o Tauran was especially dangerous, deserted of settlement, and referred to by travelers as the "Marches of Terror." Even as recently as the 1960s, a group of Basseri entered from northwest of the area, set themselves up in the village of Baghestan, and attempted to take over control of local water holes. They were finally ousted by the local population, who took the situation into their own hands (Mary Martin, personal communication, 1978). The traditional response to such insecurity has been to erect *qal'as* and watch towers, even at the small field sites that serve as summer stations.

Government-instituted pacification and protection have undermined the power base of the local khans. The *qal'as* are falling into disrepair, and new ones are no longer being built. The social scene is much less stratified than in the past, and the built environment reflects it in less differentiated, more humble dwellings. Khar o Tauran thus contrasts with areas in Afghanistan and Pakistan, where stylistically, although not functionally, impressive *qal'a* are still being built by large landowners for the prestige they bring (Hallet and Samizay 1980; Jentsch and Loose 1980; Szabo and Barfield 1991). Khar o Tauran, a less fertile area, does not today have individuals wealthy enough or display-conscious enough to build in that manner. How long this will remain so is unpredictable, given the present state of Iran's economy. When I was there doing fieldwork, some individuals (especially in Zamanabad and Salehabad) were indeed building large, well-decorated houses—but in urban rather than traditional rural styles.

## ARCHAEOLOGICAL RECOGNITION OF SETTLEMENT TYPES

This discussion of the varied and fluid nature of settlement in Khar o Tauran holds a number of implications for archaeological analysis. Variation in the season of use, the activities carried out, and the personnel present in settlements means that one site cannot be considered representative of the whole. A well-designed survey would be essential to secure adequate coverage of the range of ways in which even this small an area is occupied. Variation in the relative longevity of different kinds of sites means that, over a period of time, the archaeological record would show a disproportionate accumulation of some sites compared with others. To avoid counting such sites more than once in archaeological data, it would be necessary to introduce a correction to account for instability. Moreover, those providing population and carrying capacity estimates must beware the influence of double counting not only sites but also the people who live in them. Drawing boundaries around people and their activities is always problematic in areas exploited by mobile populations. In a case such as this one, for example, pastoral stations should be given full weight for regional productivity estimates but not for regional population estimates when those who use them, the Sangsari, are present only seasonally.

The different degree of preservation of sites is a well-known obstacle to unbiased archaeological collection. The most ephemeral among Khar o Tauran's camps will undoubtedly be quickly destroyed by the passage of time. But assuming that some semblance of the variety once present were recoverable, how might these several types be recognized? Criteria for identifying the appearance of sedentariness in the archaeological record, such as those assessed by Rafferty (1985), are generally useful for thinking about how to proceed. Some of these indicators, especially those that apply to entire settlement patterns, are geared toward recognizing the initial or growing appearance of sedentariness in a developmental sequence. Others could be used to distinguish degrees of stability among contemporary settlements within a typologically sedentary society, such as the one in Khar o Tauran. These latter include architectural indicators, such as more substantially built dwellings, the replacement of round with square houses, and the appearance of ceremonial or communal structures; artifactual indicators, such as a greater variety and quantity of material goods, especially those involving storage and trade; and indicators of adaptive strategies, such as evidence for year-round occupation and agricultural technology (Rafferty 1985, 128–37).

Previous sections of this chapter described the physical, locational, and occupational differences among the several types of settlement in Khar o Tauran (see also Horne 1993). Compared with pastoral stations, villages in Khar o Tauran have buildings that are more expensive to build, more permanent, and of greater functional variety. Dwellings are square in villages, round in winter and summer stations (when built for that purpose). Only villages have communal structures such as *hammāms* and *hoseiniyas*. Villages certainly have a much wider range of artifacts, including ones that are more costly or decorative, than those used at pastoral stations. Distinctions based on settlement morphology, the form and layout of the site, work well for winter stations. Because so many summer stations were once year-round settlements, however, they are less easily differentiated from villages. In this present context, indicators that emphasize seasonality of occupation and degree of pastoral activity will probably be the most useful for distinguishing these special-use settlements. Among these are portable or temporary substitutes for standard village features, such as skins, cloth, woven sacks, and shallow hearths for making bread. Unfortunately, many of these indicators are perishable, and only the absence of their permanent equivalents (*kondus*, pottery, *tanurs*) would be noted. Supplementing architectural and artifactual study, therefore, should be the sometimes ingenious technical analyses of mineral deposits and organic remains, including characteristic minerals from animal dung or carbonized layers of deposit from the disinfectant burning of animal shelters (see Brochier, Villa, and Giacomarra 1992). These technical analyses are applicable especially to the identification of seasonal and pastoral activities. The identification of agricultural fields and terraces was discussed in Chapter 3.

Thus, for areas of transhumance such as this one, it could be possible, archaeologically, to identify sites that are occupied seasonally and to recognize their place within a settlement pattern type of base and satellite special-purpose habitation sites. But being able to construct a settlement typology is of limited use to understanding what went on and why. In order to reconstruct in useful detail the kinds of activities that actually took place at these several kinds of settlements, an archaeologist would need to have more specific on-site information.

# CHAPTER 5

# VILLAGE SPACES

he architectural holdings of Baghestan consist of the occupied and unoccupied remains of what were once three separate residential settlements—Gauju, Kalata, and Qal'a Baghestan (see Figures 9 and 10).[1] Each area has its own *qanāt* and field system. Today two of the areas have no households in residence; everyone lives in the central settlement, Gauju. The surviving structures of the other two are used only for storage facilities and animal shelter and are still owned for the most part by descendants of the original inhabitants. Such shifts in residence appear to be characteristic of settlement in the area.

Nearly all the spaces and structures of Baghestan are used for residential or production activities and are privately owned by their individual users. Only rarely is ownership shared by members of several households; in those cases the owners are said to be *sharik* (partners) with one another (in each case the co-owners are brothers). A small part of the village is, nevertheless, not in private hands—for example, the *hoseiniya,* the *hammām,* and the alleys that serve as pathways through the village. Villagers say these places are owned by either no one (for example, alleys) or everyone (the *hoseiniya*). None of these serves as a focal point around which structures are oriented because of common use, symbolic meaning, or any other such quality. They neither attract nor repel private construction.

Privately owned structures in the village are generally either mud brick, domed buildings, which are permanent and are used for both people and animals, or else mud-walled shelters roofed with brush and mud, which are less permanent and are used only for animals. In plan the

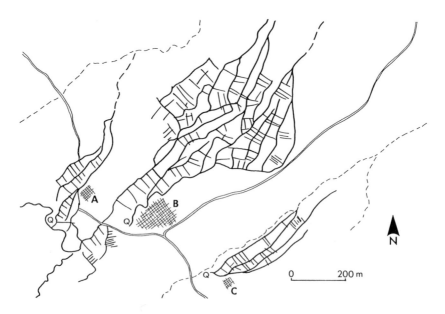

Figure 9. The three areas that make up Baghestan village and their irrigated field systems. A = Qal'a Baghestan, B = Gauju (the core area), C = Kalata, and Q = *qanāt* outlet at head of irrigation channels.

two types are easily distinguishable from each other both by shape and wall thickness. Between 1976 and 1978 two new animal shelters of a more permanent nature were built. These are the same type that are built at winter stations out on the rangeland for sheep and goats. At the winter stations they are dug into the ground, but in the village they merely sit on the surface.

The village in its entirety contains 170 permanent domed or vaulted structures that I refer to as rooms even though the local term is the Persian *khāna,* usually glossed as "house." Of these rooms, 141 are in Gauju, 5 are in Kalata, and the remaining 24 are in Qal'a Baghestan. Also in Gauju but not tallied in the above count are a mill, *hoseiniya,* shop, and four *eivāns* (also called *salon* or *hashti* in Baghestan), or entrance porches, often used as rooms in the summer (see Appendix, Figures A-2, A-7).

With the exception of the vaulted roof, which is always built by a specialist (who may be a fellow villager, working part or full time at

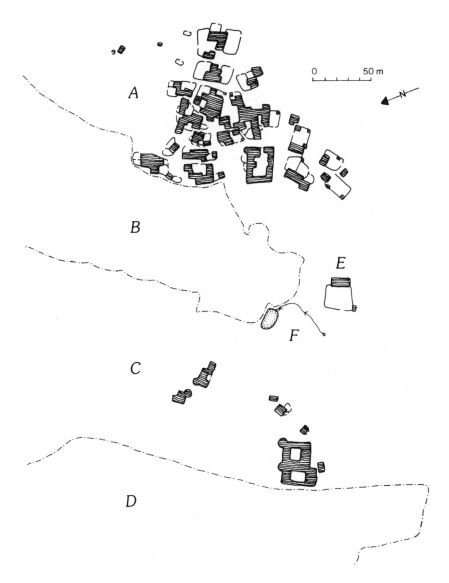

Figure 10. The village of Baghestan in relation to two of its field systems. A = the central core, B and D = irrigated field systems, C = the residentially abandoned area of Qal'a Baghestan, E = the government schoolhouse, and F = the nearest *qanāt* outlet and its storage pond. Shaded areas indicate buildings.

building), all the work of design, building, and maintenance and alterations can be, and often is, undertaken by the owner and his family. More and more frequently, a specialist from the village of Eshqvan or from the villages outside Sabzevar is called in to build the entire structure with labor supplied from within the village. Most of the materials of construction are local in origin, although windows and doors are increasingly purchased in the city.

Individual rooms are the basic building unit in this area; they rarely lead into one another but, rather, open directly onto courtyards or alleys. There are four basic types of rooms—living rooms, storerooms, straw storage rooms, and animal rooms—distinguished more by function than by form. Living rooms are used for eating, sleeping, entertaining, tea making, some cooking, and miscellaneous noncommercial craft activities. One kind of storeroom is used for household chores such as cooking, and for storing food, domestic equipment, and clothing. The other kind is used to store agricultural equipment, fertilizer, fodder, firewood, or straw. Animal rooms are stables for oxen and donkeys, and sometimes for sheep, goats, chickens, and agricultural equipment. (Sheep, goats, and chickens are also kept in courtyard pens.) A few families have rooms used exclusively as kitchens, but these are similar enough in use and contents to be classified as storerooms.

Several public and community buildings complete the inventory of building types. A small store inside the part-time shopkeeper's compound holds yardgoods, copy books, batteries, soap, and other small items that are not locally produced. The shopkeeper also butchers and sells meat for other villagers. The diesel-powered village mill is housed next to the miller's compound at the edge of the village, where patronage from villages without mills does not interfere with village privacy (although it is located there because that is where the miller lives, not vice versa; the previous mill was right in the heart of the village, in a room in the *qal'a*). There is a single *hoseiniya*, where sermons and commemorative rites are held for Hosein and Hasan, the foremost martyrs of the Shi'i sect of Islam. The government-sponsored schoolhouse consists of two rooms flanking an *eivān* and a large courtyard outside the village core, near the head of the *qanāt*. It is built of mud brick with a white gypsum-plastered interior. Its courtyard has a small garden, a volley ball net, two latrines side-by-side, and a well. The schoolteacher, a member of the literacy corps (*sepāh-e dānesh*), is not from the village and is in residence only in the winter, during which time he rents an empty room. In 1978 he rented the compound vacated by one of the households. In theory, both boys and girls attend school, which goes up to fifth grade. In practice, few boys and even fewer girls finish school.

Lastly, the old traditional bathhouse, of the type sometimes called "Turkish," is down below the schoolhouse, close to the water, which, when the building was still in use, had to be hauled to the pools inside. Built of baked brick (mud brick would melt in the humid heat) with Gothic-arched niches, sunken pools, and cement-plastered benches, it is very different in style and materials from other traditional buildings in the village. The water in the interior room was heated by brushwood burned in a specially built semidomed structure attached to the outside. This heating chamber is unusual in that it is built largely of reused baked brick, cobbles, and even grinding stones, which appear to have been taken from the early Islamic sites surrounding the village. This old *hammām* was used only in winter. In the summer, people bathe in the open at the Kalata pond or inside a low enclosure wall at the Gauju *qanāt*. A new community bathhouse of modern materials and design was under construction in the summer of 1978, paid for partly by the government and partly by subscription from each household. Use will be without charge to Baghestanis except for the running cost of fuel. Outsiders will be charged a per use fee.

Most of the other shared spaces, whether used by small groups or the entire village, lie outside the residential area proper. These areas include those that provide water: the *qanāt* mouth (*sarāb*), where dishes are washed and water is drawn; the low-walled bathing and laundry enclosure that straddles the Gauju *qanāt* channel; and the two pools (*hauz*), one at Gauju and one at Kalata, for storing irrigation water, watering animals, washing clothes, and bathing. The cemetery lies to the southwest of the village on one of a series of natural rises that are covered with cobbles and glazed sherds tentatively dated to the ninth through twelfth centuries. The cobbles, apparently remnants of earlier walls and buildings, are a convenient source for the shallow mound of stones that covers each modern grave. Six smoothly mud-plastered threshing floors, ranging in size from about 60 to 750 square meters lie at the village edges, each shared and maintained jointly by three to five households. They are used for storing unthreshed grain, threshing and winnowing, and weighing and distributing processed grain. Milking stations are also shared by several households; the animals are milked together and the yield rotated among the group's member households in turn. Grape-processing areas for boiling crushed grapes to a thick molasseslike product are near the walled grape and melon gardens found near each *qanāt* head.

*All* space in Baghestan is in fact shared in one way or another. With the single exception of an elderly widow and a bachelor, who usually stays in another village, no one lives alone. There is no such thing as "a room of one's own."

The built-up area of the village contains no productive land, such as gardens or orchards. Neither do the water channels pass through the village itself (see English 1966 for a contrasting arrangement in Kirman). Spaces between buildings are used for passage or for places to dig up earth (for construction or soil conditioning) or to dump trash. Except for unwritten agreements on free access, there is nothing to prevent the filling in of these unused spaces with new construction.

Fitting so many structures into a clustered village is achieved by sharing house and compound walls; there are also four second-story rooms (*bālākhānas*). Only sixteen rooms in the entire village are freestanding; all the others share at least one party wall (usually a long wall), and some in the interior of the village share three. The patterned way in which this happens produces strings of rooms and blocks of compounds.

A degree of common orientation of buildings can be seen just by inspection of the village plan (see Figures 11–14). The common orientation holds for other villages on the plain as well. More will be said below about the orientation of individual rooms and the reasons behind it.

## THE VILLAGE AS WORKPLACE

We saw in the previous chapter how villages are located with respect to their natural resources, these resources being (in decreasing order of locational importance) water, agricultural fields, pasture and firewood, and

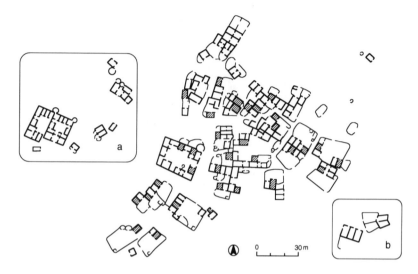

Figure 11. Distribution of summer living rooms (shaded areas) in Baghestan. Winter living rooms are used as storerooms in the summer and are shown in Figure 12. a = Qal'a Baghestan, b = Kalata.

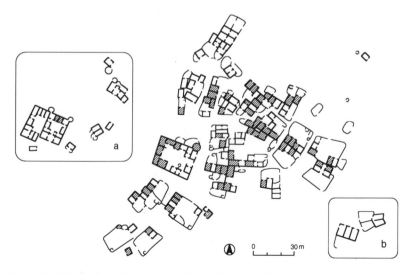

Figure 12. Distribution of storerooms (shaded areas) in Baghestan. a = Qal'a Baghestan, b = Kalata.

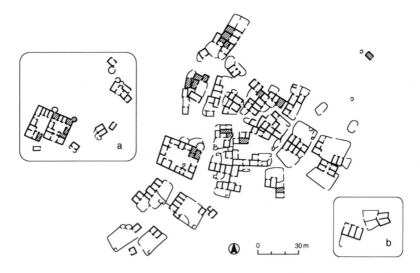

Figure 13. Distribution of straw storage rooms (shaded areas) in Baghestan. a = Qal'a Baghestan, b = Kalata.

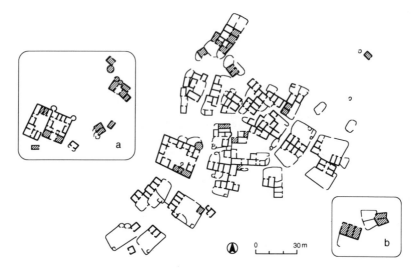

Figure 14. Distribution of animal rooms (shaded areas) in Baghestan. a = Qal'a Baghestan, b = Kalata.

building materials. Although all these resources (with the exception of building materials) are located beyond the built area of the village, many activities involving their procurement, processing, distribution, storage, and consumption take place within the village itself, often in special-purpose buildings or areas.

Figures 11 through 14 show the location of room types within the village. Table 6 shows the allocation of rooms to different functions. More than a quarter of the rooms within the core area and nearly 40 percent of rooms overall are reserved solely for agricultural and pastoral storage and stabling. When courtyard spaces, outside pens, and mixed-use storage rooms are added to these numbers, the degree to which the village is a workplace as much as a dwelling place becomes clear.

Although different types of rooms are distributed in different ways, the location of specialized structures or areas within the village rarely can be attributed to the location of the resources they depend on. For example, animal houses and straw storage rooms tend to concentrate at Kalata, Qal'a Baghestan, and the northern part of the village core. Because of the custom of recycling rooms, their distribution is more closely related to the age of the buildings than to proximity to fields or pasture. Older structures, found in these older parts of the settlement, are more likely to

TABLE 6. ALLOCATION OF VILLAGE SPACE AMONG ROOM TYPES IN
BAGHESTAN, 1976

| Area | No. of living rms | No. of store-rooms | No. of straw rms | No. of animal rms | Total no. of rooms | Total area (m²) | Mean room size (m²) |
|---|---|---|---|---|---|---|---|
| Gauju | 33 | 69 | 19 | 20 | 141 | 1,863.3 | 13.2 |
| | (23.4%) | (48.9%) | (13.5%) | (14.2%) | (100.0%) | | |
| Kalata | 0 | 0 | 0 | 5 | 5 | 97.6 | 19.5 |
| | (0.0%) | (0.0%) | (0.0%) | (100.0%) | (100.0%) | | |
| Qal'a Baghestan | 0 | 2 | 6 | 16 | 24 | 346.6 | 14.4 |
| | (0.0%) | (8.3%) | (25.1%) | (66.7%) | (100.0%) | | |
| Total | 33 | 71 | 25 | 41 | 170 | 2,307.5 | 13.6 |
| | (19.4%) | (41.8%) | (14.7%) | (24.1%) | (100.0%) | | |

be used for straw storage and animals. The block of buildings built especially as animal houses (shown at the top of Figure 14 and in the Appendix, Figure A-1) is probably an exception. These buildings are near the largest of Baghestan's three field systems, and all the owners have significant agricultural holdings there—although several of them also own the fields at Kalata. The most desirable location for storerooms is in newer structures, as near to living rooms as possible, and these are all in the residential core of the village. Living rooms are quite evenly spaced throughout Gauju, especially during the summertime. Unlike in urban Tehran, rural Kirman (English 1966), and elsewhere (Kramer 1982b, 271), newer and richer dwellings in Baghestan are not clustered higher on the slope toward the water or *qanāt* source. The eight households in the wealthiest quartile and the eight in the poorest are evenly distributed throughout the village.

Although the location of resources and products has not influenced the internal organization of the village, several activities that take place at the edge of the village are located according to their functions. Threshing, milking, and grape processing all take place in more or less permanently marked-out areas. They balance proximity to the village (the destination of the grain, straw, milk, and grape syrup) with proximity to the products' origins (fields, water source, and gardens). In addition, threshing floors are usually located so that the prevailing winds do not carry the chaff into the village.

## THE VILLAGE AS SHELTER

Shelter for people and their animals, activities, equipment, and products is unquestionably one of the most important functions of the buildings in the village of Baghestan.[2] The climate of this area of Iran (like many other temperate arid zones) is characterized by hot summers, cold winters, frequent high winds and dust storms, summer drought, and winter dampness accompanied by rain and sometimes snow. Earthquakes are an infrequent but real hazard. Survival in this climate would be impossible without temporary or permanent shelter from the elements.

In terms of need, shelter can be minimally defined as that which ensures biological survival. Beyond that bare minimum, the amount of shelter that ensures efficient work conditions, maintains general health, and provides a generally tolerable environment within an acceptable range of personal comfort is of course both culturally and individually defined. Nevertheless, in an attempt to establish a hypothetical comfort zone for Baghestan following the procedure used by Koenigsberger and his colleagues (1973), I found that, the Western picture of Iranian villages notwithstanding, the range of effective temperatures (which take humidity and air movement into account) actually falls *below* the comfort zone most of the year. It is cold, not heat, that causes greater discomfort most of the time.

That does not mean, however, that other climatic factors are unimportant or ignored. Nor does it mean that the environment is as uniform as it appears in smoothed-out curves of averages. Composite climates such as this one, with periods of heat and cold, rain and drought, pose quite different problems at different times of the year and even at different times of the day. In Khar o Tauran, the struggle is not only to keep warm and dry in the winter but to keep out of the sun's worst heat in the summer and dust-laden winds all year round. Still, among these goals, winter warmth is undoubtedly the most difficult to achieve in terms of effort, cost, and available technology.

People in Tauran apparently do not take rare events like earthquakes into account in their design of structures or of villages (see also Ambraseys and Melville 1982, 25). It is not that infrequent natural disasters are ignored but, rather, that they are more likely to be placed in the realm of ritual than in that of material control. The earthquake that leveled Tabas (Ambraseys and Melville 1982, 103–106), a city 150 kilometers to the southeast of Tauran, occurred a few days before I left the field in September of 1978. The rocking that shook the village brought people out of their houses into the alleys, where they called to each other and invoked the name of Allah (using the Koranic formula "There is no God but Allah . . ."). My neighbor across the alley refused to leave his dooryard chores, and no one could prevail upon him to come out. The talk in general concerned the earthquake as a divine comment on the revolutionary turmoil in Iran at the time and a belief that this sign would resolve the disturbance. Radio Tehran's announcement that there would be a full eclipse of the moon that night underscored the earthquake's meaning for the villagers.

Domed mud brick structures are in fact quite unsafe under severe earthquake stress, especially where the roof plaster of mud and straw has been built up through years of maintenance.[3] Location and layout are other contributing factors to building collapse and human injury or death. A village sited on firm bedrock holds up better than one on loose alluvium, and a small, open settlement offers faster escape routes than does a larger, densely compact one (Tchalenko and Ambraseys 1973). Most of Baghestan is built on a rocky spur, and the earthquake did no damage. I was told there was structural cracking in some of the other villages, but I had no opportunity to confirm the reports. In any case, the epicenter was far enough away that severe damage was unlikely on this occasion.

The more ordinary effects of the environment are controlled in a variety of ways. The simplest is spatial behavior (working behind natural windbreaks or under trees, sleeping outside in the summer). Appropriate clothing, wood-burning space heaters, and appropriate building materials and building design also contribute to making the environment tolerable. In the summer, most activities, including sleeping, take place outside. Villages at the edge of the sand sea, such as Darbahang, Zamanabad, and Talkhab, have *bādgirs,* simple roof ventilators on the top of the dome that face the wind and circulate air through the house, but Baghestanis apparently do not feel the need for this device. In the winter, drafty windows and roof vents are bricked up and plastered. Good maintenance of the mud or lime plaster on the inside and outside of the walls also helps to insulate the rooms. (Quilt-covered charcoal braziers, called *korsi* or *sandali,* are common in colder areas of Iran and Afghanistan but are not found in this area.)

Climate control can also be achieved through the layout of the settlement—the way village structures are located in relation to the environment and to one another. The clustered, wall-sharing plan characteristic of Near Eastern villages is frequently explained as an adaptation to a hot, arid environment. Such an explanation is not adequate in Khar o Tauran because, as stated above, cold, not heat, is the more severe thermal constraint. Still, what works to regulate hot temperatures works to regulate cold ones; shared walls and winding alleys provide insulation from cold, too (Clark 1980, 321). Where climates are extremely cold, in high mountains or farther north, houses change shape altogether and become multiroomed structures sheltered by a single roof.

No one in the village offered climate control as an explanation for clustered construction. Small rooms were said to be easier to heat, but the reason given for building against party walls was that it was cheaper and easier. Climate control *was* the usual explanation, however, for the way the structures are oriented. When asked which way a building should face and where the door should be, the two usual answers were either "on the south side" or "*qebla.*" Because *qebla* in Persian means both "south" and "the direction of Mecca," that is, the direction to face when praying, both the environmental and the symbolic sides of the claim ought to be considered in this discussion.

In the first place, the villagers' perception is that houses not only *ought* to be but most frequently *are* oriented in a roughly north-south direction, with the door most frequently on the short, southern wall. This perception is borne out by actual room orientations. In explanation, I was told that these doors face the sun and the most benign breezes. It is certainly the case that only rarely do any doors open to the west through north-northwest directions—the directions of the prevailing winds (north-northwest) and of both wind and rain storms (west)—and that only one of these doors belongs to a living room. The direction toward which doors in rooms other than living rooms open appears to favor southern exposures only slightly. But living-room doors do more frequently face roughly south and east than other compass directions (eleven face south or southwest; thirteen face south or southeast). If human comfort is the main goal, then the greater frequency with which living rooms face south makes sense.

In the eyes of the villagers, sun and a gentle breeze at the living-room door are an ideal combination (the door is often the only effective light source, especially in older rooms). A southern exposure for the main living quarters is reportedly widespread in urban courtyard houses, as well as in *qal'a* layouts in the countryside throughout Iran and Afghanistan.[4] When separate summer and winter quarters are available, the winter rooms face south, and the summer ones (often in the form of a *tālār,* a kind of open, ventilated room or porch) face north. Some households in Baghestan also switch living rooms seasonally, but the orientations are less predictable. Of six summer living rooms, three have (roughly) southern entrances, two northern, and one eastern; of the associated winter partners, two face south and four face east. One household built a handsome windowed room intended as a new living room, but because it faces north it is cold and drafty in winter and has probably ended up as a storeroom. These orientations support the argument below that winter comfort is of greater concern than summer comfort.

Of the village's four second-story rooms, three are used as living rooms in the summer, when they are cooler, and as storerooms in the winter, when they would be difficult to heat and exposed to drafts. The one in Gauju's *qal'a* is traded in the appropriate seasons with an adjoining and more protected second-story room. The others are alternated with a first-story room. *Eivāns* are excellent buffers against winter wind and chill and summer heat and sun.

How successful is this built environment as shelter? In 1978 I measured air temperatures over several typical days in the courtyard and living room of the compound in which I was living. Courtyard temperatures ranged from 20 degrees centigrade to 33 degrees centigrade, with the peak in mid-afternoon and the low at night and early in the morning. Living-room temperatures had a narrower range, from 25 to 27.5 degrees centigrade during the same period. These differences agree with my own and others' subjective perception that houses in the summer are warmer at night but cooler by day than are adjacent outside spaces.

The summer heat is frequently uncomfortable, but it is rarely so great that it becomes life-threatening, as it does sometimes, for example, in southwestern Iran or even on the sand sea and *kavir* near Khar o Tauran. Many activities take place in the open, and in the shade if possible. People often spend the mid-afternoon eating a large lunch and then napping until the sun is lower. Although domed mud brick houses provide passive cooling by day, even in Khar o Tauran they hold so much heat at night that for much of the summer people sleep outside in courtyards, sometimes on mud platforms, or on roofs (where they continue to sleep under quilts and covers). Even courtyards, when small, are perceptibly warmer than are more open areas on the outside.

## THE VILLAGE AS SOCIAL SETTING

Access to the small area of common pasture that surrounds the village constitutes the main rights obtained through residence. Rights and responsibilities with respect to field systems are held by virtue of private ownership in land and water, not through residence. A structure of leadership that includes a *kadkhodā* (headman) and a village council has been imposed by the central government for its own administrative purposes. The council meets in the headman's compound.

The village as a whole takes responsibility for the *hammām,* the *hoseiniya,* and the cemetery. The schoolhouse is built and the teacher hired by the central government. The village is a coherent unit in a number of other ways. Village residents gather on special occasions of religious obligation, such as those during the fasting month of Ramadan or those commemorating the death of Hosein during the month of Moharram. Tied to the religious solar calendar, the dates of religious holidays move back ten or eleven days each year. Holiday services are held in private courtyards, the *hoseiniya,* or the village cemetery, depending on the event and the sponsor. They usually include the distribution of food or at least tea. The whole village also takes part in traditional Persian New Year celebrations, which include visiting, food sharing, and games.

Although villagers typically act individually and in household units, a network of cooperation is also apparent in the form of mutual aid, milking groups, flock pooling, and other productive activities. The villagers are all related to one another through kinship or marriage, which tends to be village endogamous. There are few newcomers in the village. In all but one set of married couples, at least one member was from the village; both partners of 63 percent of the married couples were from Baghestan. They feel attached to the village, say they prefer it to others, and praise its location, water quality, and soil quality.

The layout of the village (Figure 11) reflects the social arrangements and activities of the residents. Its nucleation and the presence of a single religious structure, a single community bathhouse, one cemetery, and one schoolhouse reflect the unity of the village. The threshing floors and a number of milking sites reflect small groups that cooperate in production at a level lower than the entire village.

TABLE 7. HOUSEHOLD SIZE AND COMPOSITION IN BAGHESTAN, LATE
SUMMER, 1976

| Household | Size | Composition[a] | Est. age of head[a] | Kin relationship of wife to husband[b] |
|---|---|---|---|---|
| 2 | 7 | H, W, 5C | 30s | |
| 3 | 8 | H, W, 6C | 40s | |
| 4 | 2 | Widow, 1C | 40s | FBD and MZD |
| 5 | 4 | H, W, 2C | 20s | FBD and MZD |
| 6 | 6 | H, W, 4C | 50s | |
| 7 | 7 | H, W, 4C, HF | 40s | |
| 8 | 6 | H, W, 4C | 50s | |
| 9 | 3 | H, W, FZ | 50s | |
| 10 | 6 | H, W, 4C | 30s | |
| 11 | 4 | H, W, 2C | 50s | FBD |
| 12 | 5 | H, W, 3C | 40s | FZD |
| 13 | 4 | H, W, 2C | 20s | MMFBSD |
| 14 | 4 | H, W, 1D | 50s | |
| 15 | 7 | H, W, 4C, HM | 30s | |
| 16 | 8 | H, W, 6C | 30s | MBD |
| 17 | 2 | H, W | 50s | |
| 18 | 1 | Widow | 60s | |
| 19 | 6 | H, W, 4C | 20s | |
| 20 | 4 | Widow, 1C, 1D, 1GC | 50s | |
| 22 | 3 | H, W, 1C | 60s | |
| 23 | 6 | H, W, 4C | 30s | |
| 24 | 6 | H, W, 3C, 1D | 50s | |
| 25 | 2 | H, W | 20s | MZD |
| 26 | 7 | H, W, 4C, WM | 30s | |
| 27 | 3 | H, W, GC | 50s | |
| 28 | 7 | H, W, 4C, FM | 40s | |
| 29 | 5 | H, W, 3C | 40s | MBD |
| 31 | 4 | H, W, 2C | 20s | |
| 32 | 5 | H, W, 3C | 40s | |
| 33 | 5 | H, W, 3C | 40s | |

TABLE 7. *cont.*

| Household | Size | Composition[a] | Est. age of head[a] | Kin relationship of wife to husband[b] |
|----------|------|----------------|---------------------|----------------------------------------|
| 34 | 7 | H,W,5C | 40s | FZD |
| 35 | 1 | B[c] | 50s | |

*Note:* B = bachelor; C = child, children; D = adult daughter; FBD = father's brother's daughter; FZ = father's sister; FZD = father's sister's daughter; GC = grandchild; H = husband; HF = huband's father; HM = husband's mother; MBD = mother's brother's daughter; MMFBSD = mother's mother's father's brother's son's daughter; MZD = mother's sister's daughter; W = wife; WM = wife's mother. Blank cells = no kin relationship known.

a. Age categories are based on data collected by Mary Martin (personal communication, 1980). They are estimates because people in Baghestan do not generally know their exact ages.

b. Eight out of the 31 couples (26.8%) are first cousins—3 on the father's side, 3 on the mother's side and 2 on both (as a result of brothers marrying sisters in a previous generation).

c. A part-time resident.

No intervening agent such as the state, absentee landlords, or system of field redistribution has organized either land or settlement here, although all of these occur elsewhere in Iran. And indeed nothing in the layout suggests an imposed order, as is often seen in villages planned by outside agencies, those settled by nomads, or others that were built all at once. For the most part, Baghestan looks like the village it is—one that was built gradually through the accumulation of individual choices.

With two exceptions, the minimal residential unit is either the nuclear family (with or without children), or the nuclear family extended by an unmarried adult relative, often widows and widowers who move in with married children (Table 7). Five households include a single aged parent; these parents do not have separate facilities that reflect their presence in a material sense. It is possible, although unusual, to live alone, and one elderly widow, who has no children or siblings in the village, actually does. A bachelor lives alone part of the time (the rest of the time he lives with relatives in a neighboring village).

As is true throughout the Iranian Plateau, a single room is the minimal freestanding architectural unit. Sometimes it is the minimal residential unit as well. When resident in the village, the bachelor mentioned earlier lives in just one room; the widow who lives alone does so very nearly in a single room—her tiny back storeroom has no exterior door. In all other cases, though, a household's structures include at least two rooms; the mean is five rooms per household. Although their full spatial extent is often discontinuous, households are located in the village by what I call a core compound area (minimally a living room and a forecourt).

Although there are no clear-cut corporate kin groups beyond the household unit, a variety of patterned interactions and task-oriented, shared activities occur, a situation similar to that reported by Kramer (1982b) and Watson (1979) in western Iran. In Baghestan, kinship structures many of these relationships and activities, such as the milking groups, bread oven groups, and house-building teams. Although not expressly acknowledged by residents, trying to live next to close relatives is among these kin-structured behaviors.

### Kinship and Proximity

One way to find out how well residents succeed in living in proximity with their relatives is through statistical description and analysis of two kinds of distance—physical and social. Figure 15 maps the primary kin relationships found among Baghestan's residents.[5] Each circle represents a household's (winter) living room, placed where it appears on the village plan. The lines indicate kin relationships to a depth of one generation among adult household members in the village. Both the household head and his wife are included, but grown children and aged single parents are not, even when they live permanently with the couple.

House-to-house distances were measured from room center to room center. Living rooms rather than courtyard gates were chosen because they are built first and therefore reflect the builder's spacing decision at least as well as do courtyard gates. Also, they have the virtue of being more likely to be recovered and recognized in the archaeological record than are courtyards. In practice, direct routes are frequently blocked by intervening buildings and walls so that the actual route from house to house at ground level is longer. These routes on the ground could be plotted from the village plan, but kin and close friends take shortcuts

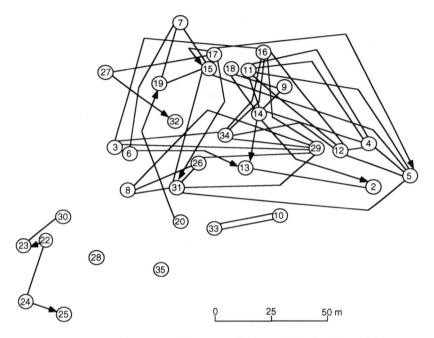

Figure 15. Kinship and proximity in Baghestan. Circles mark the location of living rooms. Lines with arrows show parent-to-child ties. Plain lines indicate sibling-to-sibling ties. Only adult household members are represented.

over the roofs. Because the actual house-to-house routes were not known in all cases, I chose the measurement from room center to room center as being at least straightforward and comparable to existing data from elsewhere.

Primary kin connections were chosen for the diagram in part because including more distant cousins and uncle-aunt pairs would create a hopeless visual tangle of connections. Everyone in the village is ultimately related through marriage or descent. Kin relationships are woven even more tightly by cousin marriage: father's brother's daughter is a young man's preferred mate. In actual practice, 26.8 percent (eight cases) of the thirty-one Baghestan marriages (see Table 7) are to first cousins, or were in 1976, although only three of these are to the father's brother's daughter. (Because two brothers married two sisters in the previous generation, two of these are also to the mother's sister's daughter.) The rest are to father's sister's daughter (two cases), mother's brother's daughter (two cases) and mother's sister's daughter (one case). This pattern of patrilateral parallel cousin marriage typifies the Islamic Near East, and, when repeated over several generations, the paternal and maternal sides in a sense become blurred. A cultural bias in favor of interpreting the relationship as patrilineal affects how the relationship is thought of and expressed. Thus, for example, the relationship I refer to literally as a mother's brother's daughter may also be put in the category of father's brother's daughters and would likely be so named in interviews.

Primary kin connections were also selected because they were expected to show the strongest spatial patterning, an expectation based on patterns of formal and informal cooperation in the village. Furthermore, given the patrilateral bias both ideologically and in practice in Near Eastern villages, it might be expected that male connections (parent-son, brother-brother) would be stronger than female connections (parent-daughter, sister-sister). Tauran women are not without say in initiating or agreeing to interactions between households, however, and some of these interactions are linked through sisters rather than brothers. The question of whether interactions result from proximity rather than vice versa is often moot here, where some of the mechanisms that lead to proximity in the first place (inheritance, kin ties) also influence cooperation in the long and short term.

In Table 8 I list mean distances and ranges of distances between households for various categories of kin and non-kin pairs, including the primary kin pairs that are diagrammed in Figure 15. Even though the database is small, kin pairs do appear to live closer together, on average, than do unrelated pairs of households. Brothers live closer together than do either sisters or parents and married children. But kin do not live as close as they might or as they might like to; only eleven pairs, or 33 percent, of nearest neighbors are primary kin.

It is difficult to say whether sons live closer to their parents than do daughters, for only two of the ten parent-child pairs are parent-son pairs. The reason for the small number of parent-son pairs compared with parent-daughter pairs is not likely to be purely by chance, however. At marriage, men are older than women, who typically are still teenagers.

TABLE 8. PROXIMITY OF HOUSEHOLD PAIRS IN
BAGHESTAN, 1976

| Category | Number | Mean distance (m) | Range (m) |
|---|---|---|---|
| All household pairs | 528 | 38.2 | 2.9–97.4 |
| Non-kin pairs | 481 | 39.5 | 3.5–97.4 |
| Primary kin pairs | 47 | 24.4 | 2.9–55.7 |
| Parent-child pairs | 10 | 23.6 | 2.9–53.9 |
| Sibling pairs | 37 | 24.6 | 5.8–55.7 |
| Brother-brother pairs | 9 | 18.9 | 11.6–34.8 |
| Brother-sister pairs | 18 | 20.8 | 5.8–46.4 |
| Sister-sister pairs | 10 | 36.5 | 18.6–55.7 |
| Nearest-neighbor pairs | 33 | 8.0 | 2.9–14.5 |
| Nearest-primary kin pairs | 31 | 14.2 | 2.9–32.5 |
| Nearest-non-kin pairs | 22 | 8.6 | 3.5–14.5 |

Thus it is less likely that a married man's parents still live, or at least remain active enough to maintain a separate household. Furthermore, because of a shortage in productive land in relation to the current population, sons tend to leave the village to work in the city or in the army. A deficit in marriageable males is beginning to be felt as parents worry about finding husbands for their daughters (Mary Martin, personal communication, 1978).

Even though a strictly parallel analysis cannot be made, it appears that households are more tightly knit spatially in the western Iranian villages of Aliabad and Hasanabad (Kramer 1982b and Watson 1978, respectively) than they are here. Kramer's architectural analysis of proximity proceeds from Aliabad's village layout, divided as it is into blocks of attached compounds. She classes household pairs according to whether they are located in the same house (that is, the same compound), in adjacent compounds, facing across the alley, in the same block, in neighboring blocks, or in even more distant blocks (Kramer 1982b, Table 4.5). As is true in Hasanabad, this layout is more clearly organized into freestanding blocks than is Baghestan's (especially the central area). Nevertheless, in an attempt to make categorical equivalents in Baghestan (Table 9), Ha-

TABLE 9. PROXIMITY OF KIN PAIRS IN BAGHESTAN, 1976

| Kin pair | Distance (m)[a] | Kin relationship | Location |
|---|---|---|---|
| 2/13 | 30.7 | Married brothers | Distant |
| 2/14 | 32.5 | Parents, married son | Distant |
| 3/16 | 44.7 | Married sisters | Distant |
| 3/29 | 47.6 | Married sisters | Distant |
| 3/34 | 25.5 | Married brother, married sister | Neighboring block |
| 4/5 | 12.2 | Married brothers | Shared courtyard |
| 4/11 | 33.1 | Married brother, married sister | Distant |
| 4/12 | 7.0 | Married brother, married sister | Across alley |
| 4/14 | 26.7 | Married sisters | Distant |
| 5/11 | 45.2 | Married brother, married sister | Distant |
| 5/12 | 16.8 | Married brother, married sister | Across alley |
| 5/15 | 53.9 | Married sisters | Distant |
| 5/17 | 53.9 | Parents, married daughter | Distant |
| 5/31 | 55.7 | Married sisters | Distant |
| 6/7 | 36.0 | Married sisters | Across alley |
| 6/13 | 27.8 | Parents, married daughter | Neighboring block |
| 7/15 | 13.3 | Married brothers | Across alley |
| 7/19 | 15.1 | Married brothers | Adjacent compounds |
| 8/26 | 18.6 | Married sisters | Across alley |
| 8/29 | 46.4 | Married brother, married sister | Distant |
| 8/31 | 11.6 | Married brother, married sister | Across alley |
| 9/14 | 7.0 | Married brother, married sister | Adjacent compounds |
| 9/18 | 13.3 | Married brother, married sister | Neighboring block |
| 10/33 | 16.2 | Married brother, married sister | Adjacent compounds |

TABLE 9. *cont.*

| Kin pair | Distance (m)[a] | Kin relationship | Location |
|---|---|---|---|
| 11/12 | 29.0 | Married sisters | Distant |
| 11/14 | 5.8 | Married brother, married sister | Across alley |
| 12/16 | 27.8 | Married brothers | Neighboring block |
| 12/34 | 27.8 | Married brother, married sister | Neighboring block |
| 13/14 | 15.1 | Parents, married son | Adjacent compounds |
| 14/18 | 11.6 | Married brothers | Across alley |
| 15/17 | 2.9 | Parents, married daughter | Adjacent compounds |
| 15/19 | 11.6 | Married brothers | Across alley |
| 15/31 | 28.4 | Married sisters | Neighboring block |
| 16/29 | 24.9 | Married sisters | Neighboring block |
| 16/34 | 23.2 | Married brother, married sister | Neighboring block |
| 17/27 | 24.4 | Married brother, married sister | Distant |
| 17/31 | 31.3 | Parents, married daughter | Neighboring block |
| 19/20 | 32.5 | Widow, married daughter | Neighboring block |
| 22/23 | 5.8 | Parents, married daughter | Adjacent compounds |
| 22/24 | 12.8 | Married brother, married sister | Across alley |
| 23/30 | 12.8 | Married brothers | Same block |
| 24/25 | 9.9 | Widow, married daughter | Across alley |
| 26/29 | 29.0 | Married brother, married sister | Neighboring block |
| 26/31 | 8.1 | Married brother, married sister | Neighboring block |
| 27/32 | 23.8 | Parents, married daughter | Distant |
| 29/31 | 34.8 | Married brothers | Neighboring block |
| 29/34 | 22.0 | Married brother, married sister | Across alley |

a. Measured from living room to living room.

sanabad, and Aliabad, I found some differences in residential patterns that are probably significant, in spite of the small sample size.

Thirty-eight of Aliabad's sixty-seven compound units (57 percent) hold families that are either co-resident with, next to, or across from parents, sons, and brothers of the male head of household (Kramer 1982b, 139). If counted by family rather than compound unit, then fifty-four of the eighty-three families in Aliabad, or 65 percent, live in the same compound with, next to, or across from parents, sons, and brothers of male heads of households. In Hasanabad, the comparable figure is fifteen of thirty-nine families, or 38 percent (calculated from data in Watson 1979); in Baghestan, eight of thirty-three families, or 24 percent in 1976.

In Aliabad, twenty-two of the thirty married men with married brothers in the village live very near at least one other brother, either in the same compound, an adjacent one, or across an alley (see Kramer 1982b, Table 4.5 and Figure 2.1). In Hasanabad, with a single exception, all fourteen of the married men with married brothers in the village live as close as possible to at least one other brother, either in the same compound or in an adjacent one. In Baghestan, in contrast, only seven of the fourteen married men with married brothers live in the same compound, an adjacent one, or across an alley.

In addition to general patterns, particular cases are revealing. Although there are no fully joint family households in Baghestan, there are three pairs of brothers said to be *sharik*. These are households 4/5, 12/16, and 15/19. While these individual households also fall short of forming full-fledged, economically joint households, they share tools and spaces and work closely and frequently together. All live relatively near each other, but only one of the three pairs of brothers (4/5), actually shares a compound and can be classified as nearest neighbors. (One of the brothers in this pair recently died; his widow continues to live with her daughter on their side of the compound.) Other combinations of households, not referred to as *sharik,* nevertheless share resources, usually in pairs. *Sharik* households 4 and 5 work closely together with households 11 and 12 at the residentially abandoned Kalata structures and fields and share its water. (The heads of households 11 and 12 take part by virtue of their wives' inheritances.) Households 4/5 and 12 live very near each other; household

11, while on the same side of the village, is not obviously close. Households 29 and 34, who live across an alley from each other, pool their resources into pastoral and agricultural portions: Household 29 tends the animals of household 34 at a pastoral station, and household 34 provides agricultural labor for the fields of household 29. Households 6/13, 2/14, and 27/32 are father-son or father–son-in-law pairs that work closely together.

Of all these households, only households 4/5 and 12 both work together and live in neighboring compounds. The rest, while they all live closer together than the average unrelated pair or even the average related pair, are not close enough for their relationship to be read on the map.

The public face in Baghestan is one of harmony and equality. Most people denied differences among their neighbors and emphasized their common lot, even when this stance was at odds with other evidence. The only social unit beyond the household readily acknowledged by villagers is the village as a whole, membership in which is based on residence rather than kinship. On the basis of observed interactions (such as the sharing of bread ovens and milking stations, visiting patterns, and mutual aid in construction or planting), marriage patterns, residential decisions, and the location of agricultural plots, however, a case can be made for the presence of two separate social groups even though they have no corporate or formal existence.

To explore this separation further and seek others, I show in Figure 16 my own attribution of household and kin alignments. Each household has been assigned one of four labels, determined by which of the three main village surnames—A, B, or C—the couple has, separately or jointly. (Wives do not take their husbands surnames.)

The lower cluster is occupied largely by members and relatives of the once-powerful A family. It was their forebears who built Qal'a Baghestan, now abandoned across the gully. The northern block cannot be so easily characterized, although surnames B and C do dominate. Although today the two blocks could not be distinguished by obvious differences in status or material culture between their residents, the spatial distribution of A families continues to reflect differences that were once economically and politically significant. The B and C families differentiate A families as being tribal (using the term *tāyefa* or *il*), and the members of that group

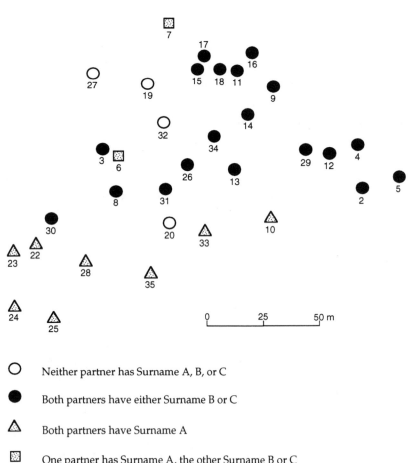

Figure 16. Kinship and proximity in Baghestan displayed by surnames of husband and wife.

○   Neither partner has Surname A, B, or C

●   Both partners have either Surname B or C

△   Both partners have Surname A

▦   One partner has Surname A, the other Surname B or C

are in fact descended from tribal groups forcibly moved from their southern homeland to the north by Naser-ud-din Shah in the nineteenth century (Martin 1980b, 32).

A lack of intermarriage between A families and the B and C families
and a social coolness evinced in a general lack of everyday interaction
underlines the physical isolation of the two clusters today. Their spatial
isolation reflects present realities accurately. But if past generations of ties
were added, the nine households across the bottom of the plan would all
become connected, and ties to households 28, 33, and 35 would attach
this lower cluster to the main part of the village. These ties are not to the
B and C families but to the distantly related A families, who once owned
the Qal'a Reza Qoli in the main part of the village (Area E; see Appendix). The surname has died out in the upper cluster, because there were
no male heirs. The female heirs have married outside the A family. In the
recent past, however, at least two failed marriages connected the A families in the lower cluster with the B and C families in the main cluster. In
both, the wife died young; in one case it was said that grief over the
husband's taking a co-wife was a contributing factor (Mary Martin, personal communication, 1977).

### Changing Places

When asked about the relative advantages and disadvantages of house
locations in Baghestan, most people denied there *were* any differences and
claimed that one place was as good as another. Some who mentioned
specific advantages ("fewer mosquitoes at the east end of the village")
added a qualifying disadvantage ("but further from the water source").
Their comments reflect the compromising nature of house location in
relation to conflicting environmental and economic goals, such as proximity to water, fields, or protection from exposure to pests or the elements. Their comments also reflect an egalitarian ideology, which is
revealed even more strongly in the way they talk about social relationships and economic competition, but which is not necessarily upheld by
actual behavior.

This point is well illustrated by the case of a family who came to the
village in 1977 from Nur, a Tauran village on the other side of the

Peighambar mountain. Initially, they moved into the core compound vacated by household 13, next to several families of B's and C's. The owner, a B, had sold his house to them and bought another compound nearby. The newly arrived couple were both closely related to the A's, who live on the southern side of the village. When I asked their neighbors in the north if it mattered that the newcomers had landed in the thick of the B's and C's, I was assured that people lived just anywhere, and it really made no difference. When I went back the following year, however, the new couple were building a compound among the A's. This story illustrates how spatial behavior can provide social and cultural information that may be difficult or impossible to elicit from informants. At the least, it suggests questions that might not otherwise have been asked.

There is another side to the picture. Now that the A families are in greater proximity to the B and C families, they are forced, or at least willing, to interact more frequently than they did when they lived across the gully. Even though the ideal marriage pattern is between patrilateral parallel cousins, marrying inside the village is also preferred. Before I left, a marriage between the two unrelated groups was being arranged. It takes only one such alliance to pave the way for more. People may attempt to use kinship to structure proximity, but proximity also affects kinship. Within another generation the village network will probably be a single one.

## THE VILLAGE AS CULTURAL SETTING

In some parts of the world, notably parts of Southeast Asia and Africa, people think and speak of their dwellings and settlements as microcosmic representations of a universal cosmic order.[6] It is not always obvious from written analyses to what extent this mental elaboration finds an "on-the-ground" expression in the ways houses are built and settlements are laid out, but in some cases, a very tangible correlation is apparent.

It is difficult, however, to read cosmological meaning into the physical characteristics of Khar o Tauran villages. The villagers themselves offer mostly practical, occasionally aesthetic, explanations for why they build as they do. Yet whether or not their inhabitants acknowledge it, houses and settlements *are* shaped by ideas about the social and natural order. Even without conscious metaphor and exegesis, the village and its houses are tied to the ritual and spiritual life of the villagers. Because they are Muslims, it is appropriate to ask how their houses and village reflect and transmit their Islamic religious beliefs and practices. Because they are Muslims in a particular social and historical setting, local and folk inter-pretations of Islam as well as pre- or non-Islamic customs also find mate-rial or behavioral expression in the built environment.

Many writers have grappled with what constitutes an "Islamic" settle-ment or architecture, without agreeing on an answer.[7] In spite of these difficulties, Petherbridge (1978) succinctly characterizes what many would agree typifies vernacular architecture in the "Islamic world": courtyard houses that grow by accretion, men's reception and guest quarters, flexible and nonspecialized interior spaces, diurnal and seasonal shifts in the loca-tion of activities, openings oriented toward (or away from) Mecca, en-trances that are offset to block direct line-of-sight into private spaces, courtyard walls, low or windowless building walls that cannot overlook another's courtyard, blank facades and embellished interiors, and a histori-cal need for fortification. Settlement in Khar o Tauran includes local ver-sions of all these elements. The spatial expression of values said to underlie these architectural forms are ritual, privacy, and the seclusion of women.

### Explicitly Religious Space

Houses in Baghestan so far have been treated as secular space. Yet because they are built and used by practicing Muslims, they are secular only for the purpose of analytical convenience. Activities that take place within domestic structures are ordered by beliefs about appropriate behavior and by ritual requirement, both of which derive from local understanding and practice of Islam. The requirements of pilgrimage and prayer, for example, find material reflection in the display of souvenir photographs taken at the Shi'i shrine and pilgrimage center in Mashad (some 300 kilometers to the northeast of Khar o Tauran) and in the rugs and tiles of holy clay used at prayer. Some of these behaviors (those surrounding eating, prayer, or childbirth, for example) routinely take place within the house. Others take place with reference *to* the house. The latter are

largely protective in intent, aimed at the physical integrity of the structure and the well-being of the residents. Their verbal expression, such as
invoking the name of God on crossing a threshold or a blessing upon
beginning the day's work of laying mud brick walls, draws on Islam.
Their material expression incorporates folk belief: rue burned daily during new construction or white plaster splashed on newly built walls to
protect against the evil eye and, in the words of the villagers, to keep the
house from falling into ruin.

In addition, the village has a building reserved for religious gatherings.
The *hoseiniya* is used primarily for Shi'i religious services, especially those
called *rauzakhāni,* held in commemoration of the martyrdom of Hosein.
There are a number of specialized buildings such as this that are explicitly
Islamic in the Shi'i world. Among them are mosques, religious schools,
*takkiyas* (used for passion plays that focus on the events surrounding the
battle of Kerbala and the martyrdom of Hosein), *emāmzādas* (shrines
associated with holy men), and houses for washing the dead. As is probably common is small settlements, however, the only such building in
Baghestan is the *hoseiniya*. In urban settings, *hoseiniyas* carry out many of
the multiple functions of a mosque (see, for example, Kheirabadi 1991).
They are apparently common in Shi'i villages, although very little information has been published on their rural distribution, appearance, and
use.[8] They are not used for Friday prayers and appear in villages with
mosques as well as those without.

The *hoseiniya* in Baghestan is the longest room in the village and the
second largest, large enough to hold all the village males if not the entire
adult community. Participants in the *rauzakhāni* sit in a semicircle facing
the sheikh, some with their backs to *qebla,* the direction of Mecca. The
sheikh faces the wall with the door, a position of honor and one that in
this building faces *qebla*. Women sit in the positions of least honor near
the door. The service includes a sermon, often with lively comment from
members of the audience, who sometimes take issue with the sheikh's
instruction. Afterward, tea might be provided by the sponsoring individual or individuals, who bring or borrow the samovar and glasses for the
occasion.

Being neither mosque nor prayer hall, the *hoseiniya* does not have a
prayer niche, minaret, or pulpit. Except when used for services, it is a

room like any other, said to have no special kind of status. It does have a wooden chair—the only one in the village—for the sheikh to preach from and religious postcards and posters on the wall.

Besides housing religious services, the *hoseiniya* in Baghestan is also used to store the religious banners used during the month of Moharram and was used to keep the lime plaster safe while the community bathhouse was being built. No kind of courtyard or gathering space is marked out in front of the *hoseiniya;* in fact during my second fieldwork season a donkey pen was built in the open space between it and the *qal'a.* It is not necessarily better kept than other structures; the year I arrived, it was badly in need of replastering and repairs and was not even in use. The following year it was refinished and back in use again with a new city-bought metal door. It is, however, set apart in plan from other village rooms because it is the largest building in the village and its door faces southwest (which means place-ment on the long side of the building, an infrequent practice).

The *hoseiniya* is on a pronounced rise, which marks the remains of the previous *hoseiniya,* which it replaced shortly before 1970. This is the only occasion I know of in which new construction took place directly on top of previous construction; probably the fact that the land and the building are a pious donation (*vaqf*), built and maintained by the entire village, keeps it rooted in place.

### Orientation to *Qebla*

Like all practicing Muslims, Tauranis are constantly aware of the direc-tion in which Mecca lies, because of its positively orienting role in ritu-ally structured activities, such as prayer, burial, and butchering, and its negatively orienting role in ritually unclean activities, such as elimination and giving birth. In these activities one avoids facing or turning one's back on Mecca. By my own observations, the former, positive, sort are always properly oriented in Baghestan; the latter, negative, sort may be less rigorously so, but I had few opportunities to observe them.[9]

Several people told me the best way for a living-room door to face is *qebla.* At first I took this comment at face value; not until later did I realize that *qebla* is frequently used instead of the standard Persian *jonub* to mean "south," which made it appear that Mecca exerts a stronger draw on house orientation than it probably does. (Mecca is actually to the south-west in this part of the country). In fact, when I pursued the question further, I was told that *qebla* is best for climatic reasons (warmth and light). In Davarabad, a village along the high road to the west of Tauran, residents also said that the main considerations in aligning a house were *qebla,* for religious reasons, and a southern exposure, for climatic reasons. In that village, however, few houses were actually oriented that way but were instead aligned according to the pragmatic considerations of previously existing houses, alleys, and canals (Alberts 1963, 155).

As mentioned in the section on shelter, summer living quarters ideally face north, and studies of urban architecture show the practice to be common in settlements on the Iranian Plateau. An exception is the Zoroastrian houses of Yazd, where a *tālār* must never face north, the direction of hell in that religion, and apparently they never do (Boyce 1971).[10]

Living rooms that were built at the village edge on freestanding plots of land, rather than in the old core of Baghestan, presumably were free to face the southwest, or *qebla,* if the owners so wished. Rather than building them to face in a particular geographic direction, however, for reasons of privacy and view, many owners chose to face them away from the village no matter the direction (although none faces west, as noted above). Thus, it appears that the religious ideal in house placement is overridden by practical and social considerations. Proper ritual orientation is in actuality more a behavioral than an architectural concern.

### Privacy

In a village this small, this isolated, and this kin-connected, distinctions between public and private spaces and behavior differ from those in larger or more central settlements. For Baghestanis, the private sector of the village is coterminous with the village itself; the public sector lies beyond the village and its fields.[11] Inside the village, there is no central public gathering space. The narrow, winding alleys preclude vehicular traffic or easy through access even on horse or donkey back. What little road traffic there is passes by at a safe distance from work and unwalled residential areas. Because everyone in the village is related by kinship or marriage, women are free to move unveiled as they go about their daily business.

Privacy is of course culturally defined. Personal or individual privacy in the sense of solitude is neither desired nor approved of in Baghestan. Wanting to be alone is regarded with suspicion. No matter its size, a family is not usually divided spatially for eating or sleeping, even when enough rooms are available. Access to certain areas, however, is restricted by gender or social relationship. Privacy can also be achieved without architectural barriers. Without leaving the room, a woman who wishes to sleep can remove herself from the presence of others by covering her face and body with her *chādor* (long veil). In an echo of Gilsenan's "as if" behavior (Gilsenan 1982, 188), bathers at the irrigation pond are treated as if they were simply not there. Bromberger's "invisible boundaries" (Bromberger (1989, 81) that separate women from men even when they are in the same room are effective here as well.

To view the walled courtyard primarily as a concession to the practice of seclusion of women in Islamic societies is to overlook its pre-Islamic origin and its other roles and meanings in contemporary life. Nor is the courtyard ubiquitous in every Iranian settlement. It is not, for example, or has not been until recently, an essential element for separating household from household or public from private space in Khar o Tauran. First of all, as we have seen, walls do not necessarily surround all the structures a household owns and, moreover, may enclose those of another household, even one that is not especially close either in kinship or cooperation. Second, villagers claim that such walls are new. They say they never built them in the past and that they are an idea imported from the city. (They do not think of *qal'as* as being walled). Alberts reports a similar change in his Garmsar village to the west; courtyard walls, high and protective at the time of his fieldwork in the 1950s, were below eye level when Davarabad was built and served only to define plots and contain livestock (Alberts 1963, 165–66). The explanation may be that there, as here, at the turn of the century whole villages were walled, or people lived in *qala's,* which made walls around individual compounds unnecessary. Third, and in contrast to the building order sometimes reported in the Near East (for example, Kamp 1982, 91; Kramer 1982b, 92; and Petherbridge 1978, 198), when a new compound is begun on an empty lot, the courtyard walls are built last, not first. And finally, the animal quarters in the northwest part of the village look very much like compound dwellings in plan, suggesting that the forecourt is as important for animal management as for social reasons.

Still, once raised, courtyard walls have much the same meaning in privacy and access as they do elsewhere in the Near East. They mark the area where domestic privacy begins, not because they literally block a view (most of them do not), but because they post the limits that set appropriate etiquettes. Their increased use is likely to be associated with the encroachment of the outside world and its customs on Baghestani life.

## PROCESSES OF GROWTH

Taken together, these village structures and their placement are the products of individual decisions rather than communal or centralized planning. The decisions are nevertheless bound by the past (via inheritance, field holdings, and kinship), and new building takes account of existing (or forecast) structures and social relationships. Once a group of structures (or a single one, such as a qal'a) has been built and oriented, for whatever reason, subsequent construction takes place in relation to those structures. In the absence of topographical irregularities, therefore, the plan of the growing village tends to repeat the previous orientations. The new freestanding compounds at the edge of Baghestan village are lined up with previously built courtyard walls. Frequently, for social and economic reasons, new rooms are attached to existing ones; when this happens there is always an already close kin connection between the two households.

The social and economic expediency of building structures near or directly attached to existing structures affects the patterning of the village layout. Crowding is densest in the center of the village and results from infilling around existing buildings. The tight nucleation of village structures may indeed provide cooler surroundings in summer and a windbreak in winter, but here those benefits seem to be by-products of social and economic goals rather than goals in themselves.

Over both the long and the short run, settlement in Khar o Tauran tends to move—gradually and in discrete jumps—rather than remain in place. The distribution of sherd scatter and other archaeological remains and the general lack of mounding or depth of deposit anywhere in the region support the proposition that building has more often taken place at new locations rather than on top of previously occupied areas. (Frequent abandonment with subsequent erosion probably plays a role in the lack of deposit as well). From aerial photos taken in 1956 and 1969, oral histories of houses, and location of new construction, similar conclusions can be drawn about the recent past and the (ethnographic) present.

Without archaeological excavation of the village, only currently standing structures, whether occupied or in ruins, can be mapped. Assigning dates of construction to existing structures is difficult. No records are kept, and people have no particular reason to remember when they were built. Associating the year of construction with that of a marriage can be of some aid, but only when the year of marriage can be unequivocably determined, which is possible only for younger couples. The oldest structures in the village are the *qal'a* and several individual rooms in the heart of the village, none of them contiguous with another. Changes during the twenty years preceding fieldwork (Figure 17) can be shown fairly accurately; those made during the three years of fieldwork are of course the most precise of all. During this twenty-year period, population growth on the plain was modest compared with national rates—probably about 9 percent from 1956 to 1976. Some Tauran villages experienced a greater increase, whereas others actually decreased in size.

Even when a village population is not actually growing larger, however, new construction continues as young people marry and set up their own households, or as older couples decide to improve their living conditions. For any settlement, hypothetical rates of construction could be set up for known or estimated population parameters, cultural timing of the formation of new houses, availability of new house lots, and rates of migration in or out. In actual practice, building probably takes place not at steady yearly rates but in fits and starts. Economic conditions often have an across-the-board effect that leads to a rash of marriages as the wherewithal to set up housekeeping becomes available. Conversely, hard economic times or political crisis with the conscription of men into military service can postpone all marriages for the duration. During the three-year fieldwork period, no marriages took place. In 1976, some

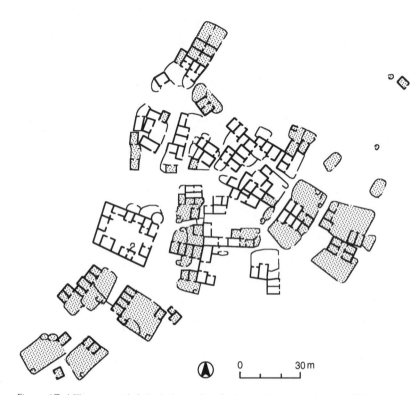

Figure 17. Village growth (stippled areas) in Baghestan between the late 1950s and the late 1970s (based primarily on oral histories).

structures that had been started in previous years (by older married couples) were still not ready for their intended uses (a living room, a guest room, and a storage room), needing interior finishing in two cases and a roof in the third. In the winter of 1976 a storeroom and a living room were begun and finished. In the summer of 1978, however, two new compounds were under construction and major additions (nearly the equivalent of an entirely new compound) were being installed at a third. Four engagements had been announced, although only one young man was already building his house (it was not clear whether the other couples would remain in the village and if so where they would live).

Other kinds of construction were also taking place. With the aid of the government and with master builders brought from Shahrud, a new community bathhouse was being built. With a government loan, several men had combined efforts to construct a storage shed for tobacco leaves awaiting sale to government agents.

All in all, eleven new rooms—living rooms, storerooms, *eivāns,* and *āghols*—were built in the core part of the village between 1976 and 1978. Only two buildings in the core went permanently out of use or collapsed. Most of the deterioration that occurred was on the neighboring ridge within the Qal'a Baghestan complex.

Like Baghestan, the other villages of Khar o Tauran, although highly nucleated, are not circumscribed by walls or other boundaries; neither is there a village gate or any other obvious entrance into the settlement. Particular kinds of activity areas and structures are found in every village, but they are not necessarily arranged in similar ways either in relation to the site or in relation to one another. Structures are not arranged around or oriented toward any kind of focal area, such as a public space or community structure.

With the single exception of Rezabad, villages in Khar o Tauran are unplanned; that is, they have not been laid out according to a preconceived design, whether executed by communal agreement, dictated by ideological or symbolic orientation, or instituted by some higher authority or planner. Rather, they are the outcome of several generations of individual decisions, albeit decisions that are not independent of one other. Two villages (Zamanabad and Salehabad) on the Tauran Plain *look* planned because of their gridlike layout, but the look is misleading; in fact, the grid reflects the pattern of abandoned fields onto which the villages are still expanding. That grid was itself shaped originally by the flat terrain, the requirements of irrigation technology, and local tenure arrangements; the house lots replicate the block-shaped fields. In Baghestan, the terrain is more rolling, the water courses more circuitous, and the village less regular. In addition, the fields on which some of the village's new construction is taking place went out of use so long ago that their boundaries are no longer visible. (See Bonine 1979 and 1989 for urban and rural examples of the effects of water flow and irrigated fields on settlement.)

Rezabad is a grid plan village designed and built in the 1960s by the Iranian government and builders from the town of Shahrud to settle a group of Chubdari, camel-herding pastoralists of tribal Baluch origin. This initially repetitious pattern is even now losing its monotony as households individually undertake alterations that better suit their particular needs and activities.

The villages on the plain, then, are "unplanned" in the sense that they do not conform to a layout drawn up in advance, whether by an outside decision maker or from within according to cultural notions of what villages should look like. Nor, given the way villages are established and grow here, is there any way of realizing such an overall conception except perhaps when a new settlement is founded, land divided up, and building proceeds all at the same time.

But although they cannot be called planned, neither are these villages haphazard or unpatterned in their growth and arrangements. There *is* a cultural notion of what a village should look like or, better, how it should be laid out no matter what it "looks" like, but that notion does not include geometric regularity of the sort that would suggest planning in most senses. Instead, individual households make locational and design decisions within a cultural framework of goals and options, taking into account the particular social and environmental settings in which they find themselves or seek out for themselves.

Because the framework for settlement is cultural and therefore shared, and because the social and environmental settings themselves are similar (although not the same) for all villagers, certain traits may be said to characterize settlement layout in the area. They indeed are likely to be characteristic of a wide area of settlement on the Iranian Plateau. Aerial photographs suggest this to be the case, although to my knowledge there are no large-scale published village plans for the area except those presented here. As we have seen in the case of Baghestan, these traits include nucleation, blocks of attached structures, a tendency to string rooms out, rooms organized in relation to a forecourt or interior court ("courtyard houses"), and a degree of common orientation among structures.

As Netting puts it, "Cultures do not normally reach the best of all possible solutions to the problems of livelihood and shelter; rather they strike one of a number of potentially viable compromises" (1977, 92). In

Khar o Tauran, as we have seen in these last three chapters, the compromise with regard to livelihood is reached through a mixed strategy of agriculture, pastoralism, and wage labor, modes that at once complement and conflict with each other. In its role of sheltering and organizing these productive activities, settlement reflects that inherent conflict and complementarity. In its role as an organizer and facilitator of communication and interaction, it is an integral part of the way that Khar o Tauranis play out their social and cultural lives.

# CHAPTER 6

# HOUSES AND HOUSEHOLDS

thnoarchaeological accounts of the Near East tend to focus on domestic architecture within villages because of its social and economic implications in archaeology. This domestic architecture is varied even in Iran. Several kinds of flat-roofed structures with mud or adobe walls are seen in the west and southwest (see Christensen 1967; Kramer 1982b; Rouholamini 1973; and Watson 1979), thatched wooden structures are the rule in the north (Bromberger 1989), and domed mud brick structures prevail on the central plateau. Generally these structural types are distributed according to zones of climate and topography, from the highlands and mountains of the west and north, to the rainy hills and plains of the Caspian Sea, to the arid desert regions of the central plateau.

In spite of the focus on village architecture in much of the literature, the rural landscape of Iran contains many other kinds of traditional structures, which serve many different purposes. The Iranian Plateau is full of examples of these special purpose buildings, many of which are found outside villages. All are built of mud brick, baked if necessary. They include the "working buildings" described at length by Beazley and Harverson (1982), particularly cisterns, icehouses, water mills, windmills, and pigeon towers. They also include caravansaries, grape-drying sheds, tobacco storage buildings, *hammāms,* watch or refuge towers, field shelters, pilgrimage stations, and houses for washing the dead.

Even Tauran has water mills and watch towers (all in a state of collapse), a pilgrim station and shrine, and *bandkhānas,* all situated on the plain outside of the villages. Most of the buildings inside the villages fill generalized and agricultural functions.

## BUILDING A HOUSE

In Tauran, people build new rooms, or houses, for many reasons—in order to marry, when changing village residence, to accommodate newly acquired animals, to create storage for agricultural products for newly acquired fields, or to improve the compound with a more modern and prestigious living or guest room.[1] Construction activity frequently continues the process of completing a compound that may have been begun some years before. Courtyard walls are added, gates are installed (Figure 18), animal rooms and privies are built, and city-bought doors and windows

Figure 18. In the foreground, the gates to the courtyards of households 10 and 29. Courtyard walls and substantial gates such as this have become every household's desire. They were spreading rapidly through the village during the three years of field study.

replace more humble homemade versions. Sometimes a new building is necessary to replace an older structure that is beyond repair, although well-tended mud houses have a longer life span than their materials suggest. A building tends to fall apart because it is abandoned; it is not abandoned because it falls apart.

Today, to build rooms used as dwellings (living rooms and storerooms) requires a cash outlay. A poor economic spell (because of drought or a slump in the central economy, for example) holds up new construction. Construction and marriage flourish in good times. Construction also tends to be seasonal. Bricks are best made during the summer and walls raised in the fall and winter before it gets too rainy. Because both the owner and local helpers usually assist in the process, work must be scheduled when they are free of competing agricultural and pastoral chores.

## Materials of Construction

Although the resources of agriculture, pastoralism, and fuel collection are not necessarily found adjacent to the settlements themselves, the primary materials of construction are invariably local in nature. Mud is the main material.[2] Great quantities go into every village settlement for every kind of structure, not only for walls, roofs, and stairs, but for features such as bread ovens, hearths, and grape-processing vats. If the village of Baghestan were packed into a solid mound, I estimate it would form a cube nearly 20 meters on each side.[3]

High-quality mud from various areas around the plain is available for the taking, but most mud comes from the builder's own land and if possible, from pits on the building site itself. The silted-in areas in or adjacent to settlements (often abandoned agricultural land) are best because the deposit there will be deep, free of rocks, and convenient. Land values and land ownership patterns make these areas also likely to be building sites. A nearby water source and a smooth level surface for laying out the bricks to dry (such as a threshing floor) are additional advantages. Because of these factors, brickmaking takes place at various locations inside and around the village.

Clods from the disintegrated remains of previous structures are also used in enclosure walls. Because of the age of the villages (some standing structures are 50 to 100 years old), the accumulated effect of removing such a quantity of earth from the landscape has been considerable. For example, a waist-high block of clay in the courtyard of household 4/5 is all that remains of the original ground level in that area. The earth around a village is in constant if subtle motion in any case, as fields silt up, canals are dug, and dirt carried into and back out of the village for fertilizing and conditioning the irrigated fields (see also Chapter 7 on mound formation). Silting of fields did not seem to be a problem in Baghestan at the time of fieldwork, but in other, similar areas, removal of the silt is sometimes necessary to keep irrigation water flowing. In one case in Pakistan, according to Douglas Merrey (personal communication, 1978), the mud removed was sold off for construction. Perhaps one reason the fields now being used for house sites on other parts of the Tauran plain were abandoned is that they had risen too high to be easily irrigated by the meager flow of irrigation water.

Stone is sometimes used for wall repair in the central part of Baghestan, but it is not used for wall construction. Generally, in Khar o Tauran, stone-walled structures are found only in villages located in rocky areas with little soil cover (as is the case at Qal'a Baghestan; see Figure 19), or in settlements (usually pastoral) where water is at an inconvenient distance for brickmaking. The rock is not quarried or dressed but used as found, usually in the form of water-worn river cobbles.

Reused materials such as baked brick fragments, old grinding stones, and thick-walled sherds scavenged from premodern settlements are common in areas where mud brick is difficult to make. Baghestan's new government-sponsored *hammām* was being constructed of limestone blocks from the mountains to the west of the plain rather than local or commercial materials.

Several kinds of plaster and *gel-e sabz* are used for protective and decorative wall and floor finishes and for lining feed troughs. Green clay of ceramic quality is also used to line bread ovens and sometimes hearths. It is dug from several pits in the area, one of which is beside Baghestan's irrigated fields. Plaster from calcareous soil (*gach-e khāk*) dug from sources near Zamanabad is prepared (roasted) by the user. Walls in the old *qal'as* were sometimes rubbed to a marble polish with polishing stones.

Figure 19. Animal stables in the group of rooms to the east of Qal'a Baghestan. The unroofed walls are built of stone rubble from earlier, perhaps medieval, Islamic occupations. At the right is a long feeding trough.

Limestone plaster (*gach-e sang*), although not much used until recently, is commercially produced and bought in Sabzevar.

Straw and dung, both agricultural products, are also used—straw for mixing with mud to make bricks and mud plaster and dung as a waterproofing material or, in packed form, as blocks for building winter pastoral stations. Wooden poles, planks, and brushwood are used in construction of doors, window frames, and roofs of shelters.

Metal, glass, plaster, cement, wood, and paint, purchased from the city, are increasingly used. Except for glass, they all have their local equivalents in the materials mentioned above.

### Labor

In these rural areas designer, builder, user, and maintainer are often the same person, especially for agricultural and pastoral utility rooms. There are four part-time builders in Baghestan. But as experienced as some of them may be, *ostāds* hired from other villages or from the city produce a squarer, more standardized building. The new construction at the compound of household 24 (see Appendix, Figure A-9) is a good example. Built with in-village labor, the plan was not clearly thought out in advance, and the new rooms sit awkwardly against the old compound's wall, in spite of the availability of space for expansion. In contrast, the rooms next to the compound of household 28 (see Appendix, Figure A-8) were being built by a specialist from the neighboring village of Eshqvan. Although he is not thought of as highly as an *ostād* from Sabzevar would be, the results are more professional (and more expensive).

Women as well as men may take on construction tasks. The father of the young woman from household 24 had recently died, and she herself was making the bricks that would be used for her brother's house; he would thus be able to return from the city to head the household. Women frequently help their husbands haul water and mud for bricks. They also have a strong voice in the planning stage and sometimes make most of the decisions. Still, men do most of the actual labor. Friends and relatives who participate in a form of mutual aid are invited for dinner in return for their help. Others may be paid day wages.

### Wall Construction

The area where a house is to be built is usually leveled by tractor brought in from outside the village. According to one builder, a room is planned and laid out according to its inside measurements. Foundations or trenches of any kind are uncommon. In the lower parts of the plain, packed mud walls in newer buildings are sometimes placed on slightly wider bases of solid silt left from cutting out soil for brickmaking. A builder in the nearby village of Zamanabad told me foundations are not necessary on silted plots reclaimed from irrigated fields. I did not see any in Khar o Tauran, although stone is sometimes added to *china* (packed mud) walls, also referred to in the literature as *pisé* or *tauf,* to reinforce them. The most casual walls, those of courtyards and animal pens, are built of earth clods and stones held together with mud and sometimes sand, but without straw.

PACKED MUD WALLS. *China* walls are used primarily for courtyard and other non-weight-bearing walls, privies, and animal pens. In Baghestan they are rarely used in dwellings or animal houses, although the new rooms at the compound of household 28 was *china* up to waist height. The rest was to be finished with mud brick, and the *china* was therefore built to the same width (65–70 centimeters) as a standard brick wall. *China* walls are not considered to be as good as brick walls, but they are less expensive because they take less time to build, use no straw, and do not need the services of an *ostād*. One older animal house had a bottom course of stone and gravel and an upper course of *china* extending to the vault, which was brick. In neighboring Zamanabad, where a good deal of construction was taking place, walls were frequently of packed mud courses alternating with several of mud brick.

*China* walls are marked out in meters, measured (somewhat variably) by the length from nose to hand. All measuring I observed was done by eye; a tautly stretched string marked out the walls and kept them straight, in theory at least. In practice, one wall I measured was 20 centimeters shorter on one side than the other. When I pointed this out to the builder, he cut back the inside of the wall with a shovel and threw more mud onto the outside to straighten it.[4]

MUD BRICK WALLS. Mud is prepared for brickmaking by digging a trench, filling it with water, piling the dirt back in to dampen it, then shoveling it over to the brickmaker who works nearby. Houses that were being built when I was in Baghestan were made of bricks measuring 23 to 25 centimeters square and 6 or 7 centimeters thick, depending on the mold at hand. Three molds (*chahār chub* ["wooden frame"] or *qāleb khesht* [mud brick mold]) in the village were borrowed as needed. They differed slightly in size, measuring 25, 23.5, and 25.5 centimeters square. Older buildings are frequently of larger bricks, up to 31 centimeters square. The villagers measure molds by finger widths: Baghestan's are said to be 14 finger widths wide, nearby Salehabad's 16–18 finger widths.[5]

The mold is a four-sided frame, open top and bottom, which makes a single brick at a time. The workers I watched slapped mud in the mold first, then topped it with a double handful of wet straw mushed in with a quick motion. Elsewhere, straw and mud are usually mixed together first (see, for example, Hall, McBride, and Riddell 1973, 255; Wulff 1966, 109–10). The frame is then lifted from the wet brick and put down beside it for the next load of mud. The lines of bricks are left flat for four or five days, then turned on edge to finish drying, which may take another week or so.[6]

With enough helpers to keep a steady supply of mud and wet straw, a brickmaker can count on producing from 600 to 1,200 bricks per day, according to villagers. I watched two men with one mold make 500 to 600 bricks per day, and I timed a skilled brickmaker working without breaking his pace at 4 bricks per minute over a period of about fifteen minutes. He could not keep up that pace for a whole day.

Brickmaking usually takes a minimum of two workers, one to bring the mud, the other to mold the bricks, but it can be done alone. Four workers are ideal: three helpers working with shovels to mix and carry the materials, and one brickmaker with the mold shaping the bricks. Although, as mentioned earlier, females occasionally make bricks, ordinarily brickmakers are adult male residents of the village, part-time specialists who also farm.

According to villagers, a freestanding room uses 4,000 bricks in the walls and 500 more in the vaulted or domed roof. Paper calculations for a typical room (13 square meters in interior area, 2 meters high to the beginning of the vault, walls 2.5 bricks thick, with allowances made for mortar and wall openings) confirm these figures. A substantial courtyard gate (*sardar*) takes 2,000 bricks.

Mud brick walls are 2.5 bricks thick, each course laid so that the bonds are staggered vertically and horizontally. The speed with which walls can be laid depends on several factors: the skill of the *ostād,* the availability of helpers to keep the builder occupied, and the need for intervals of mortar drying time during the wall raising (this appeared to be every 60 to 100 centimeters of height in Baghestan). Working at normal speeds, the *ostād* and his helpers take two to three days to raise the walls of an individual room with an interior area of 12 to 13 square meters and one more day to vault it. (I verified this reported rate by checking the fees paid the *ostāds* against their daily rates.) I calculate that walls are raised at the rate of about 5½ to 8 cubic meters per day, based on construction times in ten different cases. A day's work is difficult to pin down in hours, as progress is frequently broken by other calls on the workers' time. Unlike houses built in wetter areas, a house begun in the dry season is not always finished and roofed before the rains, although there is a risk of "meltdown" should the rains be unusually heavy. Delays are less likely when a specialist is brought in and paid by the day, of course.

The number of unskilled helpers varies, depending in large part on where the bricks and mortar are prepared and how long it takes to carry or toss them on to the *ostād*. I was told ten men were usual for building a vault, but I never saw more than six to eight working at mixing mortar and tossing bricks during wall construction.

House walls are usually 80 to 85 centimeters thick, including plaster, but range from 70 to 90 centimeters. Exterior walls of *qal'as* are 100 centimeters thick, courtyard walls only about 30 centimeters. For Aliabad's flat-roofed structures, Kramer reports walls about 50 centimeters thick, except when they support a second story, in which case they may be as much as a meter thick (Kramer 1982b, 99, 125). In Malyan, Fars Ostan, the walls of single-story rooms of flat-roofed structures were two and one-half bricks thick (50 centimeters without mortar); those supporting second-story rooms were three bricks thick, or 60 centimeters without mortar (Robert Dyson, personal communication, 1980). Dwelling walls may be thicker in Tauran because they support domes and vaults.

The wall builder usually incorporates arches in all four sides of a building (see Figure 20). I did not see an arch completed in Baghestan, but in the neighboring village of Zamanabad I observed that they were filled with bricks to support the arch until it set, after which the bricks were removed. These arches will become doorways and windows if left open and niches (*darbāns*) if walled on the outside with a single layer of bricks. One builder said that the standard size currently is 1 meter wide and 1.5 meters high. This construction method lends versatility and flexibility to the ways the room can be used and, perhaps more important, reused (see the sections on recycling in Chapter 8).

## Roofing

All brick-walled structures in Baghestan are domed, vaulted, or both. The flat roofs found in the more wooded parts of Iran are not built in

Figure 20. The rear niche in the storeroom next to the living room of household 12. The construction of arched niches makes it easy to convert them into doors. The mud brick domed and vaulted roof is built without scaffolding.

Baghestan; animal houses do have pole, mud, and brush roofs, but those structures are of different, more casual construction than that used for the standard, wooden-beamed, mud-packed flat roofs found not only in Iran but elsewhere in the Near East. In Baghestan, there is not enough water for pole wood for roofs to be grown locally, as it is in, for example, the Zagros Mountains in western Iran (Kramer 1982b, 93). Lack of technology, however, need not be why one building technique dominates. In western Iran, vaults are used for rooms over which a second story will be built and for some stables and storerooms (Kramer 1982b, 93). It would seem, then, that flat roofs are consciously chosen over vaults, since both the materials and the technology are available for either type. Flat roofs, of course, offer extra storage and work space. Especially in hillside villages, this alone would make them a preferred form.

The most common roof type in this area is the half-domed barrel vault, which begins at one end with leaning tiers of bricks (see Figure 20).[7] It finishes in what resembles half a diagonal groined vault (see Horne 1980, Figure 12). A hole for lighting or ventilation is left where the groins meet the main vault. No centering of any kind is used: mud plaster holds the bricks in place, and pebble spacers placed between the bricks ensure the curve of the arch. There are a number of variations on this theme, from circular groined and corbeled domes to wall-ended barrel vaults (see Horne 1983, 18). Wooden poles (*chub bast*) are temporarily inserted into holes at the top of the wall on which the roofer can stand. These holes are sometimes still visible on finished rooms.

## Details and Finishing

The brick surfaces of walls and roofs must be plastered to protect them (and their inhabitants) against the weather. *Kāhgel* plaster 'used for the purpose is composed of the same materials, straw and mud, as are bricks. Barley straw is used in a ratio of 1:2 straw to mud and wheat straw in a ratio of 1:3 (barley is said to be "softer" and less rain resistant than wheat, so more is needed.) *Kāhgel* is applied in a layer 1 to 3.5 centimeters thick. No one in Baghestan mentioned chaff as a material that might hold up construction. Both Watson (1979, 292) and Kramer (1979, 148), however, report that it is not always available, or at least not available to everyone, even in their heavily agricultural villages. Those without their own fields must buy it, of course.

For plastering and replastering, the materials are carried to the house and prepared in the courtyard or alley. Dirt and straw are mixed and mounded in a ring, which is then filled with water and more dirt. After an overnight soaking, the entire pile is stomped by foot to mix it thoroughly, slapped onto the walls and smoothed with a trowel or by hand.

Inside walls are finished to several degrees of fineness, depending on the type of room. Most usually, a base layer of *kāhgel* covers the floors and walls, sometimes stopping at the springing of the vault (about 100 centimeters high) with the rest of the vault left bare. Animal rooms and straw rooms may not even include this much interior finish. Older living rooms were sometimes finished with only a thin wash of *gel-e sabz*, which left the shape of the bricks exposed. *Gach-e khāk* is considered to make the hardest and most attractive finish, but it takes considerably more work than *kāhgel* or *gel-e sabz* because the earth must be carted in and prepared before it can be applied. It also requires quantities of brushwood fuel. Small amounts are burned in open pans over a courtyard hearth or an *alāddin,* but larger quantities require a properly built oven (one in deteriorated condition is visible in the courtyard of households 4 and 5). For these reasons it is often used only part way (about a meter) up the walls and around the niches of rooms. Both *gel-e sabz* and *gach-e khāk* are applied with a brush made from a local plant. Villagers are just beginning to use commercial lime plaster and cement; a specialist applies them uniformly over the entire room, including the vault.

Unless there are also utilitarian benefits, villagers spend little time or money on decoration for its own sake. However, the summer living room of household 16 was topped with the horns of wild sheep, and floral designs are occasionally hand-painted on inside walls (as, for example, in the room shown in Figure 21).

Windows come in many forms, from simple open portholes only a handspan wide to glass-paned, blue-painted wooden frames that swing open and shut. Every room, no matter what kind it is, has a door. Like windows, doors vary widely. The simplest are thick, handcut wooden planks hewn from the plane tree. These swing on wooden projections that fit into forked sticks set in the mud frame above and into sockets of

Figure 21. A *kondu*, or grain storage bin, and an out-of-use wood heater in a storeroom. The room was once a living room; a branched floral design is barely visible on the wall over the bin. The bin is made of large clay rings plastered together. It is filled from the top, lidded, and emptied from the plugged hole at the bottom.

stone or sherd bases below (the swing of the door wears a hemispherical depression in both these sockets). Better wooden doors of the older style have hinges nailed to the door and tied through the jamb. Again in old-style doors, locks with wooden keys are operated from fist-size holes beside the door. The newest and most expensive doors are commercially made metal doors with or without glass-paned windows. The doorway usually has a sunken area in which the door swings, whether it opens in or out. Nearly all doors open in.

## Maintenance

Mud brick must be plastered in order to protect it from deterioration (Figure 22). Even though the roofs are domed, they are used for storage, drying clothes, sleeping, and are walked on, especially by children and

Figure 22. An out-of-compound storeroom belonging to household 11, next to the living room of household 7. The straw-mud replastering is here strictly functional and covers the parts vulnerable to weathering. Even so, deterioration at the wall base has begun.

goats. How heavy the use is determines how frequently they need replastering. Outside *kāhgel* is needed every three years as well, but the amount of work required depends on what kind of use the roof gets and what the weather conditions have been. In one case I observed, it took three men two days to prepare the *kāhgel,* scrape off the old cracked surface, and replaster four domes.

Replastering interior walls with *gel-e sabz,* is said to be carried out yearly (and probably generally is) at the time of the vernal equinox and the beginning of the Persian New Year, Nauruz, a time of rebirth and refurbishing. Replastering with *gach-e khāk* is done every two to 'three years. In the past, when cooking and heating took place on open hearths inside rooms, the walls were covered with thick deposits of greasy soot. Layers of plaster and soot were, in some abandoned rooms, built up to at least 4 centimeters in thickness. Modern metal heaters are vented through roof pipes, and although the walls still get smoked from kerosene lanterns and burning coals, they stay much cleaner now than when open fires were used. Floors need replastering too, not only because of wear and tear, but also because of leaking roof vents in the center of the dome.

### Features and Miscellaneous Minor Structures

While men are responsible for building the walls and roofs of houses and stables, women often add the finish and the built-in features.[8] These include a variety of ovens, hearths, chicken coops, storeroom bins, and weaving facilities. The itinerant specialists who come to build more demanding features, such as bread ovens, are sometimes women.

Features found inside rooms include *bokhāris* (fireplaces and heaters), *kondus,* various kinds of wall bins, and pits and stanchions once used in weaving. There are two kinds of *bokhāri:* the older *bokhāri geli* (clay heater) and the newer *bokhāri ferengi* ("European" heater). *Bokhāri gelis* are chimneyed fireplaces built into the walls of living rooms. They are no longer used and are found only in older rooms, all now used for storage. The ones in the *qal'as* are especially fine (see Horne 1991, Figure 12, for an elaborate one, Figure 14 for a simpler one). They were never universal; the living rooms of the poorer villagers had simple floor hearths. *Bokhāri ferengis* are metal space heaters that burn brushwood and are plastered

Figure 23. A *bokhāri ferengi*, or metal space heater, plastered in place behind its hearth in the living room of household 2. Felt rugs are on the floor, the room is plastered white and looks out onto its *eivān* (covered porch). Fodder is temporarily stored by the door.

onto the floor in the center of the living room (Figure 23). A stove pipe carries smoke out through a hole in the roof. In front of the heater is a circular hearth in which coals are placed for cooking pots. The heater is usually removed in the summer, when outside hearths are used for cooking. Tea is made in a samovar year round. The floor fixture is either a raised double circle (Figure 23) or a square platform plus circular hearth.

*Kondus* (Figure 21) come in a variety of sizes, built to hold from 15 to 200 *mans* (about 45 to 600 kilograms) of unmilled wheat. Small ones tend to be spherical in shape and are designated by the number of *mans* they hold. Large ones are ovoid in shape and are designated by the number of clay rings with which they were assembled. Most are either footed or plastered to the floor and have an opening at the top that can be sealed by plastering the lid down and a plugged circular opening at the bottom through which the grain is removed. A five-ring *kondu* measures about 90 centimeters high and 65 centimeters in diameter; a 200-*man kondu* measures about 200 centimeters high and 100 centimeters in diameter. Some *kondus* are as much as 2 meters high. Some built twenty-five or thirty years ago are still in use. They once were made by villagers, including the fathers of some present-day residents, but now are commissioned from a specialist from the area around Sabzevar who comes every two or three years and makes them on the spot. The rings are made out in the open, brought into the courtyard to be plastered together, and then installed in the storeroom.

Bins of several sorts are found in storerooms and in animal houses. In animal houses they are low-walled mangers, located and sized for the animal in question. In storerooms they are used to hold loose agricultural products, such as grain, fodder, or straw. (Straw in "straw rooms" is simply dumped in loose.) Existing niches and *kondus* often form their side or back walls, in which case they are called *porkhus*. One sturdy niche of this type measured 130 centimeters wide and 40 centimeters deep with rock and clay walls 20 centimeters thick.

Weaving was once a common domestic activity, but has not been practiced in the area since the 1950s. Home-grown silk and cotton were spun and woven into cloth, including the blue-checked cotton *chādor,* worn by women before it was replaced by imported commercial fabric. Neither silkworms nor the kind of cotton that can be spun and woven at home are raised now. Heddles, loom weights, and other paraphernalia used in weaving still show up in storerooms, but weaving was carried out in living rooms as well as storerooms. Built-in features for weaving include pits cut in the floor, all of which have now been filled and replastered. One patch marking the filled-in pit measured about a meter by a meter and a half. Presumably a horizontal warp-weighted loom, such as that described as being seen elsewhere on the Iranian Plateau, was set into the pit (Wulff 1966, 202–203). The loom's warp threads were held taut through a wooden ring tied to a small pole anchored into a clay support. The support was part of a shelf built into the narrow end of the room.

Other kinds of features are found outside, usually in the courtyard. These include *tālārs* (in the local dialect, coolers for milk products), *tanurs,* troughs and feed bins, and *kalgāhs* (hearths).

*Tālārs* are made of low, thin parallel walls of clay attached to a house or courtyard wall (Figure 24). Thin poles are set in crosswise to make a

Figure 24. The paired rooms in the compound of household 22. Stairs at the left lead to the roof, which is used for sleeping, drying foods, and viewing the rest of the village. A rug-covered *tālār* keeps milk products cool in spite of the summer heat.

shelf. *Tālārs* in villages usually measure about a meter or so in width and depth; those at milking stations are much larger (see Figure 5). From two to five skins of yoghurt or cheese rest on the shelf, where they drip and condense liquid. This condensation, coupled with shade provided by rugs and quilts, has a significant cooling effect. In villages, most are in the courtyard for convenience and protection. In Baghestan, however, five were on the north or west side of roofs, shaded by the dome or a second-story room. *Tālārs* are often called simply *jā-ye mast* (place for yoghurt).

*Tanurs,* in which flat slabs of wheat bread are slapped against the inside surface of a heated clay-walled cylinder and baked until they come loose, are about 1.5 or 2 meters across the top and are waist high, with a hole diameter of about 50 to 75 centimeters. To prepare for construction (according to villagers), *gel-e sabz* for the oven's lining is dug up and soaked for three days, covered with a cloth in preparation for the arrival of the *ostād,* who will bat the clay and build the oven. The circular frame has a double wall of bricks filled in between with sand for insulation. The central hole is lined with *gel-e sabz,* which bakes to ceramic hardness. Depressions on the top of the oven let rainwater run off, and a hole at the bottom provides draft. Brushwood is used as fuel. Ovens are shared because not every household can afford to build one and because sharing saves fuel.

*Kalgāhs* are usually found outside, occasionally inside, a storeroom or kitchen. Housewives build their own. I examined one that was built of square mud bricks (30 centimeters wide) and rimmed with small stones to form a raised lip. The whole was plastered over with *kāhgel* and was about one and a half meters square in size. Others are more casual in construction (Figure 25). *Kalgāhs* are sized for the pot they will hold and often appear in pairs—large and small. Fifty centimeters is a common inside diameter of the hearth for a single one. When they are routinely used for long periods of cooking, as is the case in milk processing, large copper pots are plastered directly onto their hearths, presumably to pre-serve heat and conserve fuel.

Courtyards frequently contain pens and shaded areas for animals and closed coops for chickens. Mud and brick stairs, some paved with flat stones, are sometimes built against a house wall for access to the roof. They are often replastered until they become bumpy ramps (as in Horne

Figure 25. Wood burning *kalgāhs,* or hearths. Dung is not used for fuel in this area. Households often have hearths of several sizes to match the cooking pots. Pots are sometimes plastered down to conserve heat.

1983, 21). *Tāqcha-ye sabzi* are clay pockets attached to the courtyard wall for growing sprouts of wheat or barley, symbols of spring renewal at Nauruz. I saw only one example, in the courtyard of household 29.

Several incidental structures are found both inside and outside of courtyards. *Tavilas* (open donkey pens) are about 16 square meters in area with packed mud walls 50 to 80 centimeters high. I saw one take two days to build: one day for mud preparation and one for construction. *Dastābs* (toilets) are usually just pit privies of makeshift construction. A few have cement bases bought in the city. They can be cleaned out, but often households build a new one rather than rehabilitate the old one. Most are surrounded by a circular low wall (about a meter and a half high), about 170 centimeters in inside diameter, with the door offset so the user is somewhat hidden. Sometimes the open door is baffled with a curved wall extension. A few newer ones, attached to houses, are rectangular, about 2.2 square meters in area, with walls one brick thick. Small, casually built, brush-roofed shelters, or *sāyevāns,* are sometimes built at field sites so that the children can have shade when they guard the crops against birds.

## Cost of the Completed House

In the late 1970s inflation was proceeding apace. It is difficult to arrive at comparable figures for wages and materials even during the three-year period I was doing fieldwork in Iran, but the following values are probably not too far off. At 1978 prices, a dwelling room in new or good condition was probably worth Rls 15,000 (used) to Rls 25,000 or 30,000 (new), or from about $200 to $400 at 70 rials to the dollar.[9] Nonlocal relative values cannot be assumed for the various aspects of a house. A door brought from the city, for example, may cost almost half as much as the entire room. Some examples of costs in 1977 and 1978 were Rls 5,000 (about $70) for a good window with glass, Rls 3,000 to Rls 7,000 for a good wooden door, and Rls 10,000 for a large metal courtyard door. Hiring a specialist to plaster the inside walls of a room with *simgel* (cement) cost Rls 1,500 per day. A bread oven was Rls 300; a grain storage bin, Rls 100. Floor coverings ranged from Rls 2,000 for a felt *namad* and Rls 3,000 for a flat-woven carpet (*pelās*) to Rls 20,000–25,000 for a Baluch pile carpet 2.5 meters by 1 meter.

The building lot was one of the least expensive items. Villagers referred to land on which houses were built as either *oftāda* (empty, unused at time of purchase) or *melki* ("owned"). *Melki* land is theoretically still productive, although where houses were built the water had dried up so that the land could be planted only in years of exceptional rainfall. Land without water is of little or no agricultural value and is often referred to as "worthless" at Rls 200 to 300 per *man.*[10] No water runs through the village of Baghestan, and the price of house plots reflects this. Nevertheless, the price of land was rising fast even during the three seasons I spent there. In 1977 it was worth Rls 1,000 per *man,* yet eight or nine years before that, it was only Rls 30 per *man.*

All together, a compound, including the land, two rooms with good doors plus an *eivān,* and a courtyard wall and gate could cost about Rls 80,000. The cost is kept down by using friends and relatives for non-skilled or semiskilled labor. To put this price in perspective, consider that in 1977 a day worker was paid Rls 300 to 500 a day for local construction or field labor, more or less. Thus a room was the equivalent of about 40 days' wages; three rooms and a courtyard about 7 months' wages. For further comparison, note that in 1976 a shepherd's wage for a season of three and one-half months was Rls 70,000, or $1,000 (Martin 1980, 34), approximately the cost of a two-hour share in the irrigation cycle or twenty sheep. And in another sphere of purchase, a bought shirt in 1978 cost Rls 1,100–1,200; Iranian-made Lee-brand blue jeans, Rls 4,000.

## THE IDEAL HOUSE

An ideal house lot on the higher part of the plain, where Baghestan lies, is on level ground, higher than the natural drainage system that contains the irrigated fields. In Baghestan, land of this type lies in a semicircle around the eastern and southern sides of the village. This land was irrigated until the 1960s, when the water source began to dry up. Today some of it is still irrigated in the spring and dry farmed. Because of its irrigation history, it is deeply silted, stone free, and fairly level. It is therefore easy to level it further to make the floor of a house, and it is good for making mud bricks. I noted depths from 50 centimeters to several meters of deposit in pits where building material was being collected.

The villagers in Baghestan do not usually realize the ideal house. By the end of 1978, the compound belonging to household 2 was the only one in the village that had the full panoply of structures and spaces to which a household might aspire. These are an *eivān,* a family living room, a guest room, a storeroom-kitchen, another storeroom, an animal house, a *tanur,* a privy, and a shower, all within or right next to a large courtyard. These were built gradually over a period of fifteen years.

The order of building is a guide to how the components of a compound are ranked. A living room is the first unit to be built. *Eivāns* are clearly desirable and affordable; the three compounds under construction all include them. In Baghestan the courtyard walls and gate are the last of the major structures to be built. The husband in household 5 told me, as he added a massive new gate to his old courtyard wall, that his house was now complete. The courtyard walls had been the next to last addition. In Baghestan there seems to be no need to stake out a claim on the plot, nor to have immediate privacy, both of which would be achieved by building the courtyard first.

The village plan shows what constitutes more achievable and minimally acceptable living quarters. A living room is usually paired with a storeroom-kitchen, making a unit of two rooms plus forecourt the most common configuration of dwelling space (see, for example, Figure 24 and plans of households 4 and 5 in the Appendix, Figure A-4). Nineteen core compounds are set up this way; three consist of only one room and a forecourt area; the remaining eleven contain three or more rooms. An *eivān* connecting the two is a highly desirable space, because it is said to protect the living quarters from wind. There are, however, only four of these in the village, excepting those under construction. With the exception of *qal'as,* animal houses are never found within the walls of residential compounds.

Some core compounds, such as those of households 4, 5, 10, 15, and 17, actually realize the standard unit of two rooms-plus-courtyard on the ground. Other households, such as household 11, conform in terms of the household's own holdings but cannot be so identified from the plan because rooms belonging to other households are also included in the immediate area. In another case, household 9 appears to conform but does not because the household does not itself own both rooms in the courtyard (see Horne 1982c).

Besides two rooms side by side, there is a second kind of room arrangement, seen in full-fledged form in household 2 and in an abridged version in households 13, 33, and 35 and within the *qal'as.* Two more of this type were under construction in 1978; it appears to be the currently preferred form. In this type of arrangement, a central *eivān* is flanked by a single or double pair of rooms. This plan is more expensive to build because it adds what amounts to a third room to the pair. Since the construction of the *eivān* requires the other two rooms to be built at the same time, the units all go up at once. Thus, it also means that cash and/or labor must be available for a sizable project. How many rooms a household has and how they are distributed may also be affected by a desire, or lack of desire, for prestige. Some people, especially older ones, avoid material displays and scoff at the idea of living in a grander house than they think appropriate (Horne 1991).

These and other patterns show up clearly on the village plan. Most often, several rooms are joined together along a long side. Frequently a forecourt, defined by courtyard walls, ties the group into a larger architectural unit. The result is a kind of "courtyard house." The courtyard house in this area, however, differs in some important ways from the "typical" courtyard house as idealized in the literature or as described in particular case studies. In this area the courtyard is really only a forecourt attached to a string or cluster of rooms and is not formed by the rooms themselves (in contrast to the usual case in urban and *qal'a* housing). Moreover, this less embracing type of courtyard does not have the residential consequences of the standard type, which localizes all (or very nearly all) a household's dwelling and storage holdings within a single compound's walls. The distribution of room ownership for one household (household 11) in Baghestan is shown in Figure 26. A more detailed description and explanation for this pattern will be given in the discussion of houses and households in Chapter 8.

## VARIATION IN VILLAGE STRUCTURES

To the casual eye, Baghestan's structures appear to be very much alike, perhaps monotonously so, in size and appearance. All the mud brick structures, no matter what their function, are built to a similar plan. As yet, there are no "modern" houses or materials, such as cinder block or metal roofing, to contrast with the traditional. But on closer inspection, these structures do vary. No two are alike. Not only are there differences in detailing of finish (windows, doors, fineness of plastering), there are differences in size and in the number and kind of structures held within courtyards. Size varies not so much according to room type (animal rooms, for example, are only slightly larger on average than living rooms) but within a range for any given room type. This variation, moreover, is not constant by type. Courtyards show the greatest variability, storerooms and animal houses less, and living rooms the least (Table 10). Kramer's data (1982b) show that room types in Aliabad vary in the

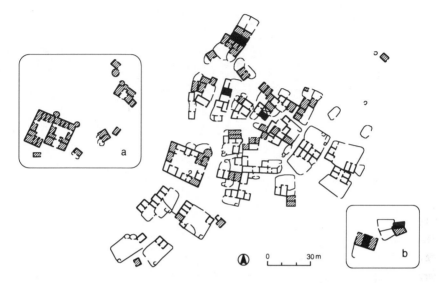

Figure 26. Location of rooms at a distance from or not opening directly onto their core compounds. As a typical example, those belonging to household 11 are marked in black; the living room (in Area C in the center of the village; see Appendix) is marked with an X. a = Qal'a Baghestan, b = Kalata.

same way as they do here.[11] The variable distribution of rooms and spaces among Baghestan's households can be seen in Table 11.

Time explains some of the variations described above, function explains others, and both time and function figure in still others. With changing times, settlement layout and architectural forms have changed dramatically in Khar o Tauran (Horne 1991 and 1993). Qal'a Baghestan (Figures 10, 11) and Qal'a Reza Qoli (Figure A-5) display an earlier style of settlement. Some obvious changes in architectural materials have occurred during the past fifty years or so, witnessed by the presence of city plaster, metal doors, and the replacement of clay fireplaces with metal space heaters. Other changes are more subtle, such as the one from polished plaster and green clay finishes to white earthen plaster. Room sizes have apparently been decreased since *qal'as* were built, as have brick sizes.

Some chronological changes are actually changes in function, such as the

TABLE 10. VARIATION IN ROOM SIZE IN BAGHESTAN, 1976

| Village rooms | N | Mean (m²) | Median (m²) | SD (m²) | Co-efficient of variation (%) |
|---|---|---|---|---|---|
| Courtyard area[a] | 32 | 95.8 | 70.0 | 72.2 | 75.3 |
| Living room | 32 | 13.2 | 13.1 | 1.9 | 14.3 |
| Storeroom (domestic) | 71 | 13.6 | 13.1 | 3.9 | 28.8 |
| Storeroom (straw) | 25 | 13.1 | 13.9 | 3.3 | 25.1 |
| Animal house or stable | 41 | 14.3 | 14.1 | 4.5 | 31.5 |

*Note:* All measurements are of interiors.

a. Courtyard areas are totals per household and in a few cases include forecourts of animal houses.

relatively abrupt disappearance of weaving features caused by a switch to American cotton grown as a cash crop rather than for local use. The different needs of agriculturalism and pastoralism are a significant functional cause of architectural variation. Even within a single village they affect storage forms (woven or skin containers versus clay bins), hearth sizes (large ones for milk processing), and room type (animal shelters).

Architecture functions in part to shelter people. It might also therefore be expected to reflect simple demographic facts such as the size and composition of the groups that dwell within or otherwise use the buildings. As discussed in Chapter 5, architecture also plays a cultural and expressive role in people's lives, including the expression of status and wealth.

## MEASURES OF WEALTH: ANIMALS, LAND, AND WATER

The primary productive investments for residents of Khar o Tauran are agricultural land and water and animals (primarily goats). These resources are not evenly distributed. Some villagers have neither irrigated land nor animals and work as shepherds or day laborers. To make ends meet, the elderly widow without children in Baghestan must depend on

TABLE 11. HOUSEHOLD SIZE AND ARCHITECTURAL SPACE IN
BAGHESTAN, 1976

| Household[a] | Household size | No. of rooms | Living room area (m$^2$) | Animal house area (m$^2$) | Total dwelling area[b] (m$^2$) | Total roofed area (m$^2$) | Court-yard area (m$^2$) |
|---|---|---|---|---|---|---|---|
| 2 | 7 | 8 | 12.3 | 21.8 | 86.4 | 108.2 | 190.0 |
| 3 | 9 | 9 | 13.5 | 34.8 | 56.7 | 114.3 | 70.0 |
| 4 | 2 | 4 | 14.7 | 16.2 | 42.4 | 58.6 | 120.0 |
| 5 | 4 | 6 | 14.4 | 33.7 | 40.9 | 94.6 | 120.0 |
| 6 | 6 | 8 | 13.0 | 27.7 | 58.3 | 94.8 | 70.0 |
| 7 | 7 | 8 | 17.9 | 19.5 | 67.1 | 117.4 | 125.0 |
| 8 | 6 | 2 | 12.9 | 0.0 | 24.9 | 24.9 | 70.0 |
| 9 | 3 | 5 | 13.2 | 0.0 | 56.0 | 68.0 | 69.4 |
| 10 | 6 | 5 | 17.4 | 16.1 | 31.6 | 78.4 | 113.8 |
| 11 | 4 | 6 | 11.4 | 44.7 | 42.6 | 5.0 | 19.5 |
| 12 | 5 | 9 | 11.1 | 58.3 | 55.3 | 128.9 | 183.0 |
| 13 | 4 | 3 | 10.8 | 0.0 | 34.1 | 44.4 | 56.2 |
| 14 | 4 | 7 | 13.9 | 31.8 | 60.7 | 104.7 | 35.0 |
| 15 | 7 | 6 | 16.6 | 13.1 | 40.5 | 70.6 | 31.2 |
| 16 | 8 | 5 | 12.0 | 0.0 | 44.3 | 55.5 | 37.5 |
| 17 | 2 | 2 | 13.6 | 0.0 | 25.2 | 25.2 | 4.7 |
| 18 | 1 | 2 | 13.2 | 0.0 | 18.5 | 18.5 | 18.8 |
| 19 | 6 | 4 | 12.4 | 31.8 | 31.0 | 58.1 | 40.6 |
| 20 | 4 | 3 | 9.7 | 0.0 | 36.7 | 36.7 | 56.2 |
| 22 | 3 | 6 | 12.6 | 23.5 | 41.3 | 77.4 | 98.4 |
| 23 | 6 | 2 | 10.4 | 0.0 | 21.9 | 21.9 | 63.6 |
| 24 | 6 | 7 | 13.9 | 40.8 | 45.0 | 100.6 | 234.4 |
| 25 | 2 | 2 | 11.6 | 0.0 | 22.5 | 22.5 | 161.7 |
| 26 | 7 | 2 | 15.0 | 0.0 | 28.4 | 28.4 | 40.6 |
| 27 | 3 | 6 | 15.4 | 28.8 | 39.7 | 78.9 | 25.0 |
| 28 | 7 | 8 | 11.7 | 42.0 | 47.9 | 106.5 | 265.6 |
| 29 | 5 | 4 | 12.4 | 0.0 | 53.4 | 53.4 | 131.2 |
| 31 | 4 | 2 | 14.0 | 0.0 | 28.5 | 28.5 | 37.5 |

TABLE 11. cont.

| Household[a] | Household size | No. of rooms | Living room area (m²) | Animal house area (m²) | Total dwelling area[b] (m²) | Total roofed area (m²) | Court-yard area (m²) |
|---|---|---|---|---|---|---|---|
| 32 | 5 | 6 | 13.5 | 12.1 | 35.2 | 71.0 | 56.2 |
| 33 | 5 | 5 | 11.6 | 22.9 | 74.0 | 81.7 | 275.0 |
| 34 | 7 | 10 | 13.2 | 40.1 | 83.6 | 134.8 | 148.4 |

a. In 1976, household 21 had not yet formed as a residential unit, household 30 had moved away, although its rooms had not been disposed of, household 33 was in the process of moving, and household 35 was resident only part-time.

b. Includes living rooms, storerooms, kitchens, and *eivāns*.

charity. Other villagers have so many flocks or fields that they must, and can afford to, hire fellow villagers as assistants. No one is so rich that they need not work at all.

When villagers have accumulated cash or capital beyond their ordinary subsistence needs, they tend to put it into productive investments: land (with water) and sheep or goats (Martin 1980a). These two kinds of holdings are good measures of traditional wealth in the Near East, where land and animals are highly valued. Moreover, indigenous rankings of wealth tend to agree with rankings based on land and animals (Kamp 1982, 343; Kamp 1987, 290; Kramer 1982b, 52–57). Table 12 is a list of household wealth as measured in animals and in hours of irrigation water. Only sheep and goats are counted in the calculations, although there are other farm animals in the village, including cows (for a supplementary family milk supply), oxen (for plowing), donkeys (for loads and sometimes for plowing), and dogs (for guarding the flocks). These animals are not included because people do not invest in them the way they do in fields and flocks. They are more appropriately placed in the category of plows and carts, part of the paraphernalia of farming.[12]

Agricultural holdings are more difficult to deal with. Trying to force the various systems of traditional Iranian land measure into comparability with each other or with the metric system is a task that is difficult to impos-

TABLE 12. PASTORAL AND AGRICULTURAL WEALTH
IN BAGHESTAN

| Wealth by household | | | Ranked wealth | |
|---|---|---|---|---|
| Household[a] | Animal wealth (thousands of rials)[b] | Water wealth (thousands of rials)[c] | Household | Total wealth (thousands of rials) |
| 2 | 207.5 | 594 | 25 | 0 |
| 3 | 785.0 | 960 | 26 | 0 |
| 4 | 82.0 | 660 | 23 | 33.0 |
| 5 | 203.5 | 660 | 20 | 46.5 |
| 6 | 72.5 | 600 | 18 | 90.0 |
| 7 | 428.5 | 1,080 | 31 | 248.0 |
| 8 | 0 | 360 | 27 | 284.0 |
| 9 | 113.5 | 270 | 32 | 340.5 |
| 10 | 275.0 | 504 | 8 | 360.0[d] |
| 11 | 274.0 | 1,320 | 9 | 383.5 |
| 12 | 100.5 | 825 | 13 | 386.5 |
| 13 | 206.5 | 180 | 19 | 412.5 |
| 14 | 152.0 | 990 | 22 | 418.5 |
| 15 | 154.0 | 510 | 17 | 655.0 |
| 16 | 71.0 | 735 | 15 | 664.0 |
| 17 | 385.0 | 270 | 6 | 672.5 |
| 18 | 0 | 90 | 4 | 742.0 |
| 19 | 142.5 | 270 | 2 | 801.5 |
| 20 | 46.5 | 0 | 16 | 806.0 |
| 22 | 118.5 | 300 | 34 | 819.0 |
| 23 | 33.0 | 0 | 5 | 863.5 |
| 24 | 18.0 | 1,008 | 12 | 925.5 |
| 25 | 0 | 0 | 24 | 1,026.0 |
| 26 | 0 | 0 | 10[d] | 1,139.0 |
| 27 | 104.0 | 180 | 14 | 1,142.0 |
| 28 | 485.5 | 1,800 | 29 | 1,490.0 |
| 29 | 950.0 | 540 | 7 | 1,508.5 |

TABLE 12. cont.

| Wealth by household | | | Ranked wealth | |
| --- | --- | --- | --- | --- |
| Household[a] | Animal wealth (thousands of rials)[b] | Water wealth (thousands of rials)[c] | Household | Total wealth (thousands of rials) |
| 31 | 68.0 | 180 | 11 | 1,594.0 |
| 32 | 40.5 | 300 | 3 | 1,745.0 |
| 33 | 60.0 | 360 | 33 | 1,900.0[e] |
| 34 | 339.0 | 480 | 28 | 2,285.5 |

*Source:* Data on herds from 1978 are from Martin 1987; data on water shares from 1976 are from Martin in a personal communication, 1989.

a. In 1976, household 21 had not yet formed, household 30 had moved, and household 35 was not a resident.

b. Goats were valued at Rls 2,500, sheep at Rls 3,000. Mean number of sheep and goats per household was 70.8. In the late 1970s, Rls 70 equaled $1.

c. In 1976, water shares converted at a factor of 10,000 to 60,000 rials per hour, depending on the field system.

d. Includes a diesel-powered grain mill valued at 360,000 rials. No one else had a comparable investment in productive equipment.

e. In 1976, household 33 still had large tracts of pasture the value of which could not be established. The figure here is somewhat arbitrary, designed to raise the household to its likely place as second wealthiest in the village.

sible, since they are predicated on inherently different premises. Most depend on the fact that what an Iranian farmer knows or needs to know is not the extent of a holding as it appears on a map, but rather its working characteristics, labor and seed input, and potential yield, which varies according to topography, soil type, and water availability. Metric units or other direct areal measures fail to describe these differences adequately.

Fortunately, in Tauran timed access to water is a practical surrogate for measured plots of irrigated land. Land without water has little worth; what makes it valuable is rights to irrigation water from the gravity-fed springs and *qanāts* of the area's field systems, which are traded, bought, and inherited like other commodities. Thus, when acquiring irrigated fields people speak of hours of water, not *mans*. Measuring agricultural wealth this way avoids many of the above-named problems, although it still does not make comparisons with other areas easy.

Dry-farmed landholdings are not assigned a value. Dry farming is a desirable supplementary option possible only in years of timely rain; the land is said to be of very little value, about Rls 200 to 300 per *man*. With one exception, dry-farmed land is held by those in the upper half of the wealth ranking, a result of its either having been inherited or having been purchased only after a more stable base of irrigated land was acquired.

In these dryland settlements where agriculture and pastoralism are the bases for livelihood, to concentrate on either one at the expense of the other would be a risky business. As might be expected, holdings of animals and land in Baghestan show a positive linear correlation ($r = .47$, $r^2 = .217$, $p<.01$), although it is not as pronounced as the one Kramer found in Aliabad (Kramer 1982b, 67).

## ARCHITECTURAL EXPRESSION OF WEALTH AND STATUS

In the following discussion I consider the allocation of village rooms and courtyards, that is, architectural variables, and their relation to selected socioeconomic variables (Table 13). Other kinds of correlations between material culture and wealth or status could of course be made, using, for example, portable, nonarchitectural belongings. Of these, pile rugs are certainly the most expensive and clearly considered to be prestige markers by the villagers. Furniture as well as decoration, they are spread for seating, especially when a household entertains guests. Seventeen of the thirty-two households owned from 1 to 5 pile rugs each. Two of these households were in the lowest wealth quartile (with a total of 7 rugs), seven in the second (with a total of 19 rugs), three in the third (with a total of 12 rugs) and five in the highest (with a total of 21 rugs). Rugs, somewhat surprisingly, appear to be rather evenly distributed among households.

Other potential indicators of wealth include bicycles, portable radios, portable cassette players and pressure lamps, and the more traditional tea samovars and large copper pots (*levirs*) for processing milk and cooking for

TABLE 13. CORRELATIONS OF
HOUSEHOLD WEALTH AND SIZE WITH
ARCHITECTURAL HOLDINGS IN
BAGHESTAN

| Correlation | $r$ | $r^2$ | $p$ |
|---|---|---|---|
| Wealth | | | |
| Household size | .401 | .161 | <.05 |
| Number of rooms | .598 | .357 | <.01 |
| Living room area | .095 | .009 | n.s. |
| Storeroom area | .55 | .302 | <.01 |
| Dwelling area | .561 | .314 | <.01 |
| Animal room area | .561 | .314 | <.01 |
| Roofed area | .67 | .449 | <.01 |
| Courtyard area | .537 | .289 | <.01 |
| Household size | | | |
| Wealth | .401 | .161 | <.05 |
| Number of rooms | .482 | .233 | <.01 |
| Living room area | .127 | .016 | n.s |
| Storeroom area | .382 | .146 | <.05 |
| Dwelling area | .397 | .157 | <.05 |
| Animal room area | .256 | .066 | n.s. |
| Roofed area | .424 | .179 | <.05 |
| Courtyard area | .218 | .047 | n.s. |

*Note:* n.s = not significant at the .05 level.

village feasts. Except for the very poorest of villagers, who have none, these items did not appear to correlate well with wealth. Once they begin to appear on the village scene, they spread quickly until most households own them and they come to be staples rather than luxury items.

Household size is not well reflected in the architectural spaces of the village, and on its own does not account for much of the variation in area ($r^2$ column in Table 13). There is no particular reason why it should. Nuclear family households vary primarily by the number of children present, and people here do not increase their living or productive spaces because of how many children they have. Children may be a burden at times, but they are also assets, especially as helpers with family chores. They can be redistributed among households to accommodate too many in one household (the parents) or too few in another (grandparents). There were two cases of this sort in Baghestan.

Wealth might come to be reflected in architectural holdings in two quite different ways. The first has to do with display and conspicuous consumption; the second, with pragmatic needs and the tools of production. Of the paired categories in Table 13, only living-room area has no significant correlation with wealth. The rest show what I judge to be moderate to good correlations. None of the results is dramatic.

Courtyards, for example, are the most public of space in Baghestan, and therefore might be expected to show off a family's status effectively. They are, however, also used for productive chores and to pen animals. They show more variation in size than any other category of space, and they do correlate positively with wealth. The correlation is not so strong, however, as to make courtyard size on its own a reliable predictor of wealth.

Every household has a living room in which to sleep (in the winter at least), eat, and entertain. Moreover, each household has only *one* living room (one living room at a time, that is; some households alternate living rooms seasonally with storerooms). Co-residence of household members means "under the same roof" in a very literal sense, for all members sleep and eat in this one room. "On the same floor" is probably more apt. In many other rural areas of the Near East, households are frequently extended or joint. In such cases (for examples, see Kamp 1982 and Kramer 1982b) each nuclear family unit occupies separate sleeping quarters within the courtyard walls, although they cook, eat, and work together. That is, a single walled compound may contain a number of living rooms even though it serves only one economic household.

In spite of this close and constant attachment of people and space, living rooms in Baghestan are all very much alike. Some are newer, and therefore more freshly or professionally finished, but all are sparsely furnished and all are relatively small and vary little in size. Living-room size does not correlate significantly with either the number of household members or wealth.[13] People in fact expressly prefer modest-size living rooms. Big ones are uncomfortable in the winter, they say, and there is no reason why one should be larger than necessary. If more space of this sort were desired, presumably it would take the form of a guest room, a separate, specialized space used for entertaining. There was only one in the village, however, installed in 1978 in a redecorated storeroom by household 2.

Total number of rooms per household and the associated total roofed area show the strongest positive linear relationship with wealth. This should not be surprising. Thirty-nine percent of the rooms in the village are animal and straw rooms (see Table 6). These rooms are really tools of production, used to house animals, to shelter food-processing tasks, and to store equipment, agricultural produce, fodder, and firewood. The wealthier the household in land and animals, the more space it needs to store and process the products. If nonagricultural income were the basis for wealth in Baghestan, another explanation would be needed.

These simple correlation procedures may help in understanding the way rooms and spaces are distributed though the village, but Baghestan's small size precludes making the kinds of intravillage comparisons that appear in other studies. There is, for example, no landless/landed dichotomy as there is in Aliabad (Kramer 1982b). Unlike Aliabad, Darnaj (Kamp 1982 and 1987), and Hasanabad (Watson 1979), Baghestan has only one co-residing household (households 4 and 5). Whereas half the households in Aliabad have second-story living rooms, only three of the thirty-two do in Baghestan. Baghestan had no guest rooms until 1978, when household 2 redecorated a storeroom for that purpose. It does not even have compounds in the sense of walled areas containing a household and its structures. This last characteristic is the most confounding for those seeking to read household economics and demographics from a village plan.

The relationship of houses and households recorded during the late 1970s probably reflects the end of a settlement style. Changes in detailing, finish, and layout of the rooms were already becoming apparent during the three years of fieldwork. As government development of rural areas, transportation, and the national and local economies improve, and as the area becomes more attached to urban opportunities, cash, and the products money buys, discretionary income may again be invested in architectural display as it was in earlier days (Horne 1991).

# CHAPTER 7

# THE VILLAGE AS AN ARCHAEOLOGICAL SITE

I n a sense, an occupied settlement acts like a living organism. Materials are gathered into it, absorbed, transformed, cycled around, and ejected again in the form of product or waste. When accumulation exceeds attrition, the result is a cultural deposit, subject to further natural and cultural transformations. In the long run, this deposit is impermanent because of the action of weathering and erosion. Geoarchaeological studies, valuable for the way they wrest information from the cultural deposit itself, emphasize the physical nature of cultural deposits and sediments. Behavioral studies, valuable for the way they connect the material with human activity, emphasize proximate causes, such as discard and recycling behaviors. Both types of study greatly increase our understanding of archaeological sites, and several works, such as those of Courty, Goldberg, and MacPhail (1989) and Schiffer (1987), carry the points made in this chapter through to down-to-earth archaeological reality.

Deposits, however, are artifacts as well as contexts, and as such provide a basis for making behavioral, cultural, and historical inferences (see, for example, Nicholas 1980). The most interesting aspects of archaeological processes, such as mound formation, are not so much the immediate behaviors and physical processes involved but, rather, the social and cultural phenomena that shape the ways that people live in settlements and therefore shape the settlements themselves and their appearance as archaeological sites.

In most of the Near East, the deposit that results from the accumulation of human activity in settled communities is most visible when it takes the form of a mound (commonly appearing, in English, as *tell* for Arabic, *hüyük* for Turkish, and *tepe* for Persian mounded sites). But accumulation of cultural deposits into mounds is not something that inevitably occurs in areas of mud or mud brick construction. It results from certain kinds of settlement activities and not others, activities that are part of particular social and cultural conditions. Furthermore, the social and cultural causes of mound formation are not everywhere the same.

While accumulation and attrition are in part functions of certain kinds of human activities coupled with natural processes, they also take place through time and are affected by duration and repetition. In fact the effects of many practices—whether natural or cultural—have less to do with what happens than with the speed with which it happens. Sites that failed to form mounds at all or to form ones high enough to withstand natural processes such as erosion or alluviation long enough to be preserved into the present, are difficult and sometimes impossible to discover archaeologically. It is, therefore, not surprising that mounds appear to be an inevitable correlate of permanent settlement in the Near East.

In spite of the fact that Khar o Tauran is known from historical and archaeological sources to have been settled for at least 1,000 years, and probably for 1,000 years or more before that, and in spite of the fact that builders throughout that period undoubtedly used the same materials that are used in the present, mounds are not typical of this area as they are in other parts of Iran. It is thus appropriate to look at the ways in which the physical rearrangement of the materials of present-day settlement occurs in Khar o Tauran, relying mostly on data from the village of Baghestan.

## THE RAW MATERIALS OF A MOUND

The materials of architectural structures, both standing and in collapse, dominate the physical composition of a living village in the Near East, as they do in archaeological mounds (see, for example, comments in Davidson 1976; Kirkby and Kirkby 1976; Lloyd 1963; Nicholas 1980; and Rosen 1986). Structures in Baghestan, as has been seen, are composed mainly of mud and straw, with mud in the greater proportion by far (at least 5:1 by volume for bricks; 2:1 or 3:1 for mud-straw plaster, depending on whether barley straw or wheat straw is used). In fact, if all this mud and straw construction (including courtyard walls, paving, and features as well as buildings) contained in the central residential area were consolidated, I estimate the resultant cube would measure nearly 20 meters on each side, or about 8,000 cubic meters of deposit. Or if, instead, the consolidation were evenly distributed across the occupied area, the resultant deposit would be about 0.4 meter deep, a significant quantity of mud. Organic matter (especially ash, straw, grains, and human and animal urine and feces) is also present in large quantities. Because much organic matter is routinely removed to fields or wasteland outside the village, the buildup inside the village is slower than might be expected, given the quantities produced.

The village of Baghestan (like several others on the plain) is built on a natural conglomerate ridge. Cross sections of the village (see Appendix, Figures A-2, A-3, and A-5; Horne 1988, Figures 5.15 and 5.16) show a gradual rise from northwest to southeast with an abrupt jump about halfway through, as the result of both cultural deposit and the shape of the bedrock below. Because the village sits on a rise, the water-laid sediments present and the biogenic and geochemical alterations that take place tend to be reworkings of the materials already there rather than of new ones brought in. Windblown dust and sand, however, do come in from outside the village to be caught by topographic elements, including built structures; both these and water-laid sediments tend to build up only in areas of relative inactivity.

## CLIMATIC FACTORS IN MOUND FORMATION

The climate of Khar o Tauran was characterized earlier as one of variable and sparse winter precipitation (mostly in the form of rain) of about 100 millimeters per year on average, with hot summers, cool winters, frequent high winds, and occasionally violent dust- or sandstorms. In maintaining their built environment, villagers must deal with infrequent but severe water erosion, wind erosion, and blown deposits of dust and sand. The toll these assaults take on mud structures in Khar o Tauran is similar to that reported for other areas by observers such as Agorsah (1985); Kirkby and Kirkby (1976); McIntosh (1975); and Schiffer (1987) and in numerous studies in the fields of architectural conservation and development.

The environment affects not only the weathering and rebuilding of an occupied settlement but also the trajectory that a site takes once it is abandoned. For example, on the Tauran Plain, the general sparseness of vegetation (owing to both human and natural causes) limits the capping effect vegetation can have on abandoned sites by sealing the surface and protecting the deposit from the full effects of erosion. Therefore, wind deflation and sheet erosion can act freely to flatten mounded sites. Still, what remains of mud features and architecture is likely to be well preserved because of the aridity.

As in other arid land settings, geomorphological characteristics of the environment also have their effects. The instability of river systems as they shift course and alternate regimes of cutting and filling frequently buries or washes away sites not protected by height.[1]

The effects of climate and environment on site formation are not only of the direct sort. As shown in this and earlier chapters, these factors also operate indirectly in the shaping of settlements and, eventually, archaeological sites. This second kind of effect is more situationally specific because of the socially and culturally variable ways that people take the physical environment into account when they build their settlements.

## THE SOCIAL SIDE OF MOUND FORMATION

In interaction with the environment, the main variables that more or less directly relate settlement and occupational activities to mound formation (or the lack of it) in Khar o Tauran and other parts of the Near East are settlement size, within-settlement density and the degree of circumscription, occupational and locational stability, construction technology, life cycle of structures, and pastoral and agricultural technologies. The following discussion emphasizes the built environment because, as noted above, in the arid Near East most of the deposits that lead to mound formation come from construction material and because the shape of a village is largely formed by the processes of construction.

## Settlement Size

In size of population the villages in central Tauran range from 27 to 178, small compared with many other areas of Iran. In physical size they are probably also smaller, ranging from 0.5 to 2.25 hectares, although comparative figures are scarce (but see Kramer 1982b, Table 5.3).[2] This range in physical size, however, is typical of estimates for those prehistoric villages that have been identified through survey and excavation. Villages of this range are large enough in area to be recoverable as archaeological sites if there is enough buildup of deposit and enough protection from erosive action and activities.

Obviously, a minimal (if unspecified) extent and intensity of activity is necessary in order to create a site of any but the most ephemeral sort. The ability of the environment to recover from the effects of human activity, the likelihood that sites will be buried by alluvium or erased by washouts, and the chance of artifactual material making its way to the surface of multicomponent sites are all dependent on the size of the area. The areal extent of the settlement of the activity, however, must be seen in conjunction with factors of density and length of occupation.

## Density within Settlements

Because of the way mud construction melts down and flattens out, structures that are packed closely together will leave a deeper deposit than those that are more scattered, not only for geometric reasons, but also because by offering less surface, a compact mass of buildings and material will be better protected from exposure and erosion. Also, more densely constructed villages will build up a deposit at a faster rate than ones that are less densely constructed.

Rural Near Eastern settlements in general may be circumscribed in a number of ways that constrain residents from building beyond the perimeters and therefore increase density. First, walls may be built around part or all of the settlement to control access and ensure privacy or defense (but probably not to act as barriers between social groups or to contain residents in quarters, as was apparently sometimes the case in Near Eastern cities; see, for example, Grabar 1978, 66). Even when its original purpose no longer applies, a wall continues to present a barrier that may discourage growth outside the perimeter until no other choice remains, as in the example of Tell-i Nun in southwestern Iran (Jacobs 1979). According to Sumner (1989, 637), most settlements in the Kur River Basin valley (where Tell-i Nun is located) are walled and compact. These walls help to explain why rural settlement densities in this valley (about 160 persons per hectare) are so much higher than they are in Tauran (about 70 persons per hectare).[3]

Second, the value of different categories of land may constrain the spread of settlement. Irrigated land may be too valuable to build on; dry-farmed land or pasture, unless it is in short supply for topographic or other reasons, may be worth little if anything more than nonagricultural house lots.

Third, social or political circumscription can also occur. For example, sharecropping residents are dependent upon landlords who control the village fields, and sometimes residential land as well, and prevent their use for building sites.

Another sort of circumscription occurs when sites are chosen for their height to avoid flooding, which occurs even in the arid Near East (near rivers or wadis, for example), to provide lookout points, to restrict access, or to provide military advantage. Also, in times of insecurity, densities may increase so that property may be more easily protected and assistance may be close at hand. When nucleation is no longer necessary for security, dispersal of activities and property becomes feasible, and, for example, animal stables and pens may safely be located at some distance from their owners' residences.

Short-term economic and political issues can cause rapid if short-lived increases or decreases in settlement density. Sumner (1989) cites a proposed dam project in southeastern Iran that resulted in increased densities as people in the affected area became unwilling to invest in new housing yet were reluctant to leave and forgo compensation for their land. Rapid increases, as he suggests, could also result from the sudden expansion in a labor market or from refugees fleeing warfare, civil unrest, or natural disaster.

Variation in social or material homogeneity within settlements contributes to variation in density within and between settlements. Whether settlements that perform social, economic, or administration functions for other settlements are more densely settled than those they serve has been discussed but not resolved (Kramer 1982b, 169; Sumner 1989, 638). Particular features, natural or constructed, may attract or repel building; particular relationships, social or economic, may do the same. Social or cultural spacing, defined by how far apart residences or other structures are from one another based on what is considered proper or comfortable, influences density. Within societies or communities, ideas about spacing are in many places complex and contingent, and therefore are revealing about the conditions that held at the time the locational decisions were made.

Villages in Khar o Tauran are not circumscribed by walls, land values, or environmental factors. (Courtyard walls for privacy are a recent phenomenon, found in all new construction but not necessarily in older ones.) In spite of residents' claims to the contrary, the villages are heterogeneous both socially and environmentally; new structures appear not only on the unoccupied fringes of the village but also in the interior as people seek proximity to near relatives. The people also try to consolidate their fragmented holdings by constructing new utility rooms (for storage or animals) nearer their living quarters if space becomes available. These activities result in increasing densities in the center as existing settlements age, as Kramer suspects may happen in both villages and cities (1982b, 174). At the same time, however, more sparsely occupied areas are appearing at the periphery.

## Occupational and Locational Stability

Settlement stability and continuity of occupation have important implications for site formation and archaeological recognition. Obviously, given a combination of activities that produces a net accumulation of deposit, the greater the occupational and locational stability, the greater the resulting deposit. But besides increasing the height or depth of deposit, later occupations place a cap on earlier ones and protect them from erosion. For both cultural and geophysical reasons, continually occupied sites preserve earlier levels better than ones periodically abandoned and reoccupied. At the same time, the activities of later occupations tend to disturb earlier materials and raise them to the surface, thus increasing the likelihood of their identification by archaeologists. This effect is of course balanced by the effect of depth of burial. The model constructed by Kirkby and Kirkby (1976) suggests a 5-meter depth to be at or near the limit for recovering sherds on mound surfaces without special conditions such as cuts or erosion.

The factors contributing to occupational and locational stability in Khar o Tauran were explored in some detail in Chapter 4 and earlier in this chapter and illustrate what kinds of things encourage or discourage repeated or continuous occupation at any given site location. Among the most important on the local level were the degree of investment in agricultural improvements, the nature of *qanāt* technology, the pastoral alternative, settlement size, the effect of random demographic fluctuations, private ownership of land and water with transfer by sale or trade possible, partible inheritance, open communities, and local security.

Even when sites are occupied for long periods of time, the tendency in Khar o Tauran is to shift location rather than to level existing ruins and rebuild in the same places. Previous areas of settlement, especially around Baghestan and Zamanabad, identified by sherd scatter and other artifactual remains, show how settlements move over the years.

## Construction Technology

As has already been noted, in Near Eastern settlements the structures of the built environment are the source of the bulk of any future archaeological deposit and important determinants both of the kinds of materials that form archaeological deposits and of the volume and distribution of those materials. By providing a three-dimensional framework for the site, the built environment also shapes the distribution of other kinds of sediments (wind-blown or water-washed, for example) and influences the final form that the mound takes. The steep-sided tells of fortified settlements are a striking example.

As similar as packed mud and mud brick villages of the Near East may appear, variation in the form and production of structures is great enough to have a potential effect on site formation processes. Structures vary in their permanence, speed of construction, and the quantity of material used and how much of it is perishable. They also vary in degree of excavation or lack of it, age of materials, wall thickness, roof construction, number of stories, and building design, including floor plans. All these elements affect both the speed with which deposits form and their absolute depth.

All but two of the buildings in Baghestan are of *china* or mud brick construction with barrel-vaulted or domed roofs. The exceptions are brush-roofed animal houses. Kramer (1982b) suggests that the use of wooden beams in the flat-roofed construction of the Zagros Mountains contributes to the speed with which houses collapse because the wood is removed at abandonment for reuse in new construction, exposing the roofless house to the elements. The domed houses of Baghestan are always used until the roof caves in. Each collapsed house then forms a small mound about 1.5 meters high (judging by field measurements of recently collapsed structures), with a "packed house volume" of about 35 cubic meters (Ammerman, Cavalli-Sforza, and Wagner 1976). As noted above, the entire contemporary village is built of some 8,000 cubic meters of mud. Potsherds are rarely included in construction materials, and stones are not used in much quantity, so neither is available to to cap the site and protect it from erosion.

The earth for construction is excavated from both inside and outside the village. In Baghestan it is not taken from the house site itself. (This practice was observed, however, in the nearby village of Zamanabad, where houses were sometimes raised on platforms carved from their surroundings. The reason may be the low-lying location of Zamanabad and the need to avoid rising salts and groundwater.) Construction materials are not reused for residences, but they may be reused for courtyard walls, animal houses, and pens. All structures (with the exception of the abandoned semisubterranean bathhouse) are built on top of the surface, without foundation trenches. Second stories are generally rare in Khar o Tauran (although they were common in *qal'as*)—there are only three in Baghestan.

The life of a mud brick house in Khar o Tauran, if well maintained, can span one hundred years or more. Its "social life" affects its utility, however, and therefore whether it is going to be maintained for its natural life span or allowed to deteriorate. Based on a sample of seventy-three rooms whose ages were estimated by their owners, in 1977 slightly more than half of the buildings in the central, residential area of the village were less than twenty years old; most were less than thirty years old, and only a very few were built more than fifty years previously.

## Social Life of the Built Environment

The timing and frequency of construction and changes in ownership, user, or use of built structures are part of the pattern of social life in human settlements. They affect not only where new construction is located but how frequently older structures are replaced and the way in which the replacement occurs. Both factors must be taken into account in the exploration of the processes of site formation.

On the basis of oral histories and observations of existing and new construction, an idealized life cycle of architecture in Baghestan might be summarized as follows: Construction begins before marriage and is undertaken by or hired out by the groom or his family. Although an entire compound might be built at once, time and money usually mean piecemeal construction in the following order: living room, storeroom-kitchen, compound wall, privy, and gate. A bread oven, additional storerooms, and animal houses are desirable, but they may never be realized. These additional structures may be shared with others. Storerooms and animal houses can be bought or inherited, in which case they will probably be located elsewhere in the village. Couples may live in inherited or purchased rooms until they can afford to build new ones, but they may not share a room with either set of parents. Rooms are recycled in a process that keeps them in use even when they are no longer considered suitable for their original purpose (Horne 1983). Old buildings are not usually pulled down and leveled but are allowed to collapse on their own (Figure 27). There are no rules of abandonment such as are found in other parts of the world (for example, abandonment at the death of the owner, or as part of a domestic or ritual cycle). Neither are there rules of primogeniture or ultimogeniture that might hold a younger household in the family compound or on the family lot down through the generations.

Figure 27. An abandoned room in the group of buildings to the east of Qal'a Baghestan. The room has begun to fill with debris from the walls and roof, exposing consecutive layers of plaster and soot. Two years later the roof had completely collapsed and only a mound of rubble remained. Note the wall niches, one of which had been plastered over.

## Farming Technology

In this area settlements are themselves part of the technology of production. Farming practices therefore affect site formation processes not only out in the fields and pastures but also within villages. As has already been noted, for example, 24 percent of village rooms house animals rather than people. Dirt is routinely carried into these rooms to be improved by the animals' urine and straw-laden manure, mixed in by the animals hoofs. Yearly this floor buildup is dug out and carried down to the fields to fertilize them and improve their condition. I measured several depths of buildup in Baghestan just before they were carried out to the fields; 50 to 60 centimeters appears to be a typical yearly amount of accumulation.

Straw, used mainly for fodder and in construction, is stored over the winter, when it fills storerooms to the roof. Straw and stable manure increase matter brought into the village only temporarily, because they will both be carried out again or used up. If, however, a building collapses or is abandoned before the material is removed, a significant quantity will appear in the archaeological record.

Trash and ash piles are also used to improve the soil. They are owned by individual households and are located just outside or near the household's core compound. Before the piles of trash are carried to the fields, sherds and other nonperishables are usually picked out and discarded at the village periphery.

Farming activities probably do not alter the density of construction within the village. Animal houses are built the same way as are human dwellings and even have courtyards, so they cannot be distinguished purely by observation of the village plan. They do, however, alter the density of occupation; a purely residential village will be more densely occupied than one that also provides shelter for animals.

In this chapter I have summarized some of the site formation processes in arid lands such as Khar o Tauran. I have emphasized the socioeconomic factors behind the movements of materials in and out of mounds. Accumulation and attrition are continually occurring, both intentionally (to create the built environment) and accidentally (as by-products of other kinds of activities) and by both natural and human agency. On balance, however, an occupied mud brick village shows a net accumulation of material. Indeed, this is true of Near Eastern settlements in general except for those excavated directly from rock or earth (for example, pit houses, cave dwellings, loess subterranean compounds). Variation in the rate of buildup derives from particular local circumstances, such as rebuilding rates, density of construction (for example, the number of second-story rooms), and cultural spacing of residences. Villages in Khar o Tauran are smaller, less densely settled, and unbounded by walls or other factors that constrain expansion, all of which undoubtedly contribute to the absence of mounded deposits in the area. It seems most likely, though, that the main reason for the (apparently) shallow accumulation of cultural deposit in Khar o Tauran, at least compared with other parts of Southwest Asia, lies in the instability of settlement, both at the intrasite scale and at the larger, regional scale. As I pointed out in earlier chapters, the factors behind the historical instability of settlement are mainly technological (*qanāt* irrigation and pastoralism in particular), economic (land values and investment of effort), and political (insecurity and lack of local central places).

# CHAPTER 8

## ASSESSING THE FIT

ost archaeologists hold the conviction, grounded in one of a number of quite different theories, that a relationship exists between material culture and society. This conviction is based on assumptions about the shared, patterned nature of human thought, human behavior, material culture, and therefore, ultimately, the residues that archaeologists take as their data. The nature of that relationship, however, and how each element acts upon or interacts with the others are subject to debate.[1]

This relationship, or at least certain aspects of it, is sometimes referred to by archaeologists as "fit" (David 1971). The search for different kinds of fit among different social or cultural traits underlies many cross-cultural studies, for example, those relating architectural space and population size and other attempts at establishing "magic" numbers or estimators. By this time, however, it is clear that not only will a fit never be perfect but that even to speak of a "degree" of fit must be undertaken with clear statements about how the relevant traits are defined and what constitutes a "satisfactory" degree of fit in the first place. In the following discussion, *fit* is defined solely for the convenience of the readers. It has no reference to how suitable a Taurani resident might find or have found the spaces in question, or whether or not the fit was intended.

In this final chapter I take three examples from previous chapters in order to look at some methodological and interpretive implications of the ways in which space is used at different scales of village settlement. The scale of the examples shifts from rooms and activities to houses and households to the village and its relationship with its fields. The kinds of fit considered have been chosen to accord with those of current interest in the literature as well as those that were of interest during my research. Thus they serve to sum up the approach I have taken here as well as to attach the results to those reported elsewhere.

Proceeding in this manner superficially resembles what Gould (1980) has called "arguing by anomaly," and Binford (1987) has called "researching ambiguity," in the sense that by tracking down the causes of unexpected results, one is likely to learn more than one was asking in the first place (Wylie 1985). The "anomaly" thus becomes a positive contribution to understanding and not simply a cautionary tale or rejected proposition.

Furthermore, the three different cases of discrepancy between expected and observed fits represented by these examples turn out to be not unrelated to each other. Recycling and dispersed holdings derive from common social and cultural practices, as do dispersed holdings and fragmented fields. Considering the three examples together has the benefit of permitting a look at how a general underlying pattern of arranging space and holdings creates common specific patterns at different spatial levels.


## ROOMS AND ACTIVITIES

Rooms as activity areas, or as settings for activity areas, are among the most common contextual units in archaeological analyses. Where architecture is constructed of permanent (as opposed to perishable) materials, as is the case in most past and present Near Eastern villages, rooms are clearly bounded both materially and culturally. They are highly visible and recoverable archaeologically and provide multiple kinds of information, serving as context as well as data in their own right. The identification of rooms according to specific individual or grouped activities may be useful in characterizing intrasite layouts and comparing settlements in different places or at different times, or in exploring spatial complexity or homogeneity. As will be seen later in this chapter, at the very least being able to identify the core dwelling unit—the living room—is an important step in identifying and characterizing households.

In most of the rural Near East, rooms in dwellings are frequently if not typically multifunctional. In Baghestan, for example, no mud brick rooms are permanently dedicated to a single unchanging purpose—both users and uses of any particular room vary in both the short and the long term. It is nevertheless feasible to assign different rooms to general descriptive types according to function. In Khar o Tauran the villagers do so themselves; the categories used by Baghestan residents are in accord with and helped determine the types used in this study.

These four main functional types of room—living rooms, storerooms, straw rooms, and animal houses—were described ethnographically in Chapter 5. There, village-wide distributions of room types were discussed as they related to broadly grouped types of activities. In order to do the same sort of distributional analysis archaeologically, it would be necessary first to be able to establish room types. In archaeological settings where activities cannot be directly observed, ascertaining whether distinct room types exist and, if they do, how they are distributed depends upon physical evidence alone; hence the desirability of being able to assume some kind of fit between structures and the activities they encompass.

## The Issue of Reuse

As was shown in Chapter 6, size, proportions, basic materials, construction techniques, and exterior appearance of all village rooms in Baghestan are very much the same. But in spite of the structural similarity among rooms built for different purposes, broadly defined types of rooms are highly recognizable ethnographically and are rather specialized, even while being multifunctional. The traits that best characterize different kinds of rooms are the features, decoration, and furnishings or equipment that are added to the original basic structure, rather than the original structure itself. For rooms that have never been used for purposes other than the ones for which they were intended at construction, there is little chance, given adequate preservation, that one type would be mistaken for another in a hypothetical archaeological future (Table 14).

Replastering or painting a room to freshen and repair it is common in Baghestan. Remodeling a room, in the sense of making structural renovations (such as adding shelves or altering niches) simply in order to make it

TABLE 14. FEATURES ASSOCIATED WITH PARTICULAR ROOM TYPES,
INCLUDING RECYCLED ROOMS

| | Room types in which the feature is found | | |
|---|---|---|---|
| **Feature** | **Always** | **Sometimes** | **Rarely or never** |
| Large windows | | Living rooms<br>Animal houses | Storerooms |
| No niches | | Animal houses<br>Storerooms | Living rooms |
| Very low door | | Storerooms<br>Animal houses | Living rooms |
| White or green plaster | Living rooms | Storerooms<br>Animal houses | |
| Mud and straw plaster | | Storerooms<br>Animal houses | Living rooms |
| No plaster | | Storerooms<br>Animal houses | Living rooms |
| Storage bins | | Living rooms<br>Storerooms | Animal houses |
| Walled-up niches | | Storerooms<br>Animal houses | Living rooms |
| Feed bins | Animal houses | | Living rooms<br>Storerooms |
| Chicken coops | | Storerooms<br>Animal houses | Living rooms |
| Dung on floor | | Animal houses | Living rooms<br>Storerooms |
| Straw, firewood | | Storerooms<br>Animal houses | Living rooms |
| Wheat and other grain | | Storerooms | Living rooms<br>Animal houses |
| Human food | | Living rooms<br>Storerooms | Animal houses |
| Tobacco and cotton | | Storerooms | Living rooms<br>Animal houses |
| Rugs in place | Living rooms | | Storerooms<br>Animal houses |
| Wall hangings in place | Living rooms | | Storerooms<br>Animal houses |

TABLE 14. *cont.*

| Feature | Room types in which the feature is found | | |
| | Always | Sometimes | Rarely or never |
|---|---|---|---|
| Heater plastered in place | | Living rooms | Storerooms Animal houses |
| Heater stored | | Storerooms | Living rooms Animal houses |
| Agricultural tools | | Storerooms Animal houses | Living rooms |

more attractive without changing the room's function, is not common. For this purpose, people usually build an entirely new structure to replace the old, probably because a large part of the desired effect comes from the newness of the building or the employment of a city builder with his ability to use urban materials and to build in a visibly more precise manner than local builders.

In contrast, remodeling for the purpose of reuse, that is, in order to change a room's function or activities, is common practice in Baghestan. Fully half of the village's rooms are currently being used for purposes other than the ones for which they originally were built. The fit between rooms and room use in Baghestan might be expected to be considerably diminished by reuse, since the current function of a room, with its implied activities and personnel, is now at odds with what the structure was designed for. As stated above, however, room types are still easily recognizable, and the fit between a room and its activities is a good one because the contents and decoration (or lack thereof) change with the changing function of the room. In an archaeological context, however, if reuse has not adequately erased evidence of previous functions (as in Baghestan it usually has not), or when excavation is not meticulous enough to identify *which* are the most recent functions of a structure, then a conflation of what were actually chronologically discrete activities will be recorded.

The consequences are important. Unless one can recognize reuse archaeologically, inaccurate functional identifications of rooms and activities are certain (see below and Horne 1983). Furthermore, inferences based on these identifications, such as population estimates or the relative importance of animal husbandry at a site, will also be subject to error.

To see how reuse takes place, let us look first at villages, or, more specifically, at the permanent, domed units that constitute the majority of village structures in this area, and then, for contrast, at pastoral stations, where both activities and architecture differ from those in villages.

## The Effects of Reuse

For Baghestan, as for other parts of the Near East, three kinds of architectural reuse can be observed: that which is seasonal, that which fluctuates with demand, and that which is devolutionary. The first two kinds are based on the nonspecific structural characteristics of rooms. Seasonal or periodic reuse sometimes begins at construction, as in the case of a winter-summer switch between living rooms and storerooms; there are six of these pairs in Baghestan. Fluctuating reuse does not simply switch back and forth seasonally but temporarily dedicates a room's use to a special purpose. For example, a room may be used as a guest room, as a family room, or for religious services, depending on the needs of the moment. Like seasonal reuse, any changes to the room tend to be temporary and reversible, and in the latter case usually involve only movable equipment.

Of the three, devolutionary reuse is perhaps of greatest consequence to archaeological inference. The term, first used by David (1971) in his ethnoarchaeological discussion of Fulani architecture, refers to a downward spiral of reuse with decreasing requirements of structural soundness and quality of finish. Most of this sort of reuse in Baghestan takes place over a long period of time, even up to a hundred or more years in the case of *qal'as*. It is not generally reversible; animal houses do not get converted back to food storage rooms, nor storerooms to living rooms. People do not generally make the effort to remove earlier features. New ones may be added, but the old ones remain.

In Baghestan, a building's life can be and often is sustained as long as possible through attentive maintenance, ideally carried out every year. With proper maintenance, many structures last for fifty years or more, outliving the original owners themselves. Still, although the four walls

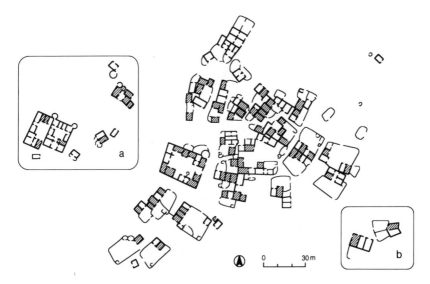

Figure 28. All rooms originally built for or used as living rooms in Baghestan. a = Qal'a Baghestan, b = Kalata. Not shown are the four second-story rooms found in the village core.

and the roof remain in place, the activities, artifacts, and features within change substantially over such a long period of time.

For comparison, contrast the plan of living-room types according to present use (Figure 11) with the one showing all the rooms ever used for that purpose (Figure 28). (This second plan of course collapses multiple events; there is no actual time at which the village ever appeared like this.) Other room types would show similar but less dramatic differences; the greatest discrepancy occurs in the case of living rooms. More living rooms are built than any other kind of structure because a living room is the minimal necessary structure and is at the top of the "dwelling chain," so to speak. An animal house is at the bottom of the chain. Seventy-six units were built as living rooms, but only thirty-three are presently used (at least at one time) for that purpose. The remainder have been recycled as another type of room—storeroom, straw room, or animal house. Room types at the top of the chain risk being overcounted by archaeologists and those lower down undercounted.

### Reuse at Pastoral Stations

Seasonal settlements, that is, pastoral stations used only in the winter or summer, might be contrasted to villages with respect to recycling, since their architecture differs in life span, cost of construction and materials, and construction skills required. To a lesser extent, they also differ in function, which means there are fewer types of structures at seasonal stations than in villages. As was seen in Chapter 4, for several reasons, seasonal stations are also less stable locationally than villages. And indeed, the fit between buildings and activities at a seasonal station is potentially excellent because of the lack of reuse and because of the narrow range of activities and personnel in the first place.

But that potential tends to be realized only when the station is of the "ideal" type, designed and fitted out to be a pastoral station at initial construction. This is almost always so for winter stations, which have stringent economically defined requirements for construction if they are successfully to shelter animals and people in the hazardous winter season. As was also seen in Chapter 4, many summer stations are not built for the purpose but are situated at abandoned villages or *qal'as*. The same kinds of interpretive problems appear at these settlements as in permanent villages. Pastoral stations such as these might in fact be taken for squatters' settlements, when they are instead just seasonal settlements whose home bases are permanent settlements elsewhere.

### Some Archaeological Implications of Recycling

The degree to which architectural recycling is practiced appears to be, in many places, associated with the life span of the structures themselves (Oswald 1987, 337–38). Structural longevity, coupled with economic and inheritance practices, appears to explain recycling in Baghestan. But whether and how architectural recycling takes place is a function not only of investment in and longevity of the built environment but also of cultural ideas about the role of architecture in society. Recycling cannot be assumed unambiguously from the technology of the structures. In some instances, structures invested with ritual or memorial meaning, for example, may not be rededicated to other ends, at least not unless appropriate measures are taken to deconsecrate them. For example, dwellings may be removed from the cycle and abandoned forever upon the death of the head or other member of the household (Jett and Spencer 1981, 28; Schwerdtfeger 1982, 278). In Baghestan, the fear of jinn, or spirits, makes people hesitant to spend time alone in abandoned structures. Although that was never offered as a reason for avoiding reuse of deteriorating areas for dwellings, it may well be a factor.

It has been seen that in spite of the prevalence of recycling, the tendency not to eradicate evidence of previous uses often makes the history of a house visible ethnographically in the form of new features, decoration, or furnishings that contrast with remnants of previous ones. Such contrast will be visible archaeologically as well. Architectural recycling in a situation like Baghestan's ought to be recognizable, given excavation techniques meticulous enough to pick them up (Kramer 1982a, 671). It has also been seen that, because of the way recycling occurs, its effects are not random and misinterpretations are likely to occur in specific directions, such as overcounting structures at the top and undercounting structures at the bottom of a devolutionary cycle. On a more positive note, recycling or the lack thereof (whether of architecture or other materials) is bound to be connected to other aspects of social life. Accompanied by other kinds of evidence, how recycling occurs may help in the understanding of the role that architecture and space play in social interaction and in cultural thought.

## HOUSES AND HOUSEHOLDS REVISITED

It is a short but important move from rooms and activities to houses and their inhabitants. After all, in the kind of archaeology assumed in this book, a goal of room-type analysis should be not just the simple identification of activities but the attachment of those activities to individuals and groups and to the social contexts in which they took place.

Of course, for archaeological projects in which social organization is in itself a primary goal of research, the household group, variously defined, does undoubtedly figure as a central unit in the analytical design. But other reasons abound for the need to be able to identify and locate households archaeologically. Among them is the desire to make population estimates or to identify population change on the basis of household counts. Inferences about the nature and composition of domestic groups at a site have been used to develop further inferences about social stratification and complexity, adaptive strategies, and political organization. One might seek to relate variation in the sizes and kinds of households within a single site to growing economic specialization and complexity. A shift from one household type to another (for example, from an extended to a nuclear household) may therefore bear on reconstructions of culture history and change. Other kinds of groups have been brought into focus as well, such as plaza groups, factions, tribal sections, and task-oriented groups. But in Tauran, the household is the most important village organizing entity, and so the choice makes sense here.

### Predicting Fit between Houses and Households

Where, as it does in this section, *fit* refers to the fit between houses on the one hand and personnel and activities on the other, the following propositions have been made. David (1971) states that this fit among the Fulani is as good as it is because residential land is freely available, structures are short-lived, there is seasonal underemployment and thus time to build, and construction requires a minimal capital outlay. Building on these as general propositions, Oswald (1987) adds that recycling will reduce the fit, and that the nature of the existing built environment as well as the length of the building process affect the degree of fit. I would emphasize that using architecture to make symbolic statements about prestige or egalitarianism will affect the strictly demographic or economic relationship. People may give priority to ritually or symbolically meaningful elements in the natural or built environment and choose to use space in relation to those elements rather than to the ones an archaeologist may be seeking to infer.

One variable affecting fit is the life span of residential structures. If households are mobile, as they are, for example, among nomadic groups or in areas where houses are fragile and must be rebuilt frequently, it is easier to live where one wishes. Mud brick villages, however, are relatively substantial. Most of the buildings in the residential area of

Baghestan last for twenty or thirty years. A few were built more than fifty years ago.

House sites in Baghestan must be either inherited or bought from other individuals; so far they are easily available and inexpensive. Most new construction occurs for residential reasons, usually when young people marry and set up their own households and more rarely as older couples decide to improve their living conditions. Because married couples cannot co-reside in the same living room, marriage is delayed until quarters separate from those of the parents are available. As buildings deteriorate, new ones must replace them, but most people remain for years in the rooms where they first set up housekeeping.

Based on these existing assumptions on how different factors constrain or facilitate the creation and maintenance of domestic spaces, what kind of fit might be expected in Baghestan? The life cycle of domestic structures is tied to the life cycle of the household. At the onset of a building's career in Baghestan, the owner, user, and builder are usually the same person. Even when ownership changes, the new owner occupies and maintains the house directly; absentee owners are a rarity. There are thus no intervening agents between the owner and whatever rearrangements of space and facilities are deemed necessary to keep the structure useful. Moreover, village architecture here is highly flexible in design, in spite of its longevity. Although reuse may complicate archaeological recovery, thereby reducing apparent fit, in the actual ethnographic situation it ought to increase the fit between personnel and space. Recycling adds an alternative to building anew, especially useful in an ongoing settlement where existing structures or the availability of land constrain the possibilities for new building.

Factors arguing against the expectation of a good fit in Baghestan are the inherent permanence of the structures and the infrequency of new construction. The crowded nature of the center of the village coupled with the desire to live near one's closer relatives narrows the options for making changes in existing spatial arrangements or building new structures contiguously. Because of a pressure to conform and a rather egalitarian ideology, in spite of differences in wealth, the people do not use houses to express social differences to the extent that they may elsewhere.

How good in fact is the fit of household size and houses in Baghestan?

Measured by the total number of rooms or total amount of roofed space per household, the fit is not very good compared with that found by other researchers in other places. It is, for example, less good than that reported by Kamp in Darnaj (1982), Kramer in Aliabad (1982b), or Watson in Hasanabad (1979). One reason may be that there is less variation here in room size, since domed construction, more that flat roofs, constrains architectural dimensions.

In exploring this relationship between households and houses, an unexpected methodological problem arose: the difficulty of defining a house in the first place and then attaching it to its resident household. Most households in Baghestan do not live in self-contained compounds the way one might imagine from the literature and from the village plan itself. Most Baghestani households own and use additional rooms in other parts of the village, and moreover, many of them own only part of what would from the plan be identified as a single house unit. The "house" in Baghestan lacks the kind of cohesion known elsewhere.

## Identifying Houses

What is a house? Unlike the minimal architectural unit that constitutes what is called here a single structure or room, a house is not so easily defined. By Western standards, it would most likely refer to a group of rooms under a single roof. The inapplicability of that definition in Baghestan (and much of the Near East) is apparent from the village plan. Far from sharing a common roof, rooms here do not even communicate with each other; each door leads either to outside space or, in a few cases, to a connecting *eivān* rather than to another room. If there are "houses" in Baghestan, the criteria must be something other than the sharing of a common roof. The number of different types of rooms, only some of which are human dwellings, should suggest that rooms may indeed be somehow grouped into "houses." In fact, they are, if a house is defined as the architectural holdings of a group of people called a household. But how then is a household defined, if not as a group of people sharing a common house? The first question, then, is whether houses can be isolated on the basis of material evidence alone.

It is apparent from the village plan that structures in Baghestan are not distributed randomly. Differences show up in the orientation, proximity, and connectedness of rooms in relation to one another. Degrees of communication, connectivity, and boundedness are common criteria for describing architectural cohesion. Architecturally, the most striking of the patterns are probably the several large rectangular arrangements that form *qal'as*. The second most striking pattern might be what appear to be courtyard dwellings: two or more rooms opening onto a common, walled courtyard. The third might be strings of buildings and clusters of rooms opening onto the same open space or alley. Least obvious are blocks of rooms that share common walls but do not appear to share anything else.

But do any of these patterns correspond to actual houses, and how, in turn, do houses relate to social groups? Of course, for an operational definition, "house" can be defined however one might wish. Baghestanis themselves do not call all the holdings taken together a "house." There is no term that ordinarily distinguishes *room* and *house;* the standard Persian word *otāq* is rarely used in Baghestan, *khāna* being the usual expression for a single, minimal unit. The term *havāli*, in the sense of someone's "place," is the one most often used in reference to the living room and its immediate surroundings. This concept makes archaeological sense as well.

If a house were defined as all the architectural holdings of a single household, located in a single self-contained compound, then most of Baghestan's living arrangements would not qualify as houses. Twenty-six of the thirty-three households own and use one or more rooms at a distance from their living quarters (Figure 25). In an additional complication, about one-quarter have rooms owned and used by others within the walls of their own residential courtyards. The degree to which this dispersion occurs depends on location within the village. If animal houses are excluded from the list of holdings, the areas where such a definition works best are the newly built compounds at the circumference of the village. The definition would be worst among structures in the crowded village interior. Wealthier households do not manage to keep their houses together better than do the poor; indeed, they do rather worse at it. Even the most striking examples of clearly circumscribed multiroom dwellings, the three *qal'as* (one in Gauju, two in Qal'a Baghestan), are divided in ownership among six, four, and six households, respectively.

This dispersed pattern is facilitated in part by recycling. As has been seen, buildings are constructed so that it is easy to make rearrangements and to recycle them. In Gauju, which is the only residential part of the village, fifty-one rooms are detached from the owners' main living quarters. The original use of forty of these could be determined. Of the forty, twenty have been recycled; of the twenty that have been recycled, nearly all were originally, but are no longer, living rooms. The remaining twenty are known not to have been recycled, and nearly all (sixteen) are animal houses; the rest (four) are storerooms.

But social factors are even more important than are technological aspects of construction in creating and maintaining dispersed holdings. Buildings in Baghestan are usually acquired in one of three ways: purchase, construction, or inheritance. (People can also rent rooms, although none were doing so when I was there.) Of the three, inheritance is the most important mechanism by which villagers come to own rooms that are not within their own courtyard areas. Forty-four of the seventy-four displaced rooms were inherited; the remaining thirty were either bought or built by their present owners.

Inherited rooms are evenly divided between male and female heirs. Female inheritance and control of real property, although permitted under Islamic law, is unusual in those few other rural Islamic societies for which information of this sort is available. Inheritance is not a free-standing trait, however. It comes with what might be called a kind of social "package" that includes other aspects of social and economic organization (Horne 1982c). Baghestan not only has an apparently unusual inheritance pattern but differs in other ways from the usual patrilineal, patrilocal, endogamous village package depicted perhaps stereotypically in the literature. For example, although ideologically patrilineal, in practice Baghestan society is bilateral and bilocal, with nuclear rather than extended or joint households. Such conditions are likely to promote an increase in female control over property.

Although inheritance is an important way in which holdings become fragmented, other conditions might affect whether or not holdings are kept together. Among these are degree of security, size of settlement, prevalent ideas about privacy and the seclusion of women, and the relative importance of time spent moving between locations. Baghestan has been, since the mid-1970s, relatively secure; people do not live in fear that their animals or goods will be stolen if they are kept outside the compound. Its small size means that no household's structure can be very far away from its core compound. It is a homogeneous village, in which people all know each other well and are closely related. The privacy and seclusion of women is thus of less concern. Besides, there are definite benefits to out-of-compound holdings. Animal houses and rooms for agricultural storerooms can be closer to the family fields than otherwise. Social interaction is certainly enhanced and news passed quickly on as people travel to their storerooms and animal houses in the course of their daily tasks.

To judge by published material, this dispersed pattern of ownership does not appear in other areas of the Near East, at least not to this extent. The published material is very sparse, however. To my knowledge only Kramer (1982b) and Watson (1979) have published village plans (of Aliabad and Hasanabad, respectively; both in western Iran) where each individual room can be assigned an owner. Kramer found only 8 (out of 67) households that owned storerooms that did not open onto or next to their courtyards (1982b, 106). In addition, her village plan shows only 25 out of a total of at least 334 roofed rooms of all kinds that are located out of the household's compound courtyard. These rooms are owned by nineteen different households, seven of which are joint. Thus, the degree of fragmentation and the distance over which it occurs is far less in Aliabad (eighteen out of sixty-seven households, or 27 percent) than in Baghestan (twenty-six out of thirty-three households, or 78 percent). Aliabad's layout differs from Baghestan's in a number of other ways: rooms frequently communicate with each other; compounds are more tightly packed, larger, and walled; there are no specialized nonresidential quarters (for example, storage areas or stables); and rooms are more variable in size and shape. Joint households are present and co-resident. Watson's Hasanabad (1979, Figure 2.1), a village of forty households, shows only one noncontiguous room, and that one lies only a short distance away from the household's courtyard gate. Hasanabad resembles Aliabad in plan more than it does Baghestan. Courtyards are well marked out; households are joint, and there are no nonresidential quarters.

For an archaeologist, of course, the question is whether it would be possible to specify archaeologically recognizable conditions under which such dispersion of rooms might occur. On the basis of findings in Baghestan and the settlements that have been discussed, I might suggest the following. Fragmented holdings should be suspected wherever settlements contain specialized, nonresidential areas (such as animal quarters or areas used exclusively for storage), extensively recycled areas, loosely clustered rooms, and lack of communication among structures. It is less likely to occur where groups of rooms share a common, repeating pattern, structures are tightly packed together and clearly bounded from each other (for example, with compound walls), rooms are interconnected, groups of rooms appear to represent a full range or the same range of activities, and there is no evidence of purposeful destruction and razing of selected structures.

## Locating Households

As seen above, living rooms locate households within villages, no matter how dispersed other rooms may be. This is in part because of the way households are defined, but also because so many of their daily activities, as a household, take place within a core compound (living room plus courtyard area plus, sometimes, storeroom). Living rooms alone still provide good evidence for many kinds of inferences, if one can control for recycling. For the most secure attachment of households to houses, it makes sense to focus on the living room and an immediate outside area as the "house," what in local Baghestani parlance would be called the "environs" of the household. By doing so, it is possible to free ourselves from culture-bound notions about what constitutes a "house."

Living rooms locate households with respect to villages as well; that is, there is for the most part a one-to-one relationship between households and living rooms, and only very occasionally do villagers maintain living rooms in more than one permanent settlement. In Baghestan, only two cases like this occurred between 1976 and 1978. In the first case, the bachelor of household 35, who is mentally or emotionally unable to maintain himself in complete independence, frequently lives with relatives in the neighboring village of Barm. In the second case, members of household 10 move back and forth from Nahar, where the household head maintains his inherited natal house and property. The inefficiency of this arrangement will undoubtedly make it temporary. Children, and adults attached as extending members in otherwise nuclear family households, do sometimes move around from household to household within or between villages, but that entails a change in household composition, not household residence. If Baghestan is typical, these same relationships hold in other Tauran villages as well. Only three rooms (all storerooms) in Baghestan were owned by those who resided in, and had living rooms in, other villages or in the city.[2]

Last, in compensation for the discouraging discovery of weak relationships sometimes found between the household and the house, Eighmy has remarked, "Given the close relationship between habitation structures and the domestic unit of production, houses may reflect in a fairly direct fashion subsistence strategy growth, decline, and differentiation. Thus, the house site does not lose its archaeological significance in the study of prehistoric change just because it may be insensitive to household composition and size. It may still be a valuable index to shifting subsistence activity among households" (1981, 233).

## FIELDS AND COMMUNITIES

The fragmented nature of holdings in a village's field system in Tauran repeats in an even more pronounced way its village layout. Such repetition should not be surprising considering that fields share with village spaces a common pattern of tenure, inheritance, and historical trajectory. Even though fragmentation of house holdings is unusual, fragmentation of fields is common in the Near East, particularly in areas where agriculture has not yet been mechanized. Even if field systems were excavated in the Near East (which they virtually never are) it is too much to expect that it would be possible to assign field units to particular owners within a village. So leaving that issue aside, let us look very briefly at a more aggregate scale, and one that *has* been used in archaeology, especially for site catchment analyses.

As was discussed in Chapters 3 and 4, fields are located outside of villages in this area of Iran. Even the fruit and vegetable gardens are set outside of the village. Moreover, settlements do not sit in the midst of their fields; they are instead situated at one side or the other of the irrigation system, usually on higher ground and on the upstream side of the irrigation system itself.

At the most favored locations, a single irrigated field system and its surrounding pasture and dry-farmed fields conform to Martin's diagram of ideal land use (1982, Figure 3). Not every village is so well located, however. For example, the land in villages against the foothills of the Peighambar range is too sloped and rocky for dry farming next to irrigated terraces, although it can be used for grazing. Thus a simple model of declining intensity of land use with increasing distance from a site, such as predicted by Chisholm's model (Chisholm 1962) or most site catchment analysis models (see discussions in Crumley 1979; Dennell 1980; Flannery 1976; and Roper 1979), never actually holds in any particular case in Tauran.

An additional characteristic of land use in Tauran further confounds any simple model relating a site to its environment, and that is the lack of a one-to-one correlation here between field system and village. That is, the dispersion of ownership extends not just within a particular village system but also from village to village. Moreover, not only do owners of field or water units sometimes live in a village other than the one at the head of the water source, but a number of field systems have no residential component at all.

Neither a complete mapping of agricultural fields across the plain nor cadastral surveys exist for this part of Iran: much of the information on agricultural holdings is thus only subjective. Except for the well-documented case of Baghestan, therefore, it is not possible to say how much land is actually held by residents of any particular village in fields adjacent to some other village. It is clear, nevertheless, that these field systems vary in how closely they are attached to their proximate villages; some of them are wholly owned by people in a single village (which may or may not be the nearest one), others are divided among four or more villages at varying removes. As a whole, the pattern is the product of historical, ecological, and social circumstances.

The village of Baghestan illustrates the nature and dimensions of these displacements. As in other villages on the plain, residents in Baghestan make use of more than one irrigated field system. Figure 29 shows the locations of the six systems either used solely by individuals from Baghestan or shared with individuals from other villages. One Baghestan resident also has land in Asbkeshan, some 30 kilometers to the southeast (not shown on this map), where he and his family summer with their flocks.

Excepting those at Asbkeshan, all the fields owned by Baghestan residents would fit in a circle centered on the village with a radius of about 1.8 kilometers, which is within a thirty-minute walk of the village. That circle, however, extends right up and into the residential areas of Barm, Eshqvan, Nauva, and Ja'farabad (the mean nearest-neighbor distance for the plain is in fact 1.8 kilometers). In addition, it includes the whole village of Feridar within its circumference. As noted above, it also encompasses fields belonging to and worked by residents of villages other than Baghestan, in particular those of Feridar, Nauva, and Ja'farabad. In fact only four of the plain's thirteen villages do *not* somewhere hold land and water in conjunction with Baghestan. Incidentally, the circle also includes most of Baghestan's dry-farmed fields, although some additional *bands* used by Baghestanis for dry farming are located outside the circle, 3 kilometers away along the drainage running to the northeast. In brief, in this particular case, while a circle of less than 2 kilometers radius encloses most of the agricultural land farmed intensively and extensively by Baghestan residents, it also includes much that belongs to other villages.

Even more extreme are the irrigated agricultural holdings (incompletely recorded) of Salehabad, which extend at least from south of Baghestan to Kariz and halfway to Talkhab. For enclosure, these fields would need a circle with a radius of at least 4.5 kilometers, which includes most of the Tauran Plain, and so becomes useless if one is attempting to isolate Salehabad's holdings. As they do in Baghestan, a number of individual cases contribute in the aggregate to the dispersal of landholdings. Many, perhaps most, Tauran villages share this trait of dispersal, although as seen above, some villages are more circumscribed than others.

Many previous studies show how the economic assumption of declining use is skewed by failure to meet an "other things being equal" criterion. The complex situation in Tauran, however, highlights what happens to models that fail to incorporate a critical assumption, namely, that social group, economic unit, and spatial unit may not be spatially congruent.

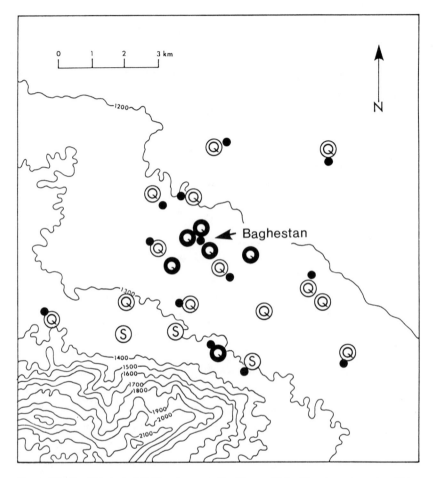

Figure 29. *Qanāt*-irrigated field systems on the Tauran Plain. The six systems in which residents of Baghestan own fields and water are circled in black. S = Spring-irrigated systems.

The distribution just described does have limits to its dispersed quality. As shown in the case of the village layout, agricultural holdings tend to remain within a reasonable distance of the owner's village. No one in Baghestan, for example, owns land in Kariz or Zamanabad, its farthest neighbors on the Plain.[3] A nonresidential site to the southwest, called Baghestan Bala, is an extreme example to the contrary; residents of only two of the six villages that surround it actually own land there. The other owners live in Salehabad and Ravazang, at a much greater distance to the east and southeast.

Although a site catchment approach would not work well to establish details of production and land use at any given site, at the regional scale, land and settlement correlate well. Thus, it appears that for catchment analysis to be useful where the condition of a singular relationship between field and community cannot be met, it would be better to focus on broad areas rather than individual sites. Nor would larger areas be inappropriate conceptually; in many ways, for example, individual villages here are only partial settlements for which the entire Tauran Plain is the settlement unit proper. Thus, even if agricultural fields could be identified, along with their sizes and some of their technological characteristics, further assumptions are necessary in order to connect any particular field system or area of land use with its associated settlement(s) and, within the settlement(s), with its owners or users. As Tringham says, in reference to the development of agriculture in Europe, "It is essential to investigate not only the site catchments themselves, but also how these were perceived; how a group organized its work force to exploit them; and how they expanded and complicated their site exploitation territories by relations and exchanges with other groups" (1985, 923).

As a whole this book has focused on human settlement—especially village spaces, fields, and pastures—in a rural area of northeastern Iran. Settlement here or anywhere is neither part of nor in itself a timeless, traditional way of life but a dynamic, flexible adaptation, adjusting to internal and external conditions with greater or less success. It is this dynamic nature of spatial and material culture that permits the study of change in the archaeological record. Upon this premise rests the usefulness of such studies to those seeking ecological interpretations of the material remains and spatial distributions of archaeological sites.

But, as also had been predicted, settlement is more than a climatic and technological solution to life in a given setting. It shapes and is shaped by social relations, expressive and communicative considerations, and ideas about the world and society. As a particular kind of material culture, one with an intrinsic spatial dimension, settlement can be profitably studied by archaeologists in many ways, not all of which have yet been taken advantage of. Among them, an ecological approach (in the broad sense) has the advantage of directly confronting this multifaceted nature of settlement.

The topic of this book has been space, with a focus on settlement and architecture as tangible orderings and orderers of space and spatial behavior. Spatial distributions and areas were seen to be multifunctional and compromised by conflicting goals. Therefore the relationship between a village or house plan, for example, and the separately sought trait, quality, or quantity should be suspected of only approximate realization or expression.

How satisfactorily the fit (or lack thereof) has been demonstrated depends on what questions one asks and how willing one is to be wrong. For example, I discovered during my research and analysis that scale can be critical to whether or how confidently or plausibly one can make certain kinds of arguments. Obviously, an appropriate choice of scale must be considered in designing a research project in order to provide either the amount of detail or breadth of data necessary to the argument. But it is important in other ways, too, for as has been seen, what works in the aggregate need not work in the particular instance. Site catchment analysis showed this up clearly. Furthermore, larger areas may be more meaningful units conceptually than those more commonly selected for their convenience and comprehensibility.

Fieldwork and analysis also brought out the extent to which the past accumulates in the present's material record. In order for the fit to be recoverable from archaeological data alone, it is further necessary that events separate in time be distinguishable from one another. Sometimes this happens historically, that is, later events erase the material events of earlier ones. Other times the burden will be on the archaeologist to make the distinction. This accumulation is not necessarily bad; indeed it is part of understanding a site and a society. For what we see in any human settlement, whether in the present or in the past, is an accumulation of past and present activities. In the most literal sense, there is no "point in time" except as a creation of the observer's mind, and yet working out these temporal relations is an essential prerequisite to understanding and interpreting the spatial dimension of archaeological remains.

"Ethnoarchaeology does not aim to show why material culture is uninterpretably complex. Quite the contrary, for ethnoarchaeology to have any place in the science of human behavior it must (a) increase our understanding of human behavior and (b) expose the behavioral order expressed in material culture" (Eighmy 1981, 233). As a practical matter, it may be added that archaeology is expensive and it is time consuming; it tends to be carried out on a scale that is costly and labor- and time-intensive. Ethnoarchaeology should also assist in setting questions that are answerable and that are best answered in an archaeological context.

I chose the subject of spatial organization and the area of northeastern Iran in part because so little ethnographic information was available about them. I hope that I have addressed questions that will engage not only archaeologists but cultural anthropologists, rural sociologists, and architects as well.

# APPENDIX

# PLANS OF THE RESIDENTIAL CORE (GAUJU) OF

# BAGHESTAN

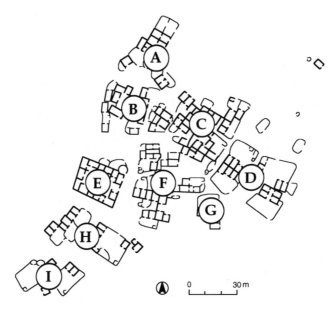

Key to Location of Areas A through I.

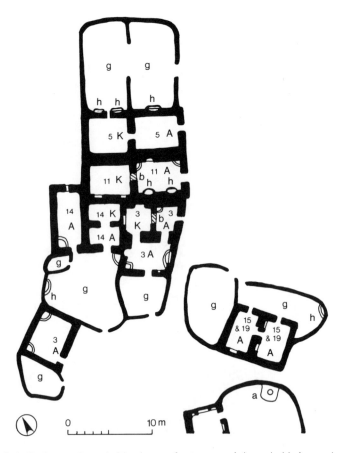

Figure A-1. Baghestan Area A. Numbers refer to owner's household. A = animal house, or stable, K = straw storage room, a = *tanur* (bread oven), b = blocked door, g = sheep or goat pen, h = feed trough.

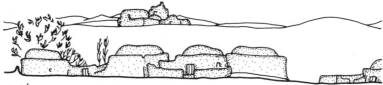

AA´

Figure A-2. Baghestan Area B. Numbers refer to owner's household. A = animal house, or stable, L = living room, K = straw storage room, S = storeroom, a = *tanur* (bread oven), e = *tālār* (milk product storage rack), g = sheep or goat pen, k = *kalgāh* (cooking hearth), m = *bokhāri geli* (old-style wall fireplace). The small double circles are *bokhāri ferengi* (metal space heater) bases with their hearths. A cross section through A-A´ is shown at the top of the figure.

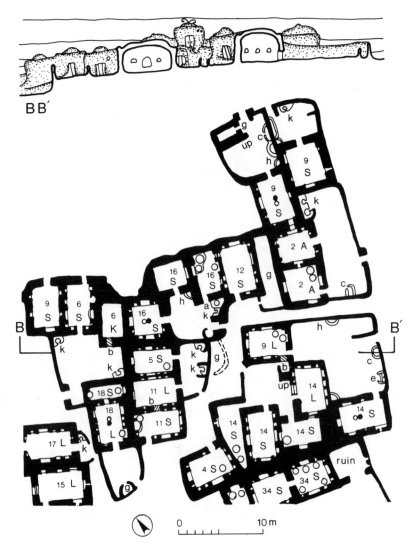

Figure A-3. Baghestan Area C. Numbers refer to owner's household. A = animal house, or stable, L = living room, K = straw storage room, S = storeroom, b = blocked door, c = chicken coop, e = *tālār* (milk product storage rack), g = sheep or goat pen, h = feed trough, k = *kalgāh* (cooking hearth). The single circles inside rooms are *kondus* (grain storage bins) and the small double circles are *bokhāri ferengi* (metal space heater) bases with their hearths. A cross section through B-B' is shown at the top of the figure.

Figure A-4. Baghestan Area D. Numbers refer to owner's household. A = animal house, or stable, E = *eivān* (covered porch), L = living room, S = storeroom, a = *tanur* (bread oven), c = chicken coop, d = privy, e = *tālār* (milk product storage rack), g = sheep or goat pen, h = feed trough, k = *kalgāh* (cooking hearth). The single circles inside rooms are *kondus* (grain storage bins) and the small double circles are *bokhāri ferengi* (metal space heater) bases with their hearths. Construction begun after 1976 is marked with dashed lines.

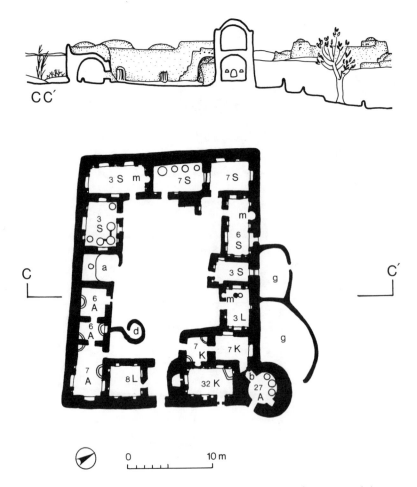

Figure A-5. Qal'a Reza Qoli in Baghestan Area E. Numbers refer to owner's household. A = animal house, or stable, L = living room, K = straw storage room, S = storeroom, a = *tanur* (bread oven), b = blocked door, d = privy, g = sheep or goat pen, m = *bokhāri geli* (old style wall fireplace). The single circles inside rooms are *kondus* (grain storage bins) and the small double circles are *bokhāri ferengi* (metal space heater) bases with their hearths. A cross section through C-C' is shown at the top of the figure.

Figure A-6. Baghestan Area F. Numbers refer to owner's household. A = animal house, or stable, E = *eivān* (covered porch), L = living room, K = straw storage room, S = storeroom, a = *tanur* (bread oven), b = blocked door, d = privy, e = *tālār* (milk product storage rack), f = gravity feed shower, g = sheep or goat pen, k = *kalgāh* (cooking hearth). The single circles inside rooms are *kondu* (grain storage bins) and the small double circles are *bokhāri ferengi* (metal space heater) bases with their hearths. Construction begun after 1976 is marked with dashed lines.

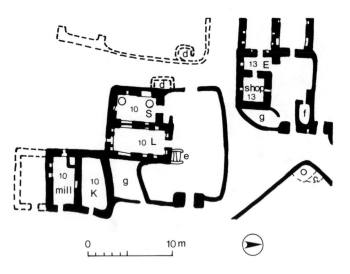

Figure A-7. Baghestan Area G. Numbers refer to owner's household. E = *eivān* (covered porch), K = straw storage room, L = living room, S = storeroom, d = privy, e = *tālār* (milk product storage rack), f = gravity feed shower, g = sheep or goat pen. The single circles inside rooms are *kondus* (grain storage bins). Construction begun after 1976 is marked with dashed lines.

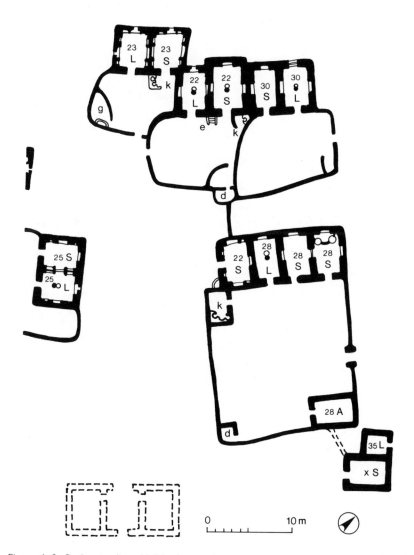

Figure A-8. Baghestan Area H. Numbers refer to owner's household; the X designates a household that resides in a nearby village. A = animal house, or stable, L = living room, S = storeroom, d = privy, e = *tālār* (milk product storage rack), g = sheep or goat pen, k = *kalgāh* (cooking hearth). The single circles inside rooms are *kondus* (grain storage bins) and the small double circles are *bokhāri ferengi* (metal space heater) bases with their hearths. Construction begun after 1976 is marked with dashed lines.

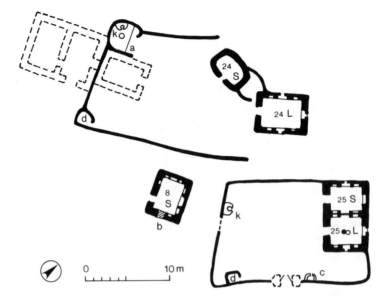

Figure A-9. Baghestan Area I. Numbers refer to owner's household. L = living room, S = storeroom, a = *tanur* (bread oven), b = blocked door, c = chicken coop, d = privy, k = *kalgāh* (cooking hearth). The small double circles are *bokhāri ferengi* (metal space heater) bases with their hearths. Construction begun after 1976 is marked by dashed lines.

# NOTES

## CHAPTER I. INTRODUCTION

1. For a comprehensive review of theoretical approaches to space and the built environment, see Lawrence and Low 1990.

2. The set of reports and studies on settlement, subsistence, and material culture, including architecture, in Iran's Caspian provinces is a remarkable exception (see, for example, Bazin 1980; Bazin and Bromberger 1982; and Bromberger 1989).

3. Kamp (1982 and 1987), Kramer (especially 1979 and 1982b) and Watson (1978, 1979) are especially important sources of data and analysis as well as bibliography and comparative comments for settlement and material culture, past and present, in the Near East and elsewhere.

4. Two important, ongoing and many-volumed works, the *Cambridge History of Iran* and the *Encyclopaedia Iranica,* provide essential information on every aspect of Iran's history and culture. As background to many of the topics covered in this book, the classic sources are Lambton's works on rural settlement and organization (Lambton 1953 and 1969) and Wulff's rich coverage of the crafts and traditional industries of Iran (Wulff 1966). For a comprehensive survey and bibliography of the languages and dialects of Iran, see Schmitt 1986, and for background in Shi'i Islam, Iran's dominant religion, see Momen 1985. Alberts's dissertation (1963) is an encyclopaedic ethnography of rural life and society in Iran. Beck (1991) provides an extremely useful, up-to-date, and complete bibliographic essay on rural and tribal history and society in Iran.

5. In addition to those included in this book, photographic illustrations of the natural setting, built environment, people, and activities of Khar o Tauran appear in Horne 1982b, 1983, 1991, and 1993; Martin 1987; and Spooner and Horne 1980.

6. Ethnoarchaeological research need not be restricted to "traditional" societies. While some ethnoarchaeological projects benefit from holding as many socioeconomic variables constant as possible, others flourish in the wide-ranging

opportunities offered by fully "modern" societies. The most famous of these is undoubtedly Rathje's Garbage Project at the University of Arizona (see, among numerous publications, Rathje and Murphy 1992).

7. The Turan Programme for Ecological Research and Management in and around the Iranian Desert was a multidisciplinary study of arid zone adaptations organized and directed by Brian Spooner. It was commissioned in Iran by the Department of the Environment in 1975 and became part of UNESCO's Programme on Man and the Biosphere (MAB). The research area, broadly speaking, was designated the Turan Biosphere Reserve under MAB Project no. 8. Khar o Tauran lies just outside the reserve proper.

*Turan* is a variant spelling of *Tauran* in English, used by the government of Iran for both the program and the Biosphere Reserve. The two words are spelled the same in Persian. In publications of the Turan Programme and its members, *Turan* refers to the entire Biosphere Reserve area; *Tauran* refers to the central group of villages on what I call the Tauran Plain. Other distinct but potentially confusing uses of the terms are discussed in Spooner and Mann 1982, 142–43n1, and Rechinger 1977, 156.

8. Geographically and historically, far more attention has been paid to the cities of the Near East than to its rural areas. For this area (and most of the rest) of Iran, the first systematic settlement and demographic data appear only with the 1956 census. What little is known of Khar o Tauran's past is summarized in Chapter 4.

## CHAPTER 2. THE NATURAL ENVIRONMENT

1. Those interested in the ecology of the area in greater detail should consult Spooner and Mann (1982) and Spooner (1984) for their content and bibliographies.

2. In 1976, when Mary Martin and then I recorded daily temperatures all year long, the mean annual temperature in Baghestan was 14° C. In the summer of 1976 the absolute high was 40° C., the absolute low not much below 18° C. In the summer of 1977, from July 23 to September 7, the absolute high recorded at Baghestan was 40° C and the absolute low 14° C, based on spot checks rather than systematic daily observations. Daily records were kept the following summer, from August 3 to September 21, 1978. In August of that year the mean high was 32.7° C, the mean low 17.8° C, the absolute high 35.0° C (in midafternoon), and the absolute low 14.0° C (just before dawn). September 1978 had a mean high of 31.2° C, a mean low of 18.0° C, an absolute high of 33.5° C, and an absolute low of 15.0° C. The summer of 1977 was thought locally to be a hot summer, that of 1978 a cool one, though neither one was exceptionally so.

3. Two basic references useful for a general understanding of the geomorphology and hydrology of Iran's desert landscapes are Mabbutt 1977 and Volume

1 of the *Cambridge History of Iran* (Fisher 1968). There has been no scientific study of the topography or hydrology of the study area, but the geology and mineral deposits of nearby areas have been described by Bazin and Hübner (1969). The description in this section is largely based on my own observations and those made by botanists in the course of their plant studies (especially Bhadresa and Moore 1982; Breckle 1979; Breckle 1982; Freitag 1977; Iran 1977; Moore and Bhadresa 1978; Moore and Stevenson 1982; and Rechinger 1977.

4. See n. 7 in Chapter 1.

5. Ways in which the natural vegetation has been altered by specific activities in Khar o Tauran are discussed in some detail in Nyerges 1982 and Horne 1982a. The following highly condensed sketch of the natural vegetation has been synthesized mainly from the work of Breckle (1982), Freitag (1977), and Rechinger (1977) and the synthesis in Iran 1977. For botanical information relevant to northeastern Iran in general or to particular species found there, see Guest 1966, Pabot 1967, Rechinger (1963–), Rechinger and Wendelbo 1976, and Zohary 1963.

6. A well-illustrated general work relevant to the mammal species of the Turan Biosphere Reserve is *Mammals of Iran* (Harrington 1977), published by the Department of the Environment. As is true of the rest of the natural ecology, only a beginning has been made in studying the mammals of the area.

## CHAPTER 3. SUBSISTENCE

1. The figure of 250 hectares was arrived at by measuring field areas on aerial photographs supplied by the Iranian government, at scales of about 1:22,000 and 1:57,000.

2. For a diagram of milk-processing techniques and products in Khar o Tauran, see Martin 1980b.

3. This suggests that they, like most of the world's populations, cannot drink fresh milk without getting cramps and diarrhea because of a deficiency in lactase, the enzyme that breaks down the sugar found in milk.

## CHAPTER 4. SETTLEMENT IN KHAR O TAURAN

1. During the period in the field, my colleagues and I had neither hydrological studies of the area nor local *qanāt* diggers (*moqānnis*) to assess for us the extent to which all available *qanāt* sites are already occupied and to explain the technology of *qanāt* construction in this area. Whatever the home base of these specialists in the past, today they are concentrated in towns such as Sabzevar and thus were unavailable for consultation.

2. Alberts (1963, 424) reports that animal shelters in the area of Garmsar, east of Tehran, are burned yearly on account of parasite infestation.

3. Black tents, woven of goat hair, are the abode of a variety of nomadic and transhumant pastoral groups found in a wide belt extending from North Africa through Southwest Asia and as far east as Pakistan. To Taurani residents, they evoke a life style (nonagricultural) and social organization (tribal) very different from their own settled, village life.

4. Dewar (1986) makes a similar contrast with his terms *spatial congruity* and *temporal continuity*. Eder's term *settlement site mobility* refers specifically to the movement of entire settlements along with all their residents (1984, 846–47). Although they tend to address hunter–gatherer and agricultural rather than pastoral and agricultural adaptations, both these and other recent discussions of seasonality and mobility, especially the references cited in Kent (1992), are of substantive as well as typological interest to those exploring regional patterns of settlement and subsistence.

## CHAPTER 5. VILLAGE SPACES

1. *Qal'a* frequently appears in Iranian place names when the settlement originally consisted of or contained a *qal'a*, or fortified dwelling. There are two unoccupied *qal'a* in Qal'a Baghestan.

The village maps and architectural plans in this book were created during the three summers of my research in Iran. In 1976 William Remson surveyed the village of Baghestan and its immediate environs and created an outline map of the village boundaries and major blocks of architecture. To this outline I added each individual courtyard and structure, measured and recorded with camera, measuring tape, and compass. I measured the size, shape, and orientation of all structures and walls along with their architectural details (niches, windows, doors, bins, floor and wall finish, and so forth). Some windowless rooms were so dark or full of straw that they could not be recorded in detail. The only room that was actually inaccessible was that coded as household 35, whose owner was away most of the time. I also collected, by interview, data on building procedures and house histories, and by observation, data on how spaces and structures are used.

2. Hassan Fathy, an advocate of traditional methods of building in North Africa and the Near East, covers a great deal of information on climate and architecture in his book *Natural Energy and Vernacular Architecture* (1986). He discusses, with examples, such design topics as building materials, orientation, shade, openings, roofs, house and settlement layouts, and specialized architectural features such as the *mashrabiya* (wooden grille), blinds, claustrum, and

windcatchers. His emphasis, like that of most who write about architecture in the Near East, is on wind, sun, and aridity.

3. No mud brick buildings are earthquake resistant, yet ironically, seismic zones and earthern building generally coincide (Agarwal 1982, 143; Yorulmaz 1982, 131). Flat-roofed mud brick structures fare even worse than domed structures. Of traditional rural options in the Near East, the best are pole-frame structures (Szabo and Barfield 1991, 12, 153).

4. For examples of orientation with regard to climate, see Beazley and Harverson 1982; Bonine 1980; Roaf 1982; and Szabo and Barfield 1991. For a more theoretical discussion in comparable climates, see Olgyay 1963.

5. Precedents for such an approach exist in a number of recent books and articles that pursue the theoretical and methodological aspects of these relationships from an archaeologist's point of view. Relevant examples include Douglas and Kramer 1992; Gamble and Boismier 1991; Gargett and Hayden 1991; Gould and Yellen 1987; O'Connell 1987; and Whitelaw 1983. As might be expected, where cooperating households make proximity desirable in the first place, it is easier to bring it about in mobile settings. For example, 76 percent of nearest neighbors among the Australian Pintubi were primary kin (Gargett and Hayden 1991, 22); 83 percent among the Australian Alywara were either primary kin or close classificatory relations (O'Connell 1987, 86).

6. Well-known examples from Oceania, Africa, North Africa, and South America appear in Cunningham 1964; Griaule 1965; Bourdieu 1973; and Hugh-Jones 1979, respectively. These and similar descriptions and analyses are discussed in Lawrence and Low 1990.

7. See, for example, the several publications of the Aga Khan Award for Architecture, especially *Architecture as Symbol and Self-Identity* and *Toward an Architecture in the Spirit of Islam* (both published by the Aga Khan Award for Architecture, Philadelphia, in 1980); Horne 1982d; and Salam 1990; also see Michell 1978 (especially the chapters by Grabar, Grube, and Petherbridge), and Mumtaz 1985, 191–196. Very little of the large body of research into Near Eastern domestic architecture, whether by architects or ethnographers, deals with religious aspects or meanings of the house. Campo's *The Other Sides of Paradise* (1991) is an outstanding exception. His fieldwork took place in Egypt, but his book includes a discussion of the relations between houses and Islam as expressed in historical context by the Koran and the hadith literature, and as expressed in ethnographic context by Muslim house-dwellers in their thought, speech, and behavior.

8. Vidal [1955] describes *hoseiniyas* in villages of the al-Hasa region of Saudi Arabia.

9. Local interpretations of orientation sometimes result in contrasting practices. For example, Petherbridge notes that Sudanese Kababish tents ideally face toward Mecca, whereas Muslim dwellings in Bosnia ideally do the opposite (1978, 202).

10. Boyce's community is an example of the architectural expression of religious belief in two ways: the first as an accommodation to their own minority Zoroastrian beliefs, the second as an accommodation to the restrictive ordinances applied to them by the Islamic community in which they reside.

11. I owe this distinction and its discussion to Mary Martin's analysis of the public and private domains of Taurani women's roles (Martin 1976).

## CHAPTER 6. HOUSES AND HOUSEHOLDS

1. Unfortunately, I never saw a room or compound built to completion, partly because very little construction of any kind took place in the first two years of fieldwork, and partly because much construction takes place in the fall, the season after I had left each year. I did see bricks made, walls built, and routine maintenance carried out. I interviewed both clients and builders.

2. Much practical and technical information about mud construction can be found in books (and their bibliographies) aimed at the development of improved techniques in construction and preservation of traditional earth buildings, such as *Construire en Terre* (le CRAterre 1979), Iowa 1985, and McHenry 1984. Wulff (1966) is a rich source of building techniques in Iran, as are Aurenche 1977 and 1981 for the Near East in general, past and present.

3. To reach this estimate, I figured a "packed house volume" (discussed in Chapter 7) of 35 $m^2$ per room and multiplied that by the number of rooms, occupied and unoccupied, in the three areas of the village. To this figure I added about 30 percent to account for courtyard walls (based on running meters), gates, and miscellaneous features such as privies and bread ovens.

4. "Can't do that to a brick wall," he said, and of course he was right.

5. Although surely not "because Salehabadis eat more fat," as one brickmaking wag claimed. They probably do eat more fat, however, because they have more sheep and goats.

6. According to Hall, McBride, and Riddell (1973, 255), in Asvan, Turkey, it takes three men one to one and a half days to make 1,000 molded bricks 30 × 30 × 10 cm or 30 × 15 × 10 cm. Sun-drying takes about two two weeks. Fathy reports two brick makers and two laborers in New Gourna, Egypt, produced 3,000 molded bricks 23 × 11 × 7 cm per day. They were put on edge on the third day and were dry enough to stack by the sixth day (Fathy 1973, 198–200). Alberts reports that in Davarabad, Iran, a good brickmaker and his assistant produced 250–300 bricks 8 in. square (about 20.3 × 20.3 cm) per hour and 1,500 per day; slower workers produced 1,000 per day (Alberts 1963, 152, 493).

7. Oates (1990) refers to this method of construction as *pitched-brick* vaulting and dates its earliest known appearance (though not its origins) to 2100 B.C. at Tell al Rimah in Mesopotamia. In his article, he reviews the archaeological evidence for several other kinds of arches and vaulting in Mesopotamia. For ancient Egypt's vaults and domes, see Van Beek (1987).

8. *Feature* is a useful term by which archaeologists refer to a miscellany of built-in elements that are not the walls or floors of buildings; I use it here in much the same sense.

9. In 1976, an *ostād*'s wages were Rls 300 per day, in 1978, Rls 1,200 per day. In 1978 an urban *ostād* took four days to build a two-room (plus *eivān* with shared wall) addition, not counting the roof, to the compound of household 33. Bricks cost Rls 11,500 just for the walls. More bricks would be needed for completion, including the roof. The total for construction then would be about Rls 23,000. Finish, doors, and so forth, would raise the figure to Rls 25,000 for the equivalent of two rooms with one shared wall, land not included. The large new tobacco house cost Rls 30,000 to build in 1978 (Mary Martin, personal communication, 1979). Older rooms and compounds sold in 1977 and 1978 for Rls 50,000 and Rls 57,000 for three rooms and an *eivān* each, or Rls 17,000 and Rls 19,000 per room. That cost included land.

10. The system of land measurement used in Tauran is in principle the same as that reported by Alberts, in which there were 40 *mans* per hectare (1963). A *man* of land refers to the area on which one *man* of seed would be sown. In the field system next to Baghestan, one *man* equals about 160 m$^2$ on average and there are about 60 *mans* per hectare (Martin, personal communication, 1980). Any particular plot within the system may vary from this depending on its location and soil condition. Seed on poor soil is sown more densely than it is on fertile soil; thus the less fertile the land the greater number of *mans* per hectare. House lots in the village are measured the same way, since the land was originally irrigated field plots. The average number of *mans* per hectare in the other field systems varies according to the productivity of the system.

There are further complications in trying to make comparisons, whether from region to region or even sometimes within single field systems. The weight of a *man,* today officially set at 3 kg in Iran, traditionally showed considerable local variation and may still do so informally in some areas. In addition, the ratio of weight to land varies with the type of crop: in Baghestan, one *man* of cotton seed is sown on a unit of land that would take two *mans* of wheat seed. A *man* of cotton land is thus twice the size of a *man* of wheat land. Imposing a standard unit, such as the hectare, over the local system in order to make comparisons is a challenging task. Further discussions of traditional field measuring systems may be found in Kramer (1982b, 64–65), Lambton (1953, 4–5, 367) and Watson (1979, 67).

11. Coefficients of variation for the areas in Aliabad comparable to those in Baghestan (Table 10) are: courtyards, 109 percent; living rooms, 35 percent; storerooms, 60 percent; and stables, 50 percent. These coefficients were calculated from means and standard deviations given in Kramer 1982b, Table 4.2. Note that the *degree* of variability for each room type in Aliabad is substantially higher than in Baghestan and that the mean size of room types differs more from type to type. This kind of variability warrants further exploration. Aliabad's absolute room sizes cannot be directly compared with Baghestan's because they include wall widths, which Baghestan's do not. Arriving at an approximate conversion is straightforward, however. Kramer's walls range from 100 to 50 cm in thickness (Kramer 1982b, 99, 125). I would suggest taking from 50 to 60 percent of Kramer's areal figures. Fifty percent would be appropriate for thicker-walled first-floor rooms (such as animal houses and many storerooms) that support rooms above them, and 60 percent for second-story rooms (many of which are living rooms). These percentages will produce smaller converted areas than those arrived at by Brown (1987, 37), who used a factor of 62 percent.

12. Twenty-four of the thirty-two households listed owned donkeys (most owned only one, but some shared with another household, and two households, 11 and 28, had three each). Thirteen households owned oxen or cows; all but two of these households are in the wealthier half of the list. In any case, incorporating the donkeys (at about Rls 4,500 each) and cattle (at about Rls 30,000 each) in the list would not have altered the rank order and would have increased any one household's wealth only by Rls 2,000 to 70,000. (Preliminary data on holdings and prices of cattle and donkeys were supplied by Mary Martin, personal communication, 1990.) Most dogs in this area are more or less free, but a good Kurdish guard dog is extremely valuable, worth perhaps four sheep. The only one in Baghestan was owned by household 29, which paid Rls 11,000 for it in 1978.

13. Second-story rooms in Baghestan cannot be tested for their relationship to household size or wealth. There are only four of them in use, all in the older areas as additions to already existing compounds. Two are in the *qal'a* and belong to household 6; the others are over storerooms in the compounds of households 16 and 34. They were built as a solution to problems of expansion and of keeping cool in the summer.

## CHAPTER 7. THE VILLAGE AS AN ARCHAEOLOGICAL SITE

1. For a discussion of the principles and processes of postdepositional preservation and attrition in arid environments, Butzer 1982 and Davidson and Shackley 1976 are especially recommended.

2. Villages in Tauran are considerably smaller and less dense than the rural

Southwest Asian settlements listed in Kramer's Table 5.3 (1982b, 160). It should be noted that Kramer's table gives lower figures than presented in this book because she was restricted to the Iran 1977 maps, which later fieldwork has shown to be inaccurate. This discrepancy points up the sometimes insurmountable difficulties in arriving at accurate areal measures and densities of settlements (see also Sumner 1989).

3. See previous note.

## CHAPTER 8. ASSESSING THE FIT

1. For recent discussions of the several viewpoints, see, for example, Binford 1987; Hodder 1986; Shanks and Tilley 1987; and Watson, LeBlanc, and Redman 1984.

2. These comments refer only to permanent village settlements. Many households, of course, move seasonally to summer living rooms in pastoral stations.

3. Contradicting this statement is the fact that residents of Kariz and Zamanabad held land in Baghestan (Mary Martin, personal communication, 1988).

# REFERENCES

Adams, R. M.
1981        *Heartland of Cities: Surveys of Ancient Settlement and Land Use on the Central Floodplain of the Euphrates.* Chicago: University of Chicago Press.

Agarwal, A.
1982        Research: Mud as a traditional building material. In *The Changing Rural Habitat*, vol. 1, edited by B. B. Taylor, 137–46. Singapore: Concept Media Pte Ltd. for the Aga Khan Award for Architecture.

Agorsah, E. K.
1985        Archeological implications of traditional house construction among the Nohumuru of northern Ghana. *Current Anthropology* 26:103–15.

Alberts, R. C.
1963        Social structure and culture change in an Iranian village. Ph.D. dissertation, Department of Anthropology, University of Wisconsin.

Ambraseys, N. N., and C. P. Melville
1982        *A History of Persian Earthquakes.* Cambridge: Cambridge University Press.

Ammerman, A. J., L. L. Cavalli-Sforza, and D. K. Wagener
1976        Toward the estimation of population growth in Old World prehistory. In *Demographic Anthropology: Quantitative Approaches,* edited by E. B. W. Zubrow, 27–61. Albuquerque: University of New Mexico Press.

Ashraf, A.
1983        Abadi. In *Encyclopaedia Iranica,* edited by E. Yarshater. London: Routledge and Kegan Paul.

Aubin, J.
1971        Réseau pastoral et réseau caravanier: Les grand'routes du Khurassan a l'époque mongole. *Le Monde Iranien et l'Islam* 1:105–30.

Aurenche, O.
1977        *Dictionnaire illustré multilingue de l'architecture du Proche Orient an-
            cien.* Lyons: Maison de l'Orient, and Paris: Diffusion de Boccard.
1981        *La maison orientale: L'architecture du Proche Orient ancien des origines
            au milieu du quatrième millénaire,* 2 vols. Paris: Librairie Orientaliste
            Paul Geuthner.

Bazin, D., and H. Hübner
1969        *Copper Deposits in Iran.* Geological Survey of Iran, report no. 13.
            Tehran: Geological Survey of Iran.

Bazin, M.
1980        *Le Tâlech, une région ethnique au nord de l'Iran.* 2 vols. Paris:
            A.D.P.F.

Bazin, M., and C. Bromberger (with A. Askari and A. Karimi)
1982        *Gilân et Âzerbâyjân oriental: Cartes et documents ethnographiques.*
            Paris: A.D.P.F.

Beaumont, P.
1982        Ab "water," iii. The hydrology and water resources of the Iranian
            Plateau. *Encyclopaedia Iranica,* edited by E. Yarshater. London:
            Routledge and Kegan Paul.

Beazley, E., and M. Harverson
1982        *Living with the Desert: Working Buildings of the Iranian Plateau.*
            Warminster, England: Aris and Phillips.

Beck, L.
1991        *Nomad: A Year in the Life of a Qashqa'i Tribesman in Iran.* Berkeley:
            University of California Press.

Bhadresa, R., and P. D. Moore
1982        Desert shrubs: The implications of population and pattern studies
            for conservation and management. In *Desertification and Develop-
            ment: Dryland Ecology in Social Perspective,* edited by B. Spooner
            and H. S. Mann, 269–76. London: Academic Press.

Binford, L. R.
1987        Researching ambiguity: Frames of reference and site structure. In
            *Method and Theory for Activity Area Research: An Ethnoarchaeological
            Approach,* edited by S. Kent, 449–512. New York: Columbia Uni-
            versity Press.

Bobek, H.
1959        *Features and Formation of the Great Kavir and Masileh.* Arid Zone
            Research Centre, University of Tehran Publication, no. 2.
1976        Enstehung und Verbreitung der Hauptflursysteme Irans—
            Gründzuge einer sozialgeographischen Theorie: Part 1. *Mitteilungen
            der Österreichischen Geographischen Gesellschaft* 118:274–309.
1977        Enstehung und Verbreitung der Hauptflursysteme Irans—

Gründzuge einer sozialgeographischen Theorie: Part 2. *Mitteilungen der Österreichischen Geographischen Gesellschaft* 119:34–51.

Bonine, M. E.

1979      The morphogenesis of Iranian cities. *Annals of the Association of American Geographers* 69:208–24.

1980      Aridity and structure: Adaptations of indigenous housing in central Iran. In *Desert Housing: Balancing Experience and Technology for Dwelling in Hot Arid Zones,* edited by K. N. Clark and P. Paylore, 193–219. Tucson: Office of Arid Land Studies, University of Arizona.

1989      Qanats, field systems, and morphology. In *Qanat, Kariz and Khattara: Traditional Water Systems in the Middle East and North Africa,* edited by M. Bonine, K. McLachlan, and P. Beaumont, 34–57. London: Middle East Center, School of Oriental and African Studies, University of London in Association with Middle East and North African Studies Press Ltd.

Bourdieu, P.

1973      The Berber house. In *Rules and Meanings,* edited by M. Douglas, 98–110. Hammondsworth: Penguin.

Boyce, M.

1969      Some aspects of farming in a Zoroastrian village of Yazd. *Persica* 4:121–39.

1971      The Zoroastrian houses of Yazd. In *Iran and Islam,* edited by C. E. Bosworth, 125–47. Edinburgh: University Press.

Breckle, S.-W.

1982      The significance of salinity. In *Desertification and Development: Dryland Ecology in Social Perspective,* edited by B. Spooner and H. S. Mann, 277–92. London: Academic Press.

1979      Cool deserts and shrub semideserts in Afghanistan and Iran. In *Ecosystems of the World,* vol. 5. Amsterdam: Elsevier Scientific.

Brochier, J., P. Villa, and M. Giacomarra

1992      Shepherds and sediments: Geo-ethnoarchaeology of pastoral sites. *Journal of Anthropological Archaeology* 11(1):47–102.

Bromberger, C.

1989      *Habitat, Architecture and Rural Society in the Gilan Plain (Northern Iran).* Bonn: Ferd. Dümmlers Verlag.

Brown, B. M.

1987      Population estimation from floor area: A restudy of "Naroll's Constant." *Behavior Science Research* 21(1–4):1–49.

Butzer, K. W.

1982      *Archaeology as Human Ecology: Method and Theory for a Contextual Approach.* Cambridge: Cambridge University Press.

Campo, E. J.
1991    The Other Sides of Paradise: Explorations into the Religious Meanings of Domestic Space in Islam. Columbia: University of South Carolina Press.

Chang, K.-C.
1972    Settlement Patterns in Archaeology. Addison-Wesley Module in Anthropology, no. 24.

Chisholm, M.
1962    Rural Settlement and Land Use. Chicago: Aldine.

Christensen, N.
1967    Haustypen und Gehöftbildung in Westpersien. Anthropos 62:89–132.

Clark, K. N.
1980    Design criteria for desert housing. In Desert Housing: Balancing Experience and Technology for Dwelling in Hot Arid Zones, edited by K. N. Clark and P. Paylore, 315–19. Tucson: University of Arizona, Office of Arid Land Studies.

Clerk, C.
1861    Notes on Persia, Khorassan, and Afghanistan. Journal of the Royal Geographical Society 31:37–65.

Courty, M.-A., P. Goldberg, and R. Macphail
1989    Soils and Micromorphology in Archaeology. Cambridge: Cambridge University Press.

Crumley, C. L.
1979    Three locational models: An epistemological assessment for anthropology and archaeology. In Advances in Archaeological Method and Theory, vol. 2, edited by M. B. Schiffer, 143–73. New York: Academic Press.

Cunningham, C. E.
1964    Order in the Atoni house. Bijdragen Tot de Taal-, Land-en Volkenkunde 120:34–67.

David, N.
1971    The Fulani compound and the archaeologist. World Archaeology 3(2):111–31.

Davidson, D. A.
1976    Processes of tell formation and erosion. In Geoarchaeology: Earth Science and the Past, edited by D. A. Davidson and M. L. Shackley, 255–65. London: Duckworth.

Davidson, D. A., and M. L. Shackley
1976 (eds.)    Geoarchaeology: Earth Science and the Past. London: Duckworth.

Dennell, R. W.
1980    The use, abuse, and potential of site catchment analysis. Anthropology UCLA 10:1–20.
1982    Dryland agriculture and soil conservation: An archaeologi-

cal study of check-dam farming and wadi siltation. In *Desertification and Development: Dryland Ecology in Social Perspective,* edited by B. Spooner and H. S. Mann, 171–200. London: Academic Press.

Dewar, R. E.

1986        Discovering settlement systems of the past in New England site distributions. *Man in the Northeast* 31:77–88.

Digard, J.-P.

1975        Campements Baxtyari: Observations d'un ethnologue sur des matrériaux intéressant l'archéologue. *Studia Iranica* 4:117–29.

1980        Chiens de campement et chiens de troupeau chez les nomades Baxtyari d'Iran. *Studia Iranica* 9:131–39.

Douglas, J. E., and C. Kramer

1992        Interaction, social proximity, and distance: A special issue. *Journal of Anthropological Archaeology* 11:103–10.

Douglas, M.

1972        Symbolic orders in the use of domestic space. In *Man, Settlement and Urbanism,* edited by P. J. Ucko, R. Tringham, and G. W. Dimbleby, 513–21. London: Duckworth.

Edelberg, L.

1966/67     Seasonal dwellings of farmers in North-western Luristan. *Folk* 8–9:373–401.

Eder, J. F.

1984        The impact of subsistence change on mobility and settlement pattern in a tropical forest foraging economy: Some implications for archaeology. *American Anthropologist* 86:837–53.

Ehlers, E., and J. Safi-Nejad

1979        Formen kollecktiver Landwirtschaft in Iran: Boneh. In *Beiträge zur Kulturgeographie des islamischen Orients,* edited by E. Ehlers, 55–82. Marburger Geographische Schriften, no. 78. Marburg: Geographischen Institutes der Universität Marburg.

Eidt, R.

1984        *Advances in Abandoned Settlement Analysis: Application to Prehistoric Anthrosols in Colombia, South America.* Milwaukee: Center for Latin America, University of Wisconsin.

Eighmy, J. L.

1981        The archaeological significance of counting houses: Ethnoarchaeological evidence. In *Modern Material Culture: The Archaeology of Us,* edited by R. A. Gould and M. B. Schiffer, 225–33. New York: Academic Press.

English, P. W.

1966        *City and Village in Iran: Settlement and Economy in the Kirman Basin.* Madison: University of Wisconsin Press.

Evans, S., and P. Gould
1982        Settlement models in archaeology. *Journal of Anthropological Archae-
            ology* 1(3):275–304.
Evenari, M.
1958        The ancient desert agriculture of the Negev. Part 3. Early begin-
            nings. *Israel Exploration Journal* 8:231–68.
Fathy, H.
1973        *Architecture for the Poor: An Experiment in Rural Egypt.* Chicago:
            University of Chicago Press.
1986        *Natural Energy and Vernacular Architecture: Principles and Examples
            with Reference to Hot Arid Climates,* edited by Walter Shearer and
            Abd-el-rahman Ahmed Sultan. Chicago: University of Chicago
            Press for the United Nations University.
Fisher, W. B.
1968 (ed.)  *Cambridge History of Iran,* vol. 1: *The Land of Iran.* Cambridge:
            Cambridge University Press.
Flannery, K. V.
1976        The village and its catchment: Introduction. In *The Early Meso-
            american Village,* edited by K. V. Flannery, 91–95. New York: Aca-
            demic Press.
Forster, G.
1970        *A Journey from Bengal to England.* 2 vols. Punjab: Languages De-
            partment. (Originally published in 1798.)
Fraser, J. B.
1984        *Narrative of a Journey into Khorasan, in the Years 1821 and 1822.*
            Delhi: Oxford University Press. (Originally published in 1825.)
Freitag, H.
1977        Notes to the provisional vegetation map of the Touran Protected
            Area in Iran 1977. Manuscript. Files of the Turan Programme.
Gabriel, A.
1935        *Durch Persiens Wüsten.* Stuttgart: Strecker und Schröder.
Gamble, C. S., and W. A. Boismier
1991 (eds.) *Ethnoarchaeological Approaches to Mobile Campsites.* Ann Arbor: In-
            ternational Monographs in Prehistory.
Gargett, R., and B. Hayden
1991        Site structure, kinship, and sharing in aboriginal Australia: Impli-
            cations for archaeology. In *Interpretation of Archaeological Spatial
            Patterning,* edited by E. M. Kroll and T. D. Price, 11–32. New
            York: Plenum Press.
Gilsenan, M.
1982        *Recognizing Islam.* London: Croom Helm.
Goblot, H.
1979        *Les qanats: Une technique d'acquisition de l'eau.* Paris: Mouton.

Gould, R. A.
1980        *Living Archaeology*. Cambridge: Cambridge University Press.
Gould, R. A., and J. E. Yellen
1987        Man the hunted: Determinants of household spacing in desert and tropical foraging societies. *Journal of Anthropological Archaeology* 6(1):77–103.
Grabar, O.
1978        The architecture of power: Palaces, citadels and fortifications. In *Architecture of the Islamic World*, edited by G. Michell, 48–79. London: Thames and Hudson.
Griaule, M.
1965        *Conversations with Ogotemmele: An Introduction to Dogon Religious Ideas*. London: Oxford University Press.
Grønhaug, R.
1978        Scale as a variable in analysis: Fields in social organization in Herat, Northwest Afghanistan. In *Scale and Social Organization*, edited by F. Barth, 78–121. Oslo: Universitetsforlaget.
Guest, E.
1966        *Flora of Iraq*. Baghdad: Ministry of Agriculture, Republic of Iraq.
Hall, G., S. McBride, and A. Riddell
1973        Architectural study. *Anatolian Studies* 23:245–69.
Hallet, S. I., and R. Samizay
1980        *Traditional Architecture of Afghanistan*. New York: Garland STPM Press.
Harrington, F. A., Jr.
1977 (comp. and ed.)     *Mammals of Iran*. Tehran: Department of the Environment, Government of Iran.
N.d.        Fauna of the Touran Protected Area. Manuscript. Files of the Turan Programme.
Harrison, D. L.
1968        *The Mammals of Arabia*. 2 vols. London: Ernest Benn.
Hartl, M.
1979        *Das Najafabadtal: Geographische Untersuchung einer Kanatlandschaft im Zagrosgebirge, Iran*. Regensburger Geographische Schriften 12. Regensburg: Institut für Geographie an der Universität Regensburg.
Helbaek, H.
1972        Samarran irrigation agriculture at Choga Mami. *Iraq* 34(1):35–48.
1986        *Reading the Past: Current Approaches to Interpretation in Archaeology*. Cambridge: Cambridge University Press.
Hodder, I., and C. Orton
1976        *Spatial Analysis in Archaeology*. Cambridge: Cambridge University Press.

Hole, F.
1979          Rediscovering the past in the present: Ethnoarchaeology in
              Luristan, Iran. In *Ethnoarchaeology: Implications of Ethnography for
              Archaeology,* edited by C. Kramer, 192–218. New York: Columbia
              University Press.

Holmes, J. E.
1975          A study of social organization in certain villages in West Khurasan,
              Iran, with special reference to kinship and agricultural activities.
              Ph.D. thesis, University of Durham (by permission of the author).

Horne, L.
1980a         Dryland settlement location: Social and natural factors in the distri-
              bution of settlement in Turan. *Expedition* 22(4):11–17.
1980b         Village morphology: The distribution of structures and activities
              in Turan villages. *Expedition* 22(4):18–23.
1982a         The demand for fuel: Ecological implications of socio-economic
              change. In *Desertification and Development: Dryland Ecology in Social
              Perspective,* edited by B. Spooner and H. S. Mann, 201–15. Lon-
              don: Academic Press.
1982b         Fuel for the Metalworker: The Role of Charcoal and Charcoal
              Production in Ancient Metallurgy. *Expedition* 25(1):6–13.
1982c         The Household in Space. *American Behavioral Scientist* 25(6):677–85.
1982d         Rural habitat and habitations: A survey of dwellings in the rural
              Islamic world. In *The Changing Rural Habitat,* vol. 2, edited by B.
              B. Taylor, 27–34. Singapore: Concept Media Pte Ltd. for the Aga
              Khan Award for Architecture.
1983          Recycling in an Iranian village: Ethnoarchaeology in Baghestan.
              *Archaeology* 35(4):16–21.
1988          The spatial organization of rural settlement in Khar o Tauran,
              Iran: An ethnoarchaeological case study. Ph.D. dissertation, De-
              partment of Anthropology, University of Pennsylvania.
1991          Reading village plans: Architecture and social change in northeast-
              ern Iran. *Expedition* 33(1):44–51
1993          Occupational and locational instability in arid land settlement. In
              *The Abandonment of Settlements and Regions,* edited by C. M. Cam-
              eron and S. A. Tomka, 43–53. Cambridge: Cambridge University
              Press.

Hugh-Jones, C.
1979          *From the Milk River: Spatial and Temporal Processes in Northwest
              Amazonia.* Cambridge: Cambridge University Press.

Hütteroth, W. D.
1968          Die Bedeutung kollektiver und individueller Landnahme für die
              Ausbildung von Streifen- und Blockfluren im Nahen Osten. In

*Beiträge zur Genese der Siedlungs- und Agrarlandschaft in Europa.* Erdkundliches Wissen (Beihefte zur GZ), Heft 18, pp. 85–93. Wiesbaden: F. Steiner.

Iowa, J.
1985     *Ageless Adobe: History and Preservation in Southwestern Architecture.* Santa Fe: Sunstone Press.

Iran, Government of
1969     *Village Gazetteer*, vol. 7. Tehran: Plan Organization, Statistical Centre of Iran.
1973a     Agricultural census. Plan Organization, Statistical Centre of Iran, Tehran. Manuscript.
1973b     *Statistical Handbook.* Tehran: National Statistics Center.
1977     *Case Study on Desertification, Iran: Turan.* Tehran: Department of the Environment.

Jacobs, L.
1979     Tell-i Nun: Archaeological implications of a village in transition. In *Ethnoarchaeology: Implications of Ethnography for Archaeology,* edited by C. Kramer, 175–91. New York: Columbia University Press.

Jentsch, C., and R. Loose
1980     *Zur Geographie der ländlichen Siedlungen in Afghanistan.* Mannheim: Geographisches Institut der Universität.

Johnson, G. A.
1977     Aspects of regional analysis in archaeology. *Annual Review of Anthropology* 6:479–508.

Kamp, K. A.
1982     Architectural indices of socio-economic variability: An ethnoarchaeological case study from Syria. Ph.D. dissertation, Department of Anthropology, University of Arizona.
1987     Affluence and image: Ethnoarchaeology in a Syrian village. *Journal of Field Archaeology* 14: 283–96.

Kent, S.
1987 (ed.)     *Method and Theory for Activity Area Research—An Ethnoarchaeological Approach.* New York: Columbia University Press.
1990 (ed.)     *Domestic Architecture and the Use of Space.* Cambridge: Cambridge University Press.
1992     Studying variability in the archaeological record: An ethnoarchaeological model for distinguishing mobility patterns. *American Antiquity* 57(4):635–60.

Kheirabadi, M.
1991     *Iranian Cities: Formation and Development.* Austin: University of Texas Press.

Kirkby, A., and M. J.
1976        Geomorphic processes and the surface survey of archaeological
            sites in semi-arid areas. In *Geoarchaeology: Earth Science and the
            Past,* edited by D. A. Davidson and M. L. Shackley, 229–53. Lon-
            don: Duckworth.

Koenigsberger, O. H., T. G. Ingersoll, A. Mayhew, and S. V. Szokolay
1973        *Manual of Tropical Housing and Building Design, Part 1: Climate De-
            sign.* London: Longman.

Kortum, G.
1975        Siedlungsgenetische Untersuchungen in Fars: Ein Beitrag zum
            Wüstungsproblem im Orient. *Erdkunde* 29:10–20.

Kramer, C.
1979a       Introduction. In *Ethnoarchaeology: Implications of Ethnography for Ar-
            chaeology,* edited by C. Kramer, 1–20. New York: Columbia Uni-
            versity Press.

1979b       An archaeological view of a contemporary Kurdish village: Domes-
            tic architecture, household size, and wealth. In *Ethnoarchaeology:
            Implications of Ethnography for Archaeology,* edited by C. Kramer,
            139–63. New York: Columbia University Press.

1982a       Ethnographic households and archaeological interpretation. *Ameri-
            can Behavioral Scientist* 25(6):663–75.

1982b       *Village Ethnoarchaeology: Rural Iran in Archaeological Perspective.*
            New York: Academic Press.

1984        Spatial organization in contemporary Southwest Asian villages
            and archeological sampling. In *The Hilly Flanks and Beyond: Essays
            on the Prehistory of Southwestern Asia,* edited by T. C. Young, Jr.,
            P. E. L. Smith, and P. Mortensen, 347–68. Chicago: Oriental Insti-
            tute of the University of Chicago.

Krinsley, D. B.
1970        *A Geomorphological and Palaeoclimatological Study of the Playas of
            Iran.* Washington, D.C.: U.S. Government Printing Office.

Kuper, A.
1980        Symbolic dimensions of the Southern Bantu homestead. *Africa* 50:8–23.

Lambton, A. K. S.
1953        *Landlord and Peasant in Persia: A Study of Land Tenure and Land
            Revenue Administration.* London: Oxford University Press.

1969        *The Persian Land Reform 1962–1966.* Oxford: Clarendon Press.

Lawrence, D. L., and S. M. Low
1990        The built environment and spatial form. *Annual Review of Anthro-
            pology* 19:453–505.

Le Craterre (P. Doat, A. Hays, H. Houben, S. Matuk, and F. Vitoux)
1985        *Construire en Terre.* Paris: Editions Alternatives.

Lienau, C., and H. Uhlig
1978 (eds.)  *Flur und Flurformen.* Vol. 1 of Materialien zur Terminologie der Agrarlandschaft. Giessen: Lenz.

Loose, R.
1980  Streifige Flurteilungsysteme als kennzeichen binnenkolonisatorischer Vorgänge in Afghanistan. In *Zur Geographie der ländlichen Siedlungen in Afghanistan,* by C. Jentsch and R. Loose, 95–119. Mannheimer Geographische Arbeiten, no. 6. Mannheim: Geographisches Institut der Universität.

Lloyd, S.
1963  *Mounds of the Near East.* Edinburgh: Edinburgh University Press.

Mabbutt, J. A.
1977  *Desert Landforms.* Cambridge: M.I.T. Press.

McHenry, P. G.
1984  *Adobe and Rammed Earth Buildings: Design and Construction.* New York: Wiley.

McIntosh, R. J.
1974  Archaeology and mud wall decay in a West African village. *World Archaeology* 6:154–71.

McLachlan, K.
1988  *The Neglected Garden: The Politics and Ecology of Agriculture in Iran.* London: Tauris.

Martin, M. A.
1976  Men and women of Tauran. Paper presented at the 75th Annual Meeting of the American Anthropological Association.

1977  On fertility and the role of women in agriculture: A case from northeast Iran. Paper presented at the 76th Annual Meeting of the American Anthropological Association.

1980a  Making a living in Turan: Animals, land and wages. *Expedition* 22(4):29–35.

1980b  Pastoral production: Milk and firewood in the ecology of Turan. *Expedition* 22(4):24–28.

1982a  Case studies of traditional marketing systems: Goats and goat prodicts in northeastern Iran. In *Third International Conference on Goat Production and Disease (Proceedings),* 45–49. Scottsdale, Ariz.: Dairy Goat Journal.

1982b  Conservation at the local level: Individual perceptions and group mechanisms. In *Desertification and Development: Dryland Ecology in Social Perspective,* edited by B. Spooner and H. S. Mann, 145–69. London: Academic Press.

1987  Production strategies, herd composition, and offtake rates: Reassessment of archaeological models. *MASCA Journal* 4:154–65.

Melville, C.
1984        Meteorological hazards and disasters in Iran: A preliminary survey
            to 1950. *Iran* 22:113–50.
Michell, G.
1978 (ed.)   *Architecture of the Islamic World: Its History and Social Meaning*. Lon-
            don: Thames and Hudson.
Momen, M.
1985        *An Introduction to Shi'i Islam*. New Haven: Yale University Press.
Moore, P. D., and R. Bhadresa
1978        Population structure, biomass, and pattern in a semi-desert shrub,
            *Zygophyllum eurypterum*, in the Turan Biosphere Reserve of north-
            eastern Iran. *Journal of Applied Ecology* 15:837–45.
Moore, P. D., and A. C. Stevenson
1982        Pollen studies in dry environments. In *Desertification and Develop-
            ment: Dryland Ecology in Social Perspective*, edited by B. Spooner
            and H. S. Mann, 249–67. London: Academic Press.
Mumtaz, K. K.
1985        *Architecture in Pakistan*. Singapore: Concept Media.
Neely, J. A.
1971        Sassanian and early Islamic water control and irrigation systems
            on the Deh Luran plain. In *Irrigation's Impact on Society*, edited by
            T. E. Downing and M. Gibson. Anthopological Papers, no. 25.
            Tucson: University of Arizona Press.
Netting, R. M.
1977        *Cultural Ecology*. Menlo Park, Calif.: Benjamin Cummins.
Nicholas, I.
1980        A spatial/functional analysis of late fourth millennium occupation
            at the TUV Mound, Tal-e Malyan, Iran. Ph.D. dissertation, De-
            partment of Anthropology, University of Pennsylvania.
Nitz, H.-J.
1971        *Formen der Landwirtschaft und ihre räumliche Ordnung in der oberen
            Gangesebene*. Heidelberger Geographische Arbeiten, Heft 28.
            Weisbaden: F. Steiner.
Noy-Meir, I.
1973        Desert ecosystems: Environment and producers. *Annual Review of
            Ecology and Systematics* 4:25–51.
Nyerges, A. E.
1982        Pastoralists, flocks and vegetation: Processes of co-adaptation. In
            *Desertification and Development: Dryland Ecology in Social Perspec-
            tive*, edited by B. Spooner and H. S. Mann, 217–47. London:
            Academic Press.

Oates, D.

1990        Innovations in mud-brick: Decorative and structural techniques in
            ancient Mesopotamia. *World Archaeology* 21: 388–406.

Oates, D., and J. Oates

1976        Early irrigation agriculture in Mesopotamia. In *Problems in Eco-
            nomic and Social Archaeology*, edited by G. de G. Sieveking, I. H.
            Longworth, and K. E. Wilson, 109–35. London: Duckworth.

O'Connell, J. F.

1987        Alyawara site structure and its archaeological implications. *Ameri-
            can Antiquity* 52(1):74–108.

Olgyay, V.

1963        *Design with Climate: Bioclimatic Approach to Architectural Regional-
            ism.* Princeton: Princeton University Press.

O'Regan, B.

1977        Ecology of *Gazella dorcas* (jebeer) and *Gazella subgutterosa*
            (goitered gazelle) in Turan Biosphere Reserve. Preliminary re-
            port. In *Case Study on Desertification, Iran: Turan,* prepared
            for the Government of Iran, 90–97. Tehran: Department of the
            Environment.

Oswald, D. B.

1987        The organization of space in residential buildings: A cross-cultural
            perspective. In *Method and Theory for Activity Area Research: An
            Ethnoarchaeological Approach,* edited by S. Kent, 295–344. New
            York: Columbia University Press.

Pabot, H.

1967        *Report to the Government of Iran on Pasture Development and Range
            Improvement through Botanical and Ecological Studies.* Rome: FAO.

Parsons, J.

1972        Archaeological settlement patterns. *Annual Reviews in Anthropol-
            ogy* 1:127–50.

Petherbridge, G. T.

1978        Vernacular architecture: The house and society. In *Architecture of
            the Islamic World,* edited by G. Michell, 176–208. London: Thames
            and Hudson.

Plog, S.

1976        Measurement of prehistoric interaction between communities. In
            *The Early Mesoamerican Village,* edited by K. V. Flannery, 255–72.
            New York: Academic Press.

Prickett, M. E.

1979        Settlement and the development of agriculture in the Rud-i Gushk
            drainage, southeastern Iran. In *Akten des VII. Internationalen*

*Kongresses für Iranische Kunst und Archäologie, Munich, September 7–10, 1976,* 47–56. Berlin: Dietrich Reimer.

Rafferty, J.

1985    The archaeological record on sedentariness: Recognition, development, and implications. In *Advances in Archaeological Method and Theory,* vol. 8, edited by M. B. Schiffer, 113–56. New York: Academic Press.

Rathje, W., and C. Murphy

1992    *Rubbish! The Archaeology of Garbage.* New York: Harper Collins.

Rechinger, K.-H.

1963– (ed.)    *Flora Iranica.* Vols. 1-. Graz: Akadmische Druk-u. Verlagsanstalt.

1977    Plants of the Touran [*sic*] protected area, Iran. *Iranian Journal of Botany* 1:155–80.

Rechinger, K.-H., and Wendelbo, P.

1976    Plants of the Kavir Protected Region, Iran. *Iranian Journal of Botany* 1(1):23–56

Roaf, S.

1982    Wind-catchers. In *Living with the Desert: Working Buildings of the Iranian Plateau,* edited by E. Beazley and M. Harverson, 57–72. Warminster, England: Aris and Phillips.

Roper, D. C.

1979    The method and theory of site catchment analysis: A review. In *Advances in Archaeological Method and Theory,* vol. 2, edited by M. B. Schiffer, 119–40. New York: Academic Press.

Rosen, A. M.

1986    *Cities of Clay: The Geoarchaeology of Tells.* Chicago: University of Chicago Press.

Rouholamini, M.

1973    L'habitation dans la region de Suse. Raddadeh, Khuzistan. *DAFI* 3:171–83.

Sajjadi, S. M. S.

1982    *Qanat/Kariz: Storia, Tecnica Costruttiva ed Evoluzione.* Teheran: Istituto Italiano di Cultura Sezione Archeologica.

Salam, Hayat

1990 (ed.)    *Expressions of Islam in Buildings.* Geneva: Aga Khan Trust for Culture on behalf of the Aga Khan Award for Architecture.

Schiffer, Michael B.

1987    *Formation Processes of the Archaeological Record.* Albuquerque: University of New Mexico Press.

Schmitt, R.

1989 (ed.)    *Compendium Linguarum Iranicum.* Wiesbaden: Reichert.

Schwerdtfeger, F. W.
1982        *Traditional Housing in African Cities: A Comparative Study of Houses in Zaria, Ibadan and Marrakech.* New York: John Wiley and Sons.

Scott, D. A., H. M. Hamadani, and A. A. Mirhosseyni
1975 (comps. and eds.)   *Birds of Iran.* Tehran: Department of the Environment. (In Persian.)

Shanks, M., and C. Tilley
1987        *Re-Constructing Archaeology: Theory and Practice.* Cambridge: Cambridge University Press.

Smith, C. A.
1976 (ed.)   *Regional Analysis.* 2 vols. New York: Academic Press.

Spooner, B.
1974        Irrigation and society: The Iranian Plateau. In *Irrigation's Impact on Society,* edited by T. E. Downing and M. Gibson, 43–57. Tucson: University of Arizona Press.

1983        Abyari, "irrigation" in Iran. *Encyclopaedia Iranica,* edited by E. Yarshater. London: Routledge and Kegan Paul.

1984        *Ecology in Development.* Tokyo: UNU.

Spooner, B., and L. Horne
1980 (eds.)   Cultural and ecological perspectives for the Turan Programme, Iran. *Expedition* 22(4): 1–47.

Spooner, B., L. Horne, M. Martin, A. E. Nyerges, and C. Hamlin
1980        *The Ecology of Rural Settlements in Arid Lands: A Pilot Study.* Final report on the Turan Human Settlements Project, in association with UNESCO's Programme on Man and the Biosphere, Project Area no. 11. UNESCO/UNEP no. 0104–76–05–748, Paris.

Spooner, B., and H. S. Mann
1982 (eds.)   *Desertification and Development: Dryland Ecology in Social Perspective.* London: Academic Press.

Stager, L. E.
1976        Farming in the Judaean desert during the Iron Age. *Bulletin of the American Schools of Oriental Research* 221:145–58.

Sumner, W. M.
1989        Population and settlement area: An example from Iran. *American Anthropologist* 91(3):631–41.

Szabo, A., and T. J. Barfield
1991        *Afghanistan: An Atlas of Indigenous Domestic Architecture.* Austin: University of Texas Press.

Tchalenko, J. S., and N. N. Ambraseys
1973        Earthquake destruction of adobe villages in Iran. *Annali di Geofisica* 26(2–3):357–89.

Tomaschek, W.
1883        Zur historischen Topographie von Persien. *Sitzungsberichte der Philosophisch-Historischen Classe der Kaiserlichen Akademie der Wissenschaften* 100:201–31.

Tringham, R.
1985        Review of *Early European Agriculture: Its Foundations and Development,* by M. R. Jarman, G. N. Bailey, and H. N. Jarman. *American Antiquity* 50(4):922–23.

Van Beek, G. W.
1987        Arches and vaults in the Ancient Near East. *Scientific American,* July: 78–85.

Vaughan, H. B.
1893        A journey through Persia (1887–1888). *Royal Geographical Society Supplementary Papers* 3: 89–115.

Vidal, F. S.
1955        *The Oasis of al-Hasa.* N.p.: Arabian American Oil Co., Local Government Relations, Arabian Research Division.

Wailes, B.
1970        The origins of settled farming in temperate Europe. In *Indo-European and Indo-Europeans,* edited by G. Cardona, H. M. Hoenigswald, and A. Senn, 279–305. Philadelphia: University of Pennsylvania Press.

Watson, P. J.
1978        Architectural differentiation in some Near Eastern communities, prehistoric and contemporary. In *Social Archaeology: Beyond Subsistence and Dating,* edited by C. L. Redman, M. J. Berman, E. V. Curtin, Jr., W. T. Langhorne, N. M. Versaggi, and J. C. Wanser, 131–58. New York: Academic Press.
1979        *Archaeological Ethnography in Western Iran.* Viking Fund Publications in Anthropology, no. 57. Tucson: University of Arizona Press.

Watson, P. J., S. A. LeBlanc, and C. L. Redman
1984        *Archaeological Explanation: The Scientific Method in Archaeology.* New York: Columbia University Press.

Whitelaw, T.
1983        People and space in hunter-gatherer camps: A generalizing approach in ethnoarchaeology. *Archaeological Review from Cambridge* 2(2):48–66.

Wilkinson, T. J.
1974        Agricultural decline in the Siraf region, Iran. *Paleorient* 2:123–32.
1982        The definition of ancient manured zones by means of extensive sherd-sampling techniques. *Journal of Field Archaeology* 9:323–33.

Wulff, H. E.
1966        *The Traditional Crafts of Persia.* Cambridge: M.I.T. Press.
Wylie, A.
1985        The reaction against analogy. In *Advances in Archaeological Method and Theory,* vol. 8, edited by M. B. Schiffer, 63–111. New York: Academic Press.
Yorulmaz, M.
1982        Earthquakes and rural construction. In *The Changing Rural Habitat,* vol. 1, edited by B. B. Taylor, 131–34. Singapore: Concept Media Pte Ltd. for the Aga Khan Award for Architecture.
Zohary, M.
1963        On the geobotanical structure of Iran. *Bulletin of the Research Council of Israel,* section D (Botany), vol. IID, supplement. Jerusalem: Weizmann Science Press of Israel.

# INDEX

*Note:* All places listed are in Iran unless otherwise noted. Figures are listed in italics.

Abandoned settlements, 40, 53, 68, 80 Table 5; reuse of, 78, 182

Abandonment, 170; effects on site preservation, 164, 167, 169, *171,* 172; and erosion, 121; reasons for, 68, 78–79, 82, 129, 170, 182; of winter stations, 53, 66

*Āghols* (animal shelters), *66,* 88

*Āghols* (winter pastoral stations), 58, *66,* 88; abandonment of, 53, 66, 79; activities at, 65; burning of, for vermin, 66, 79, 214n2; location and resources, *6,* 43, 65–66; number of in Turan, 66; ownership of, 43; personnel at, 65; structures, 65

Agricultural production, 38–41; scheduling of, 41; village-to-village variation in, 40. *See also* Dry farming; Field systems; Irrigation

Alberts, Robert C., 119, 216n6, 217n10. *See also* Davarabad

Aliabad (western Iran): compared with Khar o Tauran, 3–4, 157, 160, 186; dispersed holdings in, 189; residential patterns, 107–10; variability in room type, 150–51,

218n11; wall thickness in, 135, 218n11

Alywara (Australia), 215n5

Animal houses: acquisition, 170; activities in, 160; construction, 133, 137, 169, 172; features in, 143; functions of, 90; location of, *94,* 95, 96, 149, 189; and reuse, 180–82, 187; and settlement density, 172; variation in size, 150

Animal ownership, 69–72, 152–54, 218n12. *See also* Camels, Cattle, Donkeys, Goats, Sheep

Animal pens, 52–53, 90, 132, 133, 145, 146. See also *Āghols*

Animal products. *See* Dung, Meat, Milk products, Wool

Archaeological deposit. *See* Mound formation

Archaeological recognition: of agriculture and pastoralism, 51–54; of sedentariness, 84; of settlement types, 85

Archaeological recovery. *See* Mound formation, Potsherds

Architecture: and climate, 96–100;